Women of Color Political Elites in the U.S.

This volume presents a detailed and in-depth examination of women of color political elites in the United States in varying levels of office and non-elected positions.

Through innovative data, novel theoretical frameworks, and compelling arguments, the chapters in this book explore how women of color political elites are changing, challenging, or upending the status quo in American politics. Beyond an additive approach of either race or gender, the authors in this volume employ an intersectional lens to explore the complexities of governing, running for office, and adjudicating in a diversifying America.

This book will be of great value to upper-level students, researchers, and academics of political science interested in women's and gender studies, political leadership as well as race and ethnic studies. The chapters in this book were originally published as a special issue of the *Journal of Women, Politics, & Policy*.

Nadia E. Brown is Professor of Government and Director of the Women's and Gender Studies Program at Georgetown University, USA. She is the co-author of *Sister Style: The Politics of Appearance for Black Women Political Elites*.

Christopher J. Clark is Associate Professor of Political Science at the University of North Carolina at Chapel Hill, USA. He is the author of *Gaining Voice: The Causes and Consequences of Black Representation in the American States*.

Anna Mitchell Mahoney is Administrative Associate Professor of Women's Political Leadership at Newcomb Institute at Tulane University, USA. She is the author of *Women Take Their Place in State Legislatures: The Creation of Women's Caucuses*.

Women of Color Political Elites in the U.S.

Intersectional Political Experiences

Edited by
Nadia E. Brown, Christopher J. Clark and
Anna Mitchell Mahoney

LONDON AND NEW YORK

First published 2023
by Routledge
4 Park Square, Milton Park, Abingdon, Oxon, OX14 4RN

and by Routledge
605 Third Avenue, New York, NY 10158

Routledge is an imprint of the Taylor & Francis Group, an informa business

Chapters 1–11 © 2023 Taylor & Francis

All rights reserved. No part of this book may be reprinted or reproduced or utilised in any form or by any electronic, mechanical, or other means, now known or hereafter invented, including photocopying and recording, or in any information storage or retrieval system, without permission in writing from the publishers.

Trademark notice: Product or corporate names may be trademarks or registered trademarks, and are used only for identification and explanation without intent to infringe.

British Library Cataloguing-in-Publication Data
A catalogue record for this book is available from the British Library

ISBN13: 978-1-032-44239-6 (hbk)
ISBN13: 978-1-032-44242-6 (pbk)
ISBN13: 978-1-003-37116-8 (ebk)

DOI: 10.4324/9781003371168

Typeset in Minion Pro
by codeMantra

Publisher's Note
The publisher accepts responsibility for any inconsistencies that may have arisen during the conversion of this book from journal articles to book chapters, namely the inclusion of journal terminology.

Disclaimer
Every effort has been made to contact copyright holders for their permission to reprint material in this book. The publishers would be grateful to hear from any copyright holder who is not here acknowledged and will undertake to rectify any errors or omissions in future editions of this book.

Contents

	Citation Information	vii
	Notes on Contributors	ix
1	The Community Matters: Finding the Source of the Radical Imagination of Black Women's Political Ambition *Pearl K. Ford Dowe*	1
2	The 2018 Congressional Midterms, Symbolic Empowerment, and Ayanna Pressley's Mobilizing Effect: A Case Study for Future Analysis of Historic Firsts *Evelyn M. Simien*	17
3	Legislating as Your Full Self: Queer Women of Color in US State Legislatures *Hanna K. Brant and Jordan Butcher*	35
4	Her Honor: Black Women Judges' Experiences with Disrespect and Recusal Requests in the American Judiciary *Taneisha N. Means*	48
5	The Black Women of the US Congress: Learning from Descriptive Data *Nadia E. Brown, Christopher J. Clark and Anna Mitchell Mahoney*	66
6	Galvanizing Grief: Black Maternal Politics, Respectability, and the Pursuit of Elected Office *Aidan Smith*	85
7	"Better Too Much Than Not Enough": The Nomination of Women of Color to the Federal Bench *Laura Moyer, Allison P. Harris and Rorie Spill Solberg*	101
8	Black and Desi: Indian American Perceptions of Kamala Harris *Danielle Casarez Lemi, Maneesh Arora and Sara Sadhwani*	114
9	The Future of Black Feminism and Black Women Political Elites: A Reflexive Interview with Duchess Harris *India S. Lenear*	128

CONTENTS

10 A Conversation with Mary Hawkesworth on Intersectionality, Political Science, and Challenging the Discipline   135
Catherine N. Wineinger

11 Moving beyond Niceness: Reading bell hooks into the Radical Potential for the Discipline   143
Alex Moffett-Bateau and Jenn M. Jackson

Index   151

Citation Information

The chapters in this book were originally published in the *Journal of Women, Politics, & Policy*, volume 43, issue 3 (2022). When citing this material, please use the original page numbering for each article, as follows:

Chapter 1
The Community Matters: Finding the Source of the Radical Imagination of Black Women's Political Ambition
Pearl K. Ford Dowe
Journal of Women, Politics, & Policy, volume 43, issue 3 (2022) pp. 263–278

Chapter 2
The 2018 Congressional Midterms, Symbolic Empowerment, and Ayanna Pressley's Mobilizing Effect: A Case Study for Future Analysis of Historic Firsts
Evelyn M. Simien
Journal of Women, Politics, & Policy, volume 43, issue 3 (2022) pp. 279–296

Chapter 3
Legislating as Your Full Self: Queer Women of Color in US State Legislatures
Hanna K. Brant and Jordan Butcher
Journal of Women, Politics, & Policy, volume 43, issue 3 (2022) pp. 297–309

Chapter 4
Her Honor: Black Women Judges' Experiences with Disrespect and Recusal Requests in the American Judiciary
Taneisha N. Means
Journal of Women, Politics, & Policy, volume 43, issue 3 (2022) pp. 310–327

Chapter 5
The Black Women of the US Congress: Learning from Descriptive Data
Nadia E. Brown, Christopher J. Clark and Anna Mitchell Mahoney
Journal of Women, Politics, & Policy, volume 43, issue 3 (2022) pp. 328–346

Chapter 6
Galvanizing Grief: Black Maternal Politics, Respectability, and the Pursuit of Elected Office
Aidan Smith
Journal of Women, Politics, & Policy, volume 43, issue 3 (2022) pp. 347–362

Chapter 7
"Better Too Much Than Not Enough": The Nomination of Women of Color to the Federal Bench
Laura Moyer, Allison P. Harris and Rorie Spill Solberg
Journal of Women, Politics, & Policy, volume 43, issue 3 (2022) pp. 363–375

Chapter 8
Black and Desi: Indian American Perceptions of Kamala Harris
Danielle Casarez Lemi, Maneesh Arora and Sara Sadhwani
Journal of Women, Politics, & Policy, volume 43, issue 3 (2022) pp. 376–389

Chapter 9
The Future of Black Feminism and Black Women Political Elites: A Reflexive Interview with Duchess Harris
India S. Lenear
Journal of Women, Politics, & Policy, volume 43, issue 3 (2022) pp. 390–396

Chapter 10
A Conversation with Mary Hawkesworth on Intersectionality, Political Science, and Challenging the Discipline
Catherine N. Wineinger
Journal of Women, Politics, & Policy, volume 43, issue 3 (2022) pp. 401–408

Chapter 11
Moving beyond Niceness: Reading bell hooks into the Radical Potential for the Discipline
Alex Moffett-Bateau and Jenn M. Jackson
Journal of Women, Politics, & Policy, volume 43, issue 3 (2022) pp. 409–416

For any permission-related enquiries please visit:
http://www.tandfonline.com/page/help/permissions

Notes on Contributors

Maneesh Arora is Assistant Professor of Political Science at Wellesley College, USA. His research interests include race and ethnicity, public opinion, immigration, intergroup solidarity, and methodology.

Hanna K. Brant is Assistant Professor at SUNY Geneseo, USA. Her primary area of research and teaching is American politics, with a particular focus on legislative institutions and women in politics. Her work has been published in *Congress & the Presidency*, *Presidential Studies Quarterly*, and *Social Science Quarterly*.

Nadia E. Brown is Professor of Government and Director of the Women's and Gender Studies Program at Georgetown University, USA. She is the co-author of *Sister Style: The Politics of Appearance for Black Women Political Elites*.

Jordan Butcher is Assistant Professor at Arkansas State University, Jonesboro, USA. She studies legislative politics with an emphasis on legislative careers. Her work has been published in *The Journal of Legislative Studies*, *State Politics & Policy Quarterly*, and *American Politics Research*.

Christopher J. Clark is Associate Professor of Political Science at the University of North Carolina at Chapel Hill, USA. He is the author of *Gaining Voice: The Causes and Consequences of Black Representation in the American States*.

Pearl K. Ford Dowe is Asa Griggs Candler Professor of Political Science and African American Studies with a joint appointment between the university's Oxford College and Emory College of Arts and Sciences, USA. She is Co-editor of the *National Review of Black Politics*.

Allison P. Harris is Assistant Professor of Political Science at Yale University, New Haven, USA, where she is Research Fellow at the Institution of Social and Policy Studies and Co-Director of the Center for the Study of Inequality. Her work has appeared in the *Journal of Race, Ethnicity and Politics* and *Law & Social Inquiry*, among others.

Jenn M. Jackson is Assistant Professor of Political Science at Syracuse University, USA. They are a queer Black androgynous abolitionist and lover of all Black people. Jackson's work is concerned primarily with Black politics, racial threat and trauma, and gender and sexuality.

Danielle Casarez Lemi is Tower Center Fellow at the John Goodwin Tower Center for Public Policy and International Affairs at Southern Methodist University, University Park, USA. Lemi uses experimental and elite interview methods to apply theoretical frameworks of identity and group behavior to questions of voter behavior and legislative politics.

NOTES ON CONTRIBUTORS

India S. Lenear is currently a doctoral student at Rutgers University, New Brunswick, USA. Her work broadly studies women and politics, Black politics, and American politics. More specifically, her work focuses on Black Women's studies, Body politics, and Black feminism(s).

Taneisha N. Means is Assistant Professor of Political Science on the Class of 1951 Chair at Vassar College in Poughkeepsie, USA. Her research and teaching interests are in racial and ethnic politics, judicial politics, and American political behavior and identities. Her current research projects examine the political identities and behaviors of 21st-century Black US judges.

Anna Mitchell Mahoney is Administrative Associate Professor of Women's Political Leadership at Newcomb Institute at Tulane University, USA. She is the author of *Women Take Their Place in State Legislatures: The Creation of Women's Caucuses.*

Alex Moffett-Bateau is Assistant Professor of Political Science at John Jay College of Criminal Justice at the City University of New York, USA. She is a queer, radical, and Black feminist abolitionist, and her intellectual work focuses on how political inequality shapes the scope of political identity.

Laura Moyer is Associate Professor of Political Science at the University of Louisville, USA. Her work on gender and racial diversity in the judicial system has been funded by the National Science Foundation, cited in congressional testimony, and appeared in *Law & Society Review*, *Social Science Quarterly*, and *Politics, Groups, and Identities*, among others.

Sara Sadhwani is Assistant Professor of Politics at Pomona College, Claremont, USA. Her research examines voting behavior, elections, voting rights, public opinion, public policy, and interest groups, with an emphasis on the representation of racial, ethnic, and immigrant communities.

Aidan Smith is Director of Newcomb Scholars Program at Tulane University, USA, an interdisciplinary undergraduate feminist honors program. Her latest book project explores maternal politics from across the political spectrum.

Evelyn M. Simien is Professor of Political Science and Director of the Indigeneity, Race, Ethnicity, and Politics (IREP) Master's degree program at the University of Connecticut, USA. She is the author of *Historic Firsts in U.S. Elections* (Routledge, 2022).

Rorie Solberg is Associate Professor of Political Science at Oregon State University, Corvallis, USA. She currently serves as Co-Editor of *Politics, Groups, and Identities*. Her work on gender and racial diversity in courts has appeared in *Justice System Journal*; *Politics, Groups, and Identities*; and *Judicature*.

Catherine N. Wineinger is Assistant Professor of Political Science at Western Washington University, Bellingham, USA. Her research examines political representation at the intersection of gender, race, and partisanship.

The Community Matters: Finding the Source of the Radical Imagination of Black Women's Political Ambition

Pearl K. Ford Dowe

ABSTRACT

Previous literature on women and political ambition has shown that the ambition of potential candidates is often shaped by career paths that develop the kinds of skills useful for navigating the political environment. These studies often did not include the experiences of Black women who chose to run for office. Utilizing data from interviews with Black women elected officials across the country I offer that the key to making the decision to run for office is the unique socialization process of Black women. This process is shaped by generational examples of service, familial and community nurturing that encourages striving for excellence, and a sense of obligation to do work and not just hold a title. I find that though Black women at times initially doubt their ability to be successful in politics they often overcome these doubts as a result of encouragement by peers and community members who remind them of the skills they developed from their community and political work. They are also motivated to work to meet the needs of their communities. These experiences provide further understanding of how Black women purposefully engage within their communities and develop a standing that allows for their potential success as candidates.

Black women have a long history both of engaging with their communities to address a multitude of needs, and of shaping community consensus and support for larger social movements and political engagement through organizing, activism (Jones-Branch 2021; Robnett 1997), and voting and running for office (Alex-Assensoh and Stanford 1997; Brown 2014; Gay and Tate 1998; Junn 1997; Tate 1991). In spite of Black women being inherently less likely to have the resources that tend to be markers for increased political participation (Burns, Lehman Schlozman, and Verba 2001; Verba and Nie 1972; Smooth 2014), their community work often gives them the necessary social capital (Farris and Holman 2014). This social capital in turn enables networks to develop to cultivate both political mobilization amongst their community members and political skills that foster political ambitions (Scott et al. 2021).

As a result of the deep community ties which Black women express through a multitude of actions, I suggest that ambition for Black women entails something broader than merely wanting to seek public office: it is fueled by a "radical imagination" (Dowe 2020). This radical imagination provides them a social vision that, in the face of adversity and marginalization, propels Black women to harness their vision of justice, equality, access, and freedom into the action of seeking office.

Historically, Black women have long envisioned a more just world in which their resistance matters and benefits both those who look like them and society as a whole. Robin D. G. Kelley (2002, xiii) referred to this imagination as a way to propose a "different way out of our [social, economic and political] constrictions." For Kelley (2002, 8), "Visionary dreams of a new society don't come from little think tanks of smart people ... . Revolutionary dreams erupt [out] of political engagement; collective social movements are incubators of new knowledge." For Black women these visionary or revolutionary dreams form a "culture of resistance" articulated in family and community struggle but also in caring (Collins 2000). Black women's radical imagination convinces them that individually and collectively they can change a world that tells them they are less than. This radical imagination they express through the tangible work of networks, activism, and seeking office for a more equitable society. In short, due to this radical imagination Black women's political ambitions are often motivated by community, and also resourced and championed by it.

The cultivation of this radical imagination

What cultivates this radical imagination of Black women is their socialization to serve rather than only to achieve. The very service that Black women provide as individuals and within groups of other Black women is what ultimately releases the resources to support the women who are deciding whether to run for public office and therefore helps them overcome challenges to running. Black women are typically more likely to be discouraged from running for political positions than their white counterparts and are also less likely to be recruited. The lack of recruitment has a sizable impact on political advancement. Carroll and Sanbonmatsu (2013) show that the actual recruitment of female candidates is more influential in the outcome of political success than it is for male candidates. This hesitance by party leaders reflects their limited notion of what type of candidate is electable. Limited recruitment affects the ability of Black women to secure campaign resources necessary to establish a viable campaign early, especially resources outside of their districts (Sanbonmatsu 2006; Gamble and Gillespie, 2012) as it has been shown that Black candidates typically raise less money than do others (Bryner and Hayley 2019), rely heavily on small donations, and depend on donations outside of their districts (Sanbonmatsu 2006). This lack of resources to fund campaigns early on often poses challenges in launching and running successful campaigns.

Black women are also challenged with obstacles due to racialized and gendered stereotypes. It has been shown that the electorate utilizes a series of gender and racial stereotypes as heuristics while evaluating candidates. White women candidates are deemed to be competent, nurturing, and caring (Koenig et al. 2011) while Black women face the burden of being perceived to have personalities reflective of a variety of negative stereotypes such as being controlling, angry, and tough (Littlefield 2008; Orey and Zhang 2019). Because of these stereotypes, Black women are more susceptible to negative biases. By extension, they tend to be evaluated more negatively as political candidates, and consequently are typically less successful when running for political office.

Exploring the mechanisms through which Black women engage in the world helps us to understand how Black women overcome both these hurdles and the doubts and limited access to arenas that offer networks of support. Black women share a relatively collective political identity or world view (Cole and Stewart 1996) that defines political identity as beliefs related to the social and structural relationships that connect individuals to the larger group. Such women also tend to believe that collective actions are the best responses to social problems. A socialization forged by both race and gender, by a unique desire to advance equality while maintaining a great sense of care for their communities, and by community support that reinforces their pursuit of excellence (in this case in political office) and elevates their standing within the community (Barnes 2015; Collins 2000; Giddings 1984; Robnett 1997; Simien 2006) shapes this world view.

The cultural expectations (Fordham and Ogbu 1986) and political ideology (Stewart, Settles, and Winter 1998) that promote excellence and participation is found in racialized socialization. This process has a dual purpose: to transmit values, attitudes, and behaviors that prepare future generations for possible negative race-related experiences, and to cultivate a positive racial identity (Demo and Hughes 1990). The process of race socialization links family, identity formation, and overall socialization. Gender roles are often learned in the context of race roles (McRae and Noumair 1997). Black women have a heightened sense of race identification derived from their uniquely disadvantaged status in the United States. Linda Williams (2001) suggests that both forms of group consciousness – race and gender – reinforce each other by increasing the rate of Black women's participation in the political process.

Although Black women have other identities or statuses that affect their daily lives (e.g., social class, age, sexual orientation, profession), they are particularly conscious of their racial and gender identities (Settles 2006), and this affect not only their political views but also how they view themselves. Also influencing their work ethic is the socialization process of Black women that encourages achievement while alerting them to the limitations society places on them. The literature on the social history of African American women notes that Black women are important intergenerational resources for their communities (Berry and Gross 2020; Collins 2000; Giddings 1984; Gilkes 1988): they provide racial socialization for their children (Thornton et al. 1990), for example, which Nunnally defines as "the process by which African Americans learn about and identify with the influence of race on their social status, culture and group history in the United Sates" (Nunnally 2012, 58). Educator, activist, and Black feminist Anna Julia Cooper more specifically identifies the unique role that Black women hold as "the fundamental agency under God in the regeneration . . . of the race, as well as the [initiator of the] groundwork and starting point of its progress upward" (Giddings 1984, 81).

The race and gender status of African American women strongly influences how they define family and community, and determines for them which political strategies are best suited to meet the needs of Black women, their families, and the race (Gilkes 1988; Hine 1990; Naples 1991, 1992; Gay and Tate 1998), and therefore in which strategies and causes they should participate. Historically, African American women have viewed political participation as a means to achieve full equality and to improve the status of Blacks, more specifically of Black women and a society in which they are often excluded (Barker, Jones, and Tate 1999; Jones 2020; Shingles 1981; Simien 2005; Tate 1991).

Home socialization

Literature that explores why women are not likely to run for public office suggests that, along with career access, traditional gender socialization perpetuates a culture in which women are least likely to run (Elder 2004; Lawless and Fox 2005). According to the political ambition socialization model, women who enter politics are typically outliers. Yet this (largely white) socialization model is not particularly applicable to Black women. The limited existing literature suggests that Black women's unique socialization, politicization, and life experiences make their political activity exceptional, and some scholars posit that the double discrimination that Black women face in fact motivates their higher levels of participation – to combat the invisibility and hypervisibility of being a Black woman (Alex-Assensoh and Stanford 1997; Brown 2014; Stokes-Brown and Dolan 2010). Although Black women indeed had limited career options due to the combination of race and gender, being a traditional woman/housewife has never fit most African American women (Collins 2000; Guy-Sheftall 1995; King 1975; King 1988; Simien 2006; Stone 1979). For African American women have always played a compelling role in political socialization within their communities and have always contributed to their family's and community's economic stability (King 1988; Giddings 1984). Furthermore, African American women are more likely than white women to be heads of household, have higher labor participation rates than white women, and typically have more autonomy and decision-making authority in their homes as parents and partners than do their white counterparts (Guy-Sheftall 1995; King 1975; Prestage 1991).

Communal socialization

The autonomy that Black women hold within their homes and through their community work gives them significant social capital in Black communities (Gilkes 2001; Guy-Sheftall 1995; Prestage 1991; Simien 2006). For it has created a culture that encourages the pursuit of success and good careers, economic self-reliance, political activism, and value in effectively representing themselves to and for the Black community (Barnes 2016; Higginbotham 1994). Most educated African American women were raised in a culture that encouraged their pursuit of successful careers, their achievement of economic self-reliance, and their development as role models for the Black community (Higginbotham 2001). Barnes 2016 found that besides navigating career, marriage, motherhood, and extended family responsibilities, Black women have also long been concerned about representing the Black community. This unique race and gender status (Gay and Tate 1998; King 1988) strongly influences how they define family and community and resist gender and racial oppression, and in turn leads Black women to use political participation as a means to achieve full equality and improve the status of the group (Barker, Jones, and Tate 1999; Cooper 2017; Gilkes 1988; Gay and Tate 1998; Morris 2015; Simien 2006). The work in which Black women engage in their communities places them in prominent positions and gives them levels of prestige and influence unmatched in the lives of white women of similar class backgrounds (Gilkes 2001).

Political socialization

Black women embrace their identities and navigate the world with strength and agency, a mind-set they typically cultivate early on in girlhood. In their study, Thomas and Speight (1999) demonstrate that African American girls are socialized differently than boys, specifically that boys tend to receive messages about egalitarianism and overcoming racial barriers. Girls receive more messages on racial pride, education, premarital sex and relationships with men, psychological and financial independence, and physical beauty. The socialization processes and subsequent identity development of African American girls is unique because of the particular interaction of racism and sexism, and hence may be better conceptualized as gendered racial socialization. Ruth Nicole Brown advances our understanding of the importance and potential of this time period through her groundbreaking study of Black girlhood spaces. She contends that these spaces and this time period are not only for the process of socialization but also for the formation of creativity and relationships of accountability (Brown 2013). That, she contends, is how Black women gain an understanding of and value for relationships and community.

Smooth and Richardson (2019) show that the socialization process of Black girls shapes the development of leadership skills and political interest. The girls in their study stated that the persons they most admired were women who exhibited care for their communities, and families who valued the collective and took risks on behalf of their communities. The researchers also found that Black girls are differently inspired to pursue leadership when they encounter Black women and girls leading and championing issues about which they care, whether at the grassroots or public levels. Black girls are also exposed to images of strengths when they watch their mothers and grandmothers balance their jobs, family, and community work (Shorter-Gooden and Washington 1996). Mothers feel that is important for their daughters not to allow their gender and race to be barriers for identity development or for functioning as an adult (Thomas and King 2007). This is evident in how they praise excellence and achievement, the autonomy that African American women develop in their homes, and the ways in which they use the income and connections from their careers to give back to their communities.

The radical imagination and candidate emergence

Past research on the development of political ambition has typically focused on why someone runs for office and, once they hold an office, whether they will express ambition to run again for their current seat or for a position that is considered higher on the political hierarchy (Black 1972; Schlesinger 1966). Such research assumed monolithic calculations about political opportunity and has limited applicability to Black women (Bejarano et al. 2021; Dittmar 2020; Hardy-Fanta, Pinderhughes, and Sierra 2016; Stout, Kretschmer, and Ruppanner 2017). More recent research has focused on nascent ambition – the decision dynamics involved in moving from being a potential candidate to running and becoming an office holder. Carroll and Sanbonmatsu (2013) found that direct recruitment and encouragement is more predictive of eventual candidacy for women than for men. Others have found that exposure to women office holders might have a less direct but nonetheless encouraging effect on women's political ambition (Ladam, Harden, and Windett 2018). Though these factors are undoubtedly critical to understanding the complexity of the decision-making process, I have found that for Black women, nascent political ambition or in fact any single variable that prompts Black women to run is not a neat linear upward process for many Black women but a constellation of factors that stem from the radical imagination. As seen in Figure 1, the radical imagination is what propels the desire to enhance the standing of Black women and their communities. This desire contributed to Black women carving out spaces of their own to fellowship, edify, educate, mentor, and strategize amongst themselves.

The radical imagination of Black women along with their socialization cultivates a political behavior that incorporates the actions which Holloway Sparks calls "dissident citizenship" (Sparks 1997, 75), in which marginalized groups not only vote and lobby but also develop alternative spaces for engagement, such as protests and other ways to "address the state and the wider polity." This includes the development of community and civic organizations that disregard limits that broader society attempts to impose on Black women and their communities (Giddings 1988; Jones 2020; Simien 2006). The gendered and racial discrimination of Black women and their political, economic, and social conditions have long led them to develop non-traditional forms of engagement (Giddings 1984; Hine and Thompson 1998). Such engagement fosters in Black women the confidence to seek office, and through volunteer opportunities and networks gives them specific experiences and connections to enable their eventual campaigning and pathway to office.

Black women's radical imagination that leads to dissident citizenship often first engages and develops in alternative formal spaces, such as organizations or church auxiliaries, but can also develop in intimate social spaces such as beauty shops, book clubs, and amongst friends (Collins 2000). These spaces cultivate women's talent and provide them with opportunities to engage and develop skills that are beneficial for a political campaign. Participation through organizations provides useful political capital and resources to political leaders seeking help establishing consensus and promoting the deliberation process. Historically, Black women have had to acquire leadership and power in non-traditional ways in comparison to their male counterparts, both Black and white. Yet despite that, Black women have played an integral role in race-based movements, although history often obscures their participation (Robnett 1997) because they often do not hold formal leadership roles (Dawson 2001; Giddings 1984; Jones 2020; Ransby 2003). During an interview, former Washington, D.C. Mayor Sharon Pratt described it to me this way: "Overwhelmingly the churches are male. Overwhelmingly civil

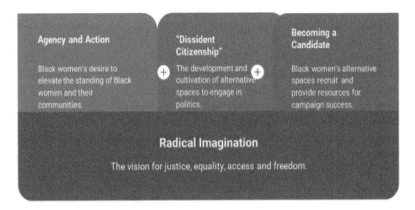

Figure 1. Candidate Emergence of Black Women.

rights organizations are male. When it is time to discuss the community and exercise power there, those positions have gone to me and other Black women." Every woman interviewed spoke of the value they placed on their community service. The majority of the women also spoke at length about how their community work put them close to the campaign process, enabled them to develop transferable skills, and helped them to overcome their hesitance to run for office.

My theoretical intervention broadens the field's understanding of how nascent ambition works for Black women. The community networks cultivated by the work and engagement of Black women mentor, recruit, and help Black women build campaigns and develop fundraising strategies among the respondents I interviewed. I discovered through interviews of Black women who serve or have served as elected officials that in addition to their unique social capital within their communities, the spaces in which Black women conduct these endeavors along with their racialized gendered identity help them to develop a unique consciousness that distinguishes them from Black men and white women. It is this continual thread of community that propels these women to sustain high levels of voter participation, political organizing, and ultimately to seek political office.

The networks of dissident citizenship give Black women opportunities and encouragement to seek office, name recognition amongst potential voters, and occasions for fundraising. Also in these spaces Black women develop skills that are transferable to the political arena, skills such as public speaking, fundraising, and a service resumé that community members respect. These women gain skills and express a heightened sense of confidence thanks to their community and volunteer work experience. It is through such perhaps nontraditional forms of participation that Black women develop social capital, and it is their network of potential voters and fundraisers that enable Black females to achieve political success. Unfortunately, this type of work is often misunderstood as signifying *lack* of ambition because it is less individual and more communal. Because such work is rarely included in how we understand Black women's motivation in seeking public office, the bulk of the literature consequently limits expressions of ambition to running and moving up the political ladder.

Data and methods

This article uses data from a sample of 35 interviews with African American women from across the country who served or currently serve as elected officials. The interviews were conducted between 2017 and 2021. These women serve(d) as US Senators, State Legislators, City Council persons, and school board members in the South, Midwest, West coast, and Northeast. The interviewees responded to an e-mail solicitation sent to 75 Black women elected officials identified by the Center for American Women in Politics and the National Black Caucus of State Legislators. Local elected officials were solicited through postings in Facebook groups that target African American women. All interviewees consented to being "on the record" and permitted the inclusion of their names in publications. Interviewees were provided with their transcript to correct, clarify, or strike any statement made during the taped interview.

During the interviews, which each ran from 45 minutes to an hour, I began by asking the women about their perceptions of politics as a young person, their observations back then of community members who engaged in politics, the source of their motivations to run for office, the fundraising process, and their experience in office. I followed up with questions about persons who inquired about them running for office or encouraged them to do so, and I asked them how they decided to run for a particular office, and to what extent community members, organizations, and political parties (had) supported them. These interviews were recorded and transcribed, then organized into themes.

The data presented here is not exhaustive. Yet the women's testimonies support my premise that Black women are socialized to serve, as evidenced in their extensive discussions of their own community work prior to seeking office. Such service provided avenues for them to be recruited and it shaped their perspectives of their political goals. The interviewees confirmed that their desire to hold office was not only or (mainly) for the position, but for impact. This desire to make an impact also helped to determine which office Black women sought. These women's testimonies also speak of their self-identity and expectations and of the importance of networks in providing support for their political campaigns.

Socialized at home and in the community for agency and action

At Delta Sigma Theta Sorority, Inc.'s 2019 "Delta Days in the Nation's Capital,"[1] then-Treasurer of the St. Louis, Missouri chapter Tishaura Jones[2] commented regarding public service that whereas "Black women run to do something; men run to be somebody." Participating on a panel of Delta members who serve in elected positions, Jones spoke of the value of Black women seeking office and noted that what drives Black women to do such work is the greater purpose of seeing change in America and in their marginalized status. Specifically, the "something" that Jones said Black women run to do is the radical imagination that offers a sense of citizenship, an imagination that is not limited to traditional forms of political engagement. Evidence of how the radical imagination for justice, equality and access was consistently expressed by the interviewees.

The respondents spoke with great passion about the influence of their families and of the persons they saw who engaged in politics. The interviewees discussed in detail working on campaigns of family members as children and teenagers. For some, this included stuffing envelopes, knocking on doors, wearing campaign t-shirts, or tagging along to campaign events. In many cases it was a family member who influenced their political paths and the work ethic they had in approaching campaigns. Former Georgia State Legislator Dee Dawkins-Haigler expressed that her political participation is in her blood, having watched her mother and grandmother participate in politics:

> I've always been in positions my entire life that dealt with some type of social justice, or political nature, even forming protests in high school, all the way up through college. And then I ran my mother's campaign for city council in South Carolina, West Columbia, South Carolina. She was the first African American, first female, and first woman ... First African American, first woman, first Democrat to hold a seat in Lexington County (South Carolina), which is like one of the strongholds of the Confederacy and white supremacy.

> The only pe[rson] that I saw really [politically] active in the community growing up was my mother, who was very active in the Democratic Party. Other than that, I didn't see Black women [being] very active, didn't even see a lot of girls my age interested in being in the political arena or even caring about social justice issues. Now, believe it or not, my grandmother was very influential in my life because she was one of the few Black women, or women, or Blacks, who was very active in the Union movement. So, she was a union officer back when it wasn't even safe to be involved, engaged in the unions, and she would ... travel to Atlanta just to go to meetings dealing with the union, because she always felt like workers should have a voice, that Black people's lives had worth.

Meredith Lawson-Rowe, who serves as a city council person in Reynoldsburg, Ohio, also participated in politics as a child. She recounted:

> [Since I was] a young girl, my mom has always been involved in social action. I've been in church, we've always been involved in community, community organizing, community building, giving back. I can remember as a young girl, maybe about 8 or 10 years old, my mother was a campaign manager for a local county commissioner, and he was our uncle. So, to me, that was, "Oh, Uncle Bob's campaign." And we wore shirts and we passed out literature. And my mom has always been political, our church has always been political, so it's always been important to me to participate in serving those that don't have equal representation.

Both Haigler and Lawson-Rowe's comments speak to an understanding that it was important to engage in community and political work but that it was also important to serve with purpose. These statements confirm the value of exposure to political examples but also the value of accessible role models and Black women engaging in politics across generations. For the socialization of Black girls, up-close and personal examples of political participation with the opportunity to participate as children have a significant effect in influencing their future involvement as candidates themselves.

In a direct expression of the impact of the radical imagination, Arkansas State Representative Vivian Flowers centered her response to why she ran for office and continues to serve on the self-worth and care with which she was raised and on the desire to ensure that other girls experience the safety and worth she experienced as a child:

> I have wonderful parents who come from really beautiful families—not that we don't have our share of issues and drama and everything that every other family experience, but I just ... I didn't grow up thinking I was less than, and I didn't grow up not getting what I needed. I grew up getting most of what I wanted, I didn't have to deal with my parents splitting up. I [have] ... never been raped, I ain't never been molested, I ain't ever been beat up. The one time my brother got into a fight and I had his back, this boy hit me in front of my father, but I knew ... I knew that no matter what, my dad was going to protect me, and it made me tough. I am safe and I'm free and I'm happy. And I just want that for everybody I represent. I just want that for them. And I want it to be where the government or white supremacists or mean, selfish, greedy people don't have any power or impact over another girl like me not being able to live her best life.

Flowers' vision for her leadership along with the other respondents informs us of an understanding that potential candidates and current candidate have of the challenges their community members face. While these women also spoke of having ambitions and goals as politicians and professionals, these ambitions are anchored in the "something" that Tishaura Jones spoke of. This is evidence of the radical imagination propelling Black women to service and a level of service by seeking office to effect change. The narratives presented are only a sample of what the women stated but they show that exposure to family members who had political lives encourages Black women to engage in politics. We also see that familial and community socialization and gendered and racialized experiences can open them to see the difficulties and obstacles involved.

Socialized to serve

As they came from communities that encouraged their achievement as a means to overcome the marginalization of racism and sexism, respondents consistently discussed the need to work at a very high level. This translated into knocking on more doors than opponents, being extremely well prepared for debates and media events, and finding ways to overcome limitations in fundraising. The memory of lessons learned as children along with campaign strategies and work ethic reflects Black women's unique societal role as both a woman and Black. For many of them, seeking excellence was closely connected with ideas both of what is necessary in order to thrive as Black women and to be in a position to win. Senator Carol Mosley Braun (D-IL, 1993–1999), the first Black woman to serve as a US Senator, recalled her mother's words to her: "I wanted to do the best job I could. That was my mother's line. Do the best job you can where you're planted. And that was my motivation[—]to do the best job I could where I was planted. And so, I just [put] one foot in front of the next. And then when it came time, I was in the US Attorney's Office." Councilwoman Strickland said it best: "If we only need 1,500 votes, you['d] better get to 2,500 votes [chuckle]. You got to work differently. You got to fundraise different. You have to have your message different to [the others who] knock on those doors."

Lydia Glaize, former city council woman for Fairburn, Georgia, was a first-time candidate when she won her seat in 2013, and later stated that her interest in running came from her community work and the knowledge she gained by engaging in that work. She recalls precisely what pushed her to consider running. She was attending a meeting for a community organization, the Voter Empowerment Collaborative, and remembers:

One of the local leaders was discussing what we called the Donut, which is the cities around [I-]285 [outside of Atlanta]. And on the south side, those cities had become minority-majority cities. But the elected positions did not reflect the makeup and the demographics of the citizens of those cities. So, when we got in the meeting that night, one of the things that was said that stuck out in my mind [and] that really prompted me to consider running, was the word 'voluntary apartheid' ... What that meant was that people of color were the majority in these cities south of the airport, and yet the mayors and city councils were reflective of the [white] minority in the city. And so, with that said, it's very similar to South Africa. There was apartheid somewhat, but [it was] voluntary because we didn't have many African Americans who had run for office. And the few that did, they lost every time, even in a [race] where [there were] at least six people running.

Glaize went on to say that upon making her decision, she found she had plenty of support to follow through, thanks to the connections she had forged through her community work in various organizations and in the local schools.

City Councilwoman Meredith Lawson-Rowe of Reynoldsburg, Ohio, was also a reluctant candidate. It was her volunteer work on a campaign that led her to being asked and accepting the call to run. She had assisted a candidate for city attorney who later ran for city council. While helping with the candidate's city council run, she also helped another candidate run for city auditor. The candidate Lawson-Rowe assisted in several campaigns would later recruit her to run for office. Lawson-Rowe explained that she deliberately had to unlearn the things that she thought would hinder her:

I told her [the city council member recruiting her] all the reasons why I couldn't do it: I didn't have the experience, I didn't have the education, I didn't have the political background, I didn't come from a political family, and all of these were the reasons why I could not do it. And she [told] me, "Well, that's not true, that's not true." She ... debunk[ed] all of [the] mess I had in my mind.

Angie Jenkins of Reynoldsburg, Ohio, who was also a reluctant first-time candidate and ran on the same slate as Lawson-Rowe, stated that her sense of community and volunteer work led her to politics. Her service gave her a keen understanding of the needs of her community and who was needed at the table to make pertinent local policy decisions:

Well, for School Board, at that time, my children were going to the Reynoldsburg school system, and I wanted to be a part of that process. Reynoldsburg went through many changes and the School Board needed some people of color to serve, and they also needed to have a voice in the community that looked like the children that were attending the schools in Reynoldsburg. Reynoldsburg was ... chang[ing] as far as minority growth [went]. From there, I went on to volunteer for the Obama campaigns, and I volunteered for the Hillary [Clinton] campaign. I also volunteered for the local city councilwoman, Kristin Bryant, who is now on City Council. Once I started volunteering with her, then I started to volunteer for Councilwoman Strickland for the election that we won. I went to her meetings and decided that I was going to sign up to volunteer and help her run. And then Kristin Bryant, who's on City Council, came to me and said, "Why don't you run?" And she gave me some options of what I could run for.

Overcoming doubts to run

Several of the women interviewed stated their hesitancy to run for elected office due to what they perceived as their lack of experience. However, they were eventually persuaded by thinking of the impact they could make. The women were conscious that their opponents would be predominantly white and male candidates. They expressed concern knowing that a white male would likely have access to far more resources than them, and were aware of the possibility for an election to become fraught with racial polarization. One such was Dr. Gethsemane Moss, who now serves as a school board trustee for the Benicia Unified School District in California, and had previously served as an appointed commissioner for her community's Arts and Culture Commission. When asked about her confidence in running and about how she made the decision to run for office, she had stated, "No, I really [didn't] feel confident." Later, she explained, "There were three white men already running for two seats. I didn't want to fight that hard and I didn't have a lot of time to think about it before the deadline to submit." Yet Moss decided to run after reflecting on the impact she could make, adding:

I think another reason why I feel compelled to do it is because . . . in the wake of everything that's been happening with things around, around systemic racism and things like that, I realize[d] . . . in some of the communication that I've had with members of the board, that if I weren't there to offer a different perspective, they would just keep on doing things the same old way. So, I just felt like, oh my God, it became very clear to me that [the board members] are almost clueless in terms of what perspectives are needed for making sure that we're serving all students.

Angie Jenkins, who serves as president of the Reynoldsburg, Ohio city council, likewise not only expressed doubt in her ability to run but was concerned about who her potential opponent would be and what the pattern of leadership in her community had been. When a friend asked her to run for council president, she said:

I thought, "Well, president? I've never [even] served on city council. How can I be president?" I wasn't really familiar with that role and didn't think that I would win, just because I wasn't really familiar with what all that entailed. And [because] there were a lot of men that were serving in that role . . . I didn't think that I would be able to beat [them] because they'd been there for so long. And they're Caucasian men, so I didn't think that was going to be possible. Running as president also was a challenge because the person that been in that position, had [previously] been on city council, and then he ran for the presidency, and he had been in that position for a while as well. But I thought maybe the city would be looking for a change and because of the growth in population with minorities, I thought I had an opportunity there to serve and to win.

The trepidation that Moss and Jenkins expressed is consistent with the lived experiences of Black women in a society in which deference is not given them. Yet both women decided to run in spite of the challenge, due to the perceived impact they felt their contributions could make on their communities.

The resources dissident citizenship provides

Central to the decision-making process to run for office, and alongside the resources available and the community work in which the respondents had previously engaged, was the role of organizations. Every politician spoke of their volunteer work with organizations as either board members, program coordinator, or someone who stuffed book bags at an annual back-to-school event. Several respondents also were responsible for forming organizations to meet a specific community need. All of these examples confirm the value of the socialization process that shapes Black women and the resources within their communities that foster the desire and value of political participation. Central to those resources are organizations that offer opportunities for Black women to gain valuable skills and the necessary skillset to become a candidate.

In addition to community service, a recurring theme that arose was the role of working on political campaigns. This type of service also gave the respondents a broader sense of policy needs for their communities, understanding of the inner workings of campaigns, and opportunities to cultivate relationships that would be useful during their own campaigns. New Hampshire State House Representative Charlotte DiLorenzo became engaged in politics through volunteering for the Obama 2008 presidential campaign and in 2011 ran for her town's new Democratic County office. She reports:

What actually got me launched into politics or even being interested in politics was the Barack Obama campaign. I joined the campaign in around April of 2007 after hearing Barack speak in Hampton, New Hampshire. Back in 2011, we were getting ready for Obama's re-election for 2012. I spoke with some folks in the Rockingham County Democrats Office . . . And my town did not have a town Democratic Committee. We formed a Town Committee. And from there, I was the Vice Chair.

In separate interviews, Sarah Anthony and Tenisha Yancey, who both serve in the Michigan House of Representatives, also noted that their interest in running for political office was piqued by doing volunteer work on campaigns. Anthony noted that she had engaged in several campaigns to preserve affirmative action in the state, and in a congressional campaign. While volunteering she:

started to realize that many of the voices that I thought should be at these tables were not being adequately represented, particularly low-income folks and Black and brown folks, that their issues just were not being uplifted with fidelity. And through that process, I was able to gain a lot of inroads into communities that would ultimately help me when I start[ed] to put my name on a ballot.

Representative Yancey's experience prior to running was very similar. She told me:

I've worked on judges' campaigns. I was exposed to the endorsement process and seeking endorsements and calling around and following up on endorsements for a few judges. On other campaigns, I did door-to-door knocking and just talking to people and getting their support. I also did phone banking and volunteering for a lot of local campaigns.

These experiences confirm that Black women participate in a variety of service opportunities and community engagement that often leads to such political participation (Alex-Assensoh and Stanford 1997; Gay and Tate 1998; Junn 1997; Scott et al. 2021; Tate 1991). Take as another example County Commissioner Sherri Washington of Rockdale County, Georgia, who has an extensive service history. She is a member of the NAACP, the local chapter of Delta Sigma Theta Sorority, Inc., and is a founder of the local bar association for Black women. She ran repeatedly but unsuccessfully for a state legislative position, but realized during those failed runs that she nevertheless always won her district. She attributed that success to her strong community engagement, which led to her winning her local election and then reelection in 2020. Not only does volunteering connect one to a variety of networks, it also provides an avenue for potential candidates to hone skills valuable as a candidate and public servant.

Amongst the interviewees, a consistent theme was the valuable role of having had experience in public service prior to seeking office in motivating women to run but also in gaining the skills required to run for office. Shanette Strickland, who serves on the Reynoldsburg, Ohio City Council, also attributed her success as a first-time candidate to her community and professional service providing her with connections:

I'm involved with this business professional club, [and that] also [helped me] to network. I was in the community at my child's football games and connected with people in my community. I learned how to communicate in a different way. Everything that *I* think is an issue may not be an issue for [everyone else]. So, having those conversations, [I'd ask], "What do you want to see change here in Reynoldsburg? What are those things that you want to see, businesses, opportunities here in Reynoldsburg?" My IT background and connection to other IT people here in Reynoldsburg allowed me to [use my communication skills] … in my position today. Communication, from an IT perspective, negotiation from an IT perspective: these are all the skill sets that I use in my job today [for] advancing the infrastructure of my city.

Brenda Gilmore stated that her experience with volunteering helped her to develop transferable skills. Gilmore began volunteering during her childhood. This enabled her to develop her strong organizational and fundraising skills. She chaired events for organizations such as the YMCA and worked in numerous women's organizations. Gilmore noted that although she did not always realize at the time that was developing particular skill sets in volunteer positions, she realized over time that skills and networks she had developed through service would prove invaluable on the campaign trail and as an elected official.

For the respondents, seeking an elected office was an extension of their commitment to serving the community. Several of the respondents conveyed that they saw the role of Black women in politics as necessary. St. Louis Mayor Tishaura Jones observed, for example, that Black women enter politics because they notice something has gone awry and that being in office is more than a career choice: it is a way to effect necessary change and to right injustice. Multiple participants shared a similar perspective about seeking different positions, saying they had other motivations besides moving up the political career ladder. Judge Sheila Calloway, who serves as Juvenile Court Judge in Nashville, Tennessee, stated when asked about her ambition to seek a higher judicial position:

> At this point in my career, I have not done all of the dreams and visions that I have for Juvenile Court, ... so I definitely will run again in two years, no question about it. After that, I don't know. ... I would like to be in a position where I'm not just influencing and changing policies for this group of kids and this family, but [doing so] on a nationwide basis, I would like to do that. I would like to be one of the decision-makers or the policymakers that are helping to decide how Juvenile Court should run and the things that we should do, and moving us away from locking up kids and sending them to the adult system, and all of those things. I want to be a part of the national conversation about it.

Respondents consistently confirmed that community and volunteer work is a strong predictor of candidate emergence. Their testimonies also help us understand that for Black women, seeking political office is not only about individual ambition but is also a form of political participation (Scott et al. 2021; Simien 2006; Smooth 2006; Tate 1991) through which to impact their communities. This desire to have impact is not just a coincidence but is a result of a socialization process that prepares Black women to overcome challenges that racism and sexism present. These responses help us understand that Black women have a deeper motivation to serve and to use their elected position to enhance the experiences of community members. This aspect of the radical imagination for something greater for the community is front and center not only in the decision to lead but also in the desire to cultivate and participate in spaces that foster leadership and encourage political participation

Conclusion

I began this article by positing that Black women have developed a *radical imagination* through which they envisage a better society – a society in which they lead, from which they benefit, and which improves the lives of their community members. The framework I have developed moves beyond the extant literature's premise that the political ambition of Black women is less than that of White women or men. In the past, it has appeared so merely because political science approaches and categorizes political participation very narrowly, typically negating and downplaying mechanisms (beyond voting) in which Black women engage, such as community and civic engagement. Such previous studies have also often ignored or devalued the rich social structures and indigenous resources within marginalized groups. Countering this, the data that my interviewees provided reveal the complex dynamics that contribute to black women's unique political socialization and resource development.

The testimonials presented confirm my theory: that the unique position of Black women in society prompts their higher levels of participation – efforts to combat the invisibility of being a Black woman (Alex-Assensoh and Stanford 1997; Stokes-Brown and Dolan 2010). This begins early in a Black girl's life with a socialization process that is shaped by home and community to have an impact on and care *for the community at large* rather than merely certain individuals. In addition, generational examples of service, the pursuit of excellence, and a sense of obligation to do something and not just to be something or to hold a title, helps women decide to run for office. This socialization has led Black women to engage in leadership and participate actively in their communities. Such engagement affects not only Black women's opinion of themselves, their identity, and their sense of agency: it also provides training mechanisms for Black women that with time empower them and influence their decision to delve into political careers, to cultivate valuable networks, and to have a greater sense of community needs once they are in office. The interviewees' reflections help us understand how and why Black women engage, and they alert us to the unique socialization and value of Black women. But their reflections also remind us of the invaluable resources in the Black community that open the door to influence in ways that compensate for Black women's limited access to other resources, such as finances and connections to political operatives. Not only that, their reflections help us understand how Black women deliberately become engaged and develop a standing within their communities that with time leads community members to recruit them to run for public office. Because they are already well known in their community, these women then attract resources through the networks of people who respect or have benefited from the women's community work.

The questions I have attempted to answer about how Black women decide to seek office and what makes their runs successful elicited other useful information too. Many of the women represented in this article and within the data set reside in communities that were proactive about facilitating the development of networks of Black women. In some communities these networks developed as a result of family members participating in certain activities. In others, through civic and social organizations women were able to develop networks and relationships in spaces reserved for Black women. Future research could usefully explore how Black women develop networks within multiracial communities, and how younger Black women without an extensive service and political background might yet cultivate networks and strategize for political success.

Notes

1. A legislative conference of Delta members that feature speakers including key policymakers, members of Congress, Congressional staff members and policy experts. Sorority members meet with congresspersons from their respective states.
2. Jones was elected mayor in April of 2021, becoming St. Louis' first African American woman mayor.

Disclosure statement

No potential conflict of interest was reported by the author(s).

References

Alex-Assensoh, Yvette, and Karin Stanford. 1997. "Gender, Participation, and the Black Urban Underclass." In *Women Transforming Politics: An Alternative Reader*, eds. Cathy J Cohen, Kathleen B. Jones, and Joan C. Tronto. New York: NYU Press, 398–411.

Barker, Lucius Jefferson, Mack H. Jones, and Katherine Tate. 1999. *African Americans and the American Political System*. Pearson College Division.

Barnes, Riché J. Daniel. 2015. *Raising the Race: Black Career Women Redefine Marriage, Motherhood, and Community*. New Brunswick, NJ: Rutgers University Press.

Barnes, Riché J Daniel. 2016. *Raising the Race*. Rutgers, NJ: Rutgers University Press.

Bejarano, Christina, Nadia E. Brown, Sarah Allen Gershon, and Celeste Montoya. 2021. "Shared Identities: Intersectionality, Linked Fate, and Perceptions of Political Candidates." *Political Research Quarterly* 74 (4):970–85. doi:10.1177/1065912920951640.

Berry, Daina Ramey, and Kali Nicole Gross. 2020. *A Black Women's History of the United States*. New York: Penguin Random House.

Black, Gordon S. 1972. "A Theory of Political Ambition: Career Choices and the Role of Structural Incentives." *The American Political Science Review* 66 (1):144–59. doi:10.2307/1959283.

Brown, Ruth Nicole. 2013. *Hear Our Truths, the Creative Potential of Black Girlhood*. Champaign: University of Illinois Press.

Brown, Nadia E. 2014. *Sisters in the Statehouse: Black Women and Legislative Decision Making*. New York: Oxford University Press.

Bryner, Sarah, and Grace Haley. 2019. "Race, Gender, and Money in Politics: Campaign Finance and Federal Candidates in the 2018 Midterms." Unpublished Working Paper. https://www.pgpf.org/us-2050/research-projects/Race-Gender-and-Money-in-Politics-Campaign-Finance-and-Federal-Candidates-in-the-2018-Midterms

Burns, Nancy, Kay Lehman Schlozman, and Sidney Verba. 2001. *The Private Roots of Public Action*. Cambridge, MA: Harvard University Press.

Carroll, Susan J., and Kira Sanbonmatsu. 2013. *More Women Can Run: Gender and Pathways to the State Legislatures*. New York: Oxford University Press.

Cole, Elizabeth R., and Abigail J. Stewart. 1996. "Meanings of Political Participation among Black and White Women: Political Identity and Social Responsibility." *Journal of Personality and Social Psychology* 71 (1):130–40. doi:10.1037/0022-3514.71.1.130.

Collins, Patricia Hill. 2000. *Black Feminist Thought: Knowledge, Consciousness, and the Politics of Empowerment*. New York: Routledge.

Cooper, Brittney C. 2017. *Beyond Respectability: The Intellectual Thought of Race Women*. Champaign: University of Illinois Press.

Dawson, Michael C. 2001. *Black Visions: The Roots of Contemporary African American Political Ideologies*. Chicago, IL: University of Chicago Press.

Demo, David H., and Michael Hughes. 1990. "Socialization and Racial Identity among Black Americans." *Social Psychology Quarterly* 53 (4):364–74. doi:10.2307/2786741.

Dittmar, Kelly. 2020. "Urgency and Ambition: The Influence of Political Environment and Emotion in Spurring US Women's Candidacies in 2018." *European Journal of Politics and Gender* 3 (1):143–60. doi:10.1332/251510819X15728693158427.

Dowe, Pearl K. Ford. 2020. "Resisting Marginalization: Black Women's Political Ambition and Agency." *PS, Political Science & Politics* 53 (4): 697–702.

Elder, Laurel. 2004. "Why Women Don't Run: Explaining Women's Underrepresentation in America's Political Institutions." *Women & Politics* 26 (2):27–56. doi:10.1300/J014v26n02_02.

Farris, Emily M., and Mirya R. Holman. 2014. "Social Capital and Solving the Puzzle of Black Women's Political Participation." *Politics, Groups, and Identities* 2 (3):331–49. doi:10.1080/21565503.2014.925813.

Gamble, Katrina, L. 2012. "Young Gifted Black and Female, Why Aren't There More Yvette Clarks in Congress?" In *The New Black Politician: Cory Booker, Newark, and Post-racial America*, ed. Andra Gillespie. New York: NYU Press, 293–305.

Gay, Claudine, and Katherine Tate. 1998. "Doubly Bound: The Impact of Gender and Race on the Politics of Black Women." *Political Psychology* 19 (1):169–84. doi:10.1111/0162-895X.00098.

Giddings, Paula. 1984. *When and Where I Enter*. Bantam Books.

Giddings, Paula. 1988. *In Search of Sisterhood: Delta Sigma Theta and the Challenge of the Black Sorority Movement*. New York: William Morrow and Company.

Gilkes, Cheryl Townsend. 1988. "Building in Many Places: Multiple Commitments and Ideologies in Black Women's Community Work." In *Women and the Politics of Empowerment*, eds. Ann Bookman and Sandra Morgen. Philadelphia, PA: Temple University Press, 53–76.

Gilkes, Cheryl Townsend. 2001. *"If It Wasn't for the Women . . . ": Black Women's Experience and Womanist Culture in Church and Community*. Orbis Books.

Guy-Sheftall, Beverly. 1995. *Words of Fire: An Anthology of African American Feminist Thought*. The New Press.

Hardy-Fanta, Carol, Dianne Pinderhughes, and Christine Marie Sierra. 2016. *Contested Transformation*. New York: Cambridge University Press.

Higginbotham, Evelyn Brooks. 1994. *Righteous Discontent: The Women's Movement in the Black Baptist Church, 1880–1920*. Cambridge, MA: Harvard University Press.

Hine, Darlene Clark. ed. 1990. *Black Women in American History: From Colonial Times through the Nineteenth Century*. Vol. 2. Carlson Pub.

Hine, Darlene Clark, and Kathleen Thompson. 1998. "The History of Black Women in America: A Shining Thread of Hope."

Jones, Martha S. 2020. *Vanguard: How Black Women Broke Barriers, Won the Vote, and Insisted on Equality for All*. Basic Books.

Jones-Branch, Cherisse. 2021. *Better Living by Their Own Bootstraps: Black Women's Activism in Rural Arkansas, 1914-1965*. University of Arkansas Press.

Junn, Jane. 1997. "Assimilating or Coloring Participation? Gender, Race and Democratic Political Participation." In *Women Transforming Politics: An Alternative Reader*, eds. Cathy Cohen, Kathleen B. Jones, and Joan C. Tronto. New York: NYU Press, 387–97.

Kelley, Robin D.G. 2002. *Freedom Dreams: The Black Radical Imagination*. Beacon Press.

King, Mae C. 1975. "Oppression and Power: The Unique Status of the Black Woman in the American Political System." *Social Science Quarterly* 56 (1): 116–28.

King, Deborah K. 1988. "Multiple Jeopardy, Multiple Consciousness: The Context of a Black Feminist Ideology." *Signs: Journal of Women in Culture and Society* 14 (1):42–72. doi:10.1086/494491.

Koenig, Anne M., Alice H. Eagly, Abigail A. Mitchell, and Tiina Ristikari. 2011. "Are Leader Stereotypes Masculine? A Meta-analysis of Three Research Paradigms." *Psychological Bulletin* 137 (4):616–42. doi:10.1037/a0023557.

Ladam, Christina, Jeffrey J. Harden, and Jason H. Windett. 2018. "Prominent Role Models: High-Profile Female Politicians and the Emergence of Women as Candidates for Public Office." *American Journal of Political Science* 62 (2):369–81. doi:10.1111/ajps.12351.

Lawless, Jennifer L., and Richard L. Fox. 2005. *It Takes a Candidate: Why Women Don't Run for Office.* New York: Cambridge University Press.

Littlefield, Marci Bounds. 2008. "The Media as a System of Racialization: Exploring Images of African American Women and the New Racism." *American Behavioral Scientist* 51 (5):675–85. doi:10.1177/0002764207307747.

McRae, Mary, and D. Noumair. 1997. *Race and Gender in Group Research: African American Research Perspectives.* Institute of Social Research, University of Michigan.

Morris, Tiyi Makeda. 2015. *Womanpower Unlimited and the Black Freedom Struggle in Mississippi.* University of Georgia Press.

Naples, Nancy A. 1991. "'Just What Needed to Be Done': The Political Practice of Women Community Workers in Low-income Neighborhoods." *Gender & Society* 5 (4):478–94. doi:10.1177/089124391005004003.

Naples, Nancy A. 1992. "Activist Mothering: Cross-generational Continuity in the Community Work of Women from Low-income Urban Neighborhoods." *Gender & Society* 6 (3):441–63. doi:10.1177/089124392006003006.

Nunnally, Shayla C. 2012. *Trust in Black America: Race, Discrimination, and Politics.* New York: NYU Press.

Orey, Byron D'Andra, and Yu Zhang. 2019. "Melanated Millennials and the Politics of Black Hair." *Social Science Quarterly* 100 (6):2458–76. doi:10.1111/ssqu.12694.

Prestage, Jewel L. 1991. "In Quest of African American Political Woman." *The Annals of the American Academy of Political and Social Science* 515 (1):88–103. doi:10.1177/0002716291515001008.

Ransby, Barbara. 2003. *Ella Baker and the Black Freedom Movement: A Radical Democratic Vision.* Chapel Hill: University of North Carolina Press.

Robnett, Belinda. 1997. *How Long? How Long?: African American Women in the Struggle for Civil Rights.* New York: Oxford University Press.

Sanbonmatsu, Kira. 2006. "Do Parties Know that 'Women Win'? Party Leader Beliefs about Women's Electoral Chances." *Politics & Gender* 2 (4):431–50. doi:10.1017/S1743923X06060132.

Schlesinger, Joseph A. 1966. *Ambition and Politics: Political Careers in the United States.* Rand McNally.

Scott, Jamil, Nadia Brown, Lorrie Frasure, and Dianne Pinderhughes. 2021. "Destined to Run? The Role of Political Participation on Black Women's Decision to Run for Elected Office." *National Review of Black Politics* 2 (1):22–52. doi:10.1525/nrbp.2021.2.1.22.

Settles, Isis H. 2006. "Use of an Intersectional Framework to Understand Black Women's Racial and Gender Identities." *Sex Roles* 54 (9):589–601. doi:10.1007/s11199-006-9029-8.

Shingles, Richard D. 1981. "Black Consciousness and Political Participation: The Missing Link." *American Political Science Review* 75 (1):76–91. doi:10.2307/1962160.

Shorter-Gooden, Kumea, and N. Chanell Washington. 1996. "Young, Black, and Female: The Challenge of Weaving an Identity." *Journal of Adolescence* 19 (5):465–75. doi:10.1006/jado.1996.0044.

Simien, Evelyn M. 2005. "Race, Gender, and Linked Fate." *Journal of Black Studies* 35 (5):529–50. doi:10.1177/0021934704265899.

Simien, Evelyn M. 2006. *Black Feminist Voices in Politics.* Albany: SUNY Press.

Smooth, Wendy. 2006. "Intersectionality in Electoral Politics: A Mess Worth Making." *Politics & Gender* 2 (3):400–14. doi:10.1017/S1743923X06261087.

Smooth, Wendy. 2014. "African American Women and Electoral Politics: Translating Voting Power into Office-holding." In *Gender and Elections: Shaping the Future of American Politics*, eds. Susan J Carroll and Richard L. Fox. New York: Cambridge University Press, 167–89.

Smooth, Wendy, and Elaine Richardson. 2019. "Role Models Matter: Black Girls and Political Leadership Possibilities." In *The Black Girlhood Studies Collection*, ed. Aria S Halliday. Toronto: Women's Press, 131–56.

Sparks, Holloway. 1997. "Dissident Citizenship: Democratic Theory, Political Courage." *Hypatia* 12 (4):74–110. doi:10.1111/j.1527-2001.1997.tb00299.x.

Stewart, Abigail J., Isis H. Settles, and Nicholas JG Winter. 1998. "Women and the Social Movements of the 1960s: Activists, Engaged Observers, and Nonparticipants." *Political Psychology* 19 (1):63–94. doi:10.1111/0162-895X.00093.

Stokes-Brown, Atiya Kai, and Kathleen Dolan. 2010. "Race, Gender, and Symbolic Representation: African American Female Candidates as Mobilizing Agents." *Journal of Elections, Public Opinion and Parties* 20 (4):473–94. doi:10.1080/17457289.2010.511806.

Stone, Pauline Terrelonge. 1979. "The Limitation of Reformist Feminism." *The Black Scholar* 10 (8/9): 24–27.

Stout, Christopher T., Kelsy Kretschmer, and Leah Ruppanner. 2017. "Gender Linked Fate, Race/ethnicity, and the Marriage Gap in American Politics." *Political Research Quarterly* 70 (3):509–22. doi:10.1177/1065912917702499.

Tate, Katherine. 1991. "Black Political Participation in the 1984 and 1988 Presidential Elections." *The American Political Science Review* 85 (4):1159–76. doi:10.2307/1963940.

Thomas, Anita Jones, and Constance T. King. 2007. "Gendered Racial Socialization of African American Mothers and Daughters." *The Family Journal* 15 (2):137–42. doi:10.1177/1066480706297853.

Thomas, Anita Jones, and Suzette L. Speight. 1999. "Racial Identity and Racial Socialization Attitudes of African American Parents." *Journal of Black Psychology* 25 (2):152–70. doi:10.1177/0095798499025002002.

Thornton, Michael C., Linda M. Chatters, Robert Joseph Taylor, and Walter R. Allen. 1990. "Sociodemographic and Environmental Correlates of Racial Socialization by Black Parents." *Child Development* 612 (2):401–09. doi:10.2307/1131101.

Verba, Sidney, and Norman H. Nie. 1972. *Participation in America*. New York: Harper and Row.

Williams, Linda Faye. 2001. "The Civil Rights–Black Power Legacy." In *Sisters in the Struggle*, eds. Bettye Collier-Thomas and V.P. Franklin. New York: NYU Press, 306–32.

Wolbrecht, Christina, and David E. Campbell. 2007. "Leading by example: Female members of parliament as political role models." *American Journal of Political Science* 51(4): 921–939

The 2018 Congressional Midterms, Symbolic Empowerment, and Ayanna Pressley's Mobilizing Effect: A Case Study for Future Analysis of Historic Firsts

Evelyn M. Simien

ABSTRACT

Ayanna Pressley was elected in 2018, becoming the first Black woman from Massachusetts to serve in the US House of Representatives and the first person of color to represent its only majority-minority congressional district (which includes three-quarters of Boston, and most of Cambridge). While Pressley was no political newcomer to the city of Boston, her campaign garnered widespread media attention on account of her victory – that is, having defeated a ten-term incumbent, Michael Capuano, of the same political party. Here I argue that the electoral context mattered, given the historic nature of the campaign and its mobilizing effect on a racially and ethnically diverse electorate. Although highlighting qualifications and experience was the preferred tactic of her opponent, it was important for Pressley to choose a strategy that best fit the electoral context. Here I offer a case study, with information that will bear on the applicability of causal generalizations to be empirically tested via formal modeling or large-N analysis in future studies. The sort of specific, intensive, and detailed information provided is necessary in advance of forecasting results across similar subjects and comparable target populations using quantitative or statistical methods.

In the months leading up to the 2018 Congressional midterm elections, journalists wrote in anticipation of several breakthrough contests. A record number of historic-first candidates had run for and won their parties' nomination for election to the US House of Representatives in 2018, with several crediting such special circumstances as Donald Trump's presidency, social movements #MeToo and #BlackLivesMatter, and Supreme Court Justice Brett Kavanaugh's Senate confirmation hearings for motivating them to seek election (Brown and Cassese 2020; Castle et al. 2020). The outcome of the 2018 midterm elections was markedly different from past ones, with Democrats gaining a total of 41 seats in the US House of Representatives and assuming control of that chamber (Brown and Cassese 2020). By all counts, voter turnout soared during the 2018 Congressional midterm elections.

Why did 2018 produce such gains for history-making firsts? A couple of factors combined to elect more diverse candidates to public office. These factors relate to the behavior of *both* the candidates *and* the voters. Arguably, the game-changing performances of historic-first candidates change the nature of political representation as we know it and challenge basic assumptions that have long advantaged white men about how, where, and which candidates can achieve electoral success (Dittmar 2017; McDonald, Porter, and Treul 2020). Take, for example, the historic victory of US House Representative Ayanna Pressley in 2018. She embraced her race-gender identities as electoral assets, not hurdles to overcome. Pressley drew upon her lived experiences and challenged the valuation and expression of stereotypically masculine credentials for office-holding with identity-based and values-laden appeals (McDonald, Porter, and Treul 2020). A high-quality challenger, Pressley skillfully blended mobilization with coalition building in a candidate-centered campaign that targeted underrepresented minorities and immigrant groups in an extremely diverse electoral environment. Pressley chose a strategy that fit the context. Few would argue, however, that race and gender were the sole factors that determined Pressley's victory. Several other influential factors interacted and functioned simultaneously to determine the outcome of this congressional race – youth turnout specifically and record high turnout generally. How this historic-first candidate used her race and gender to mobilize young voters, previously inactive voters, and newly registered voters is instructive and signals the continued significance of Black women in the Democratic Party coalition.

Here I offer a case study, with information that bears on the future of a growing number of historic-first candidates seeking public office and desiring increased electoral participation (Simien 2015, 2022; Simien and Hampson 2020). Pressley's personal story – unfortunately – is not unique for many Black women and their families; however, her election as the first Black woman to represent her district is laudable. The Congressional Black Caucus was established to represent African Americans – both inside and outside of their districts – around issues that I claim are better represented by Pressley than her White male predecessor, Michael Capuano. Correspondingly, this historic case plays an important role in knowledge production and the use of other methods in political science – statistical methods – cannot be reasonably pursued at this time absent a great deal of information gathering and marshaling of qualitative evidence for a highly context dependent subject. The sort of specific, intensive, and detailed information presented here is necessary in advance of considering what might be the right methods for forecasting results across similar subjects and comparable target populations – that is, until more data is rapidly collected for formal modeling or large-N analysis (Cartwright 2006). The case study spotlights features of an electoral system and a bi-racial contest within it that shifts our emphasis and work on evidence for future use.

Significance of the study

Not to suggest that intersectionality is shorthand for Black women, but this case study affords us a remarkable opportunity to build upon the symbolic empowerment framework, and to expand the theoretical capacity of intersectionality research by linking it to voter mobilization and electoral success. Now more than ever, research on the mobilization of American voters is vital for understanding the effect of historic firsts and their consequences for recent campaigns and elections in the United States (Simien 2015; Simien and Hampson 2020). The number of historic candidates who have been erased from larger political narratives of state and local politics, the US Congress, and presidential elections is astounding. Because of this far – too – frequent occurrence in college and university classrooms as well as high school civics or American government textbooks, this analysis elevates the status of historic firsts as subjects of scholarly importance and lays the groundwork for future studies of their candidacies. There is little evidence to suggest that the significance of such trailblazers is acknowledged by the political science discipline and the American politics subfield.

Given the psychological and social factors linked to identity (Nunnally 2012), researchers and readers alike should recognize the importance of multiple axes of identity for segments of the mass public that are far from homogenous but rather heterogeneous in the country's fastest growing areas due to increases in immigration (Collet 2008). To be sure, identity alignment between candidates and voters is symbolically empowering and mobilizing for certain populations in multicultural urban milieus like Boston, Massachusetts (Medenica and Fowler 2020). Thus, the overarching context from which such historic firsts as Ayanna Pressley emerge onto the political scene is analytically important – that being, in this case: the Trump era – and numeric gains made by Democrats at every level of office have practical implications for the substantive representation of minority interests writ large. The major takeaways are clear: the representation of those marginalized by multiple, interlocking systems of power is inextricably tied to the fate of historic-first candidates, as was shown by Georgia's 2021 run-off elections for the US Senate, and has especially important implications for voting rights legislation – namely, the For the People Act (HR 1) and the John Lewis Voting Rights Act (also known as HR 4).

Theoretical framework: symbolic empowerment

At the heart of this essay is a central, organizing concept – symbolic empowerment – that suggests historic firsts like Ayanna Pressley mobilize new segments of the American electorate. The moment in which historic-first candidates enter the electoral arena, and the campaign ensues is described in terms of contextual effects that are symbolically empowering. The cumulative effect of their multiple identities and the historic nature of their campaigns stoke the desire to vote despite problems that arise in dealing with traditional opponents, from the injection of coded racial appeals or "dog whistles" to the distortion of their legislative records and altered images in commercial ads or political cartoons (Brown and Casarez Lemi 2021; López 2015; Phoenix 2020). The presence of a historic-first candidate who mirrors a marginalized group pictorially signals greater access to electoral opportunities and motivates political behavior from the kind of voters that political analysts would describe as being on the periphery of American politics. These races are hard fought, and the stakes are high especially when historic-first candidates unite diverse electorates and establish multiracial coalitions. Loyalty, or a sense of belonging, facilitates the process whereby a strong affective intragroup emotion like pride results in an ego-enhancing appraisal of the event and public figure associated with a socially valued outcome – that being, in this case: the election of a historic first to public office (Burge 2020; Finn and Glaser 2010; Lazarus 1991; Marcus, Newman, and MacKuen 2000; Parkinson, Fischer, and Manstead 2005; Phoenix 2020; Simien 2015; Sullivan 2014). As such, historic candidacies are inextricably tied to questions of representation, electability, and performance (Mansbridge 1999; Phillips 1995).

Here I extend the theory of symbolic empowerment to the Trump era and shift the focus from a historic presidential campaign to a history-making congressional campaign. In *Historic Firsts: How Symbolic Empowerment Changes U.S. Politics*, Simien (2015) implored readers to consider the ways in which unconventional candidates use their gender and race to serve as a catalyst for Americans in the voting booths. Whether such candidates achieve group solidarity on this basis remains a hugely important and timely question, given the role women, racial and ethnic minorities, as well as younger age cohorts (many of whom were previously inactive or newly registered voters) have played in determining recent elections.

Symbolic empowerment, a theory of election campaigns involving historic-first candidates, goes beyond the traditional black-white paradigm and considers the impact of multiracial and multiethnic constituencies on American behavioral studies. Herein lies my innovation, as I advance the theory of symbolic empowerment to include the particularities of Pressley's formidable campaign and reveal the challenges faced by high quality challengers such as herself when opposing long-term incumbents who represent the default identity category in electoral politics – a white male – and when voters cannot rely on partisanship as a cue. While the study will not put to rest the debate set forth by skeptics about the usefulness of identity-based appeals and values-driven rhetoric to advance a campaign, it will inform our thinking about long-standing questions on the impact of more race neutral, deracialized electioneering techniques void of such an emphasis in comparable electoral environments (read: bi-racial contests in majority-minority districts).

Symbolic empowerment conceives of path-breaking candidates as motivational actors who are uniquely situated in an electoral system that privileges one axis of identity, either race or gender, *not* both (Simien 2015). As much as voters want to be substantively represented, they do value descriptive and symbolic representation (Tate 2001, 2003). Whereas descriptive representation is limited to the likeness of candidates in so far as they mirror constituencies based on social or demographic traits, symbolic representation is inclusive of psychological factors that evoke emotions or attitudes from which constituents might derive a sense of pride (Phillips 1995; Pitkin 1967; Simien 2015; Tate 2003). It is well understood that race and gender influence the ways in which historic firsts campaign, and the extant literature suggests that members belonging to the same identity group as their representative can bask in the glory of the political aspirant's achievements (Finn and Glaser 2010; Marcus, Newman, and MacKuen 2000; Parkison, Fischer, and Manstead 2005; Simien 2015, 2022; Sullivan 2014). The tentative or conditional terms upon which historic candidacies are viewed through the prism of race, gender, and ethnicity fortify the descriptive-symbolic link between political representation and civic engagement, as it elicits a positive intragroup emotion like pride and ignites newfound enthusiasm to actively participate in politics during the campaign (Burge 2020; Mansbridge 1999; Marcus, Newman, and MacKuen 2000; Nunnally 2012; Pitkin 1967; Simien 2015; Simien and Hampson 2017; Young 2000).

While the candidate's public visibility as it raises the salience of identities – for example, race, ethnicity, and gender shared by the candidate with American voters is important, historic-first candidates like Pressley also want members of their city, state, or home district to recognize them as one of them based on policy interests, not simply their physical characteristics (Brown 2014; Mansbridge 1999; Reingold, Haynie, and Widner 2021; Simien 2015; Tate 2001, 2003). Given the strong desire to behave in a way that would make their constituents proud – and because they stand to give prominence to issues that otherwise would be ignored – historic-first candidates build trust in government institutions (Reingold 2008; Simien 2015, 2022; Tate 2003). Such a powerful dynamic whereby historic first candidates are cognizant of their status and understand the process by which they "stand for" dispossessed subgroup members of their constituent base, can revitalize democracy and strengthen its legitimacy by virtue of *both* their presence *and* performance (Dovi 2002; Mansbridge 1999; Phillips 1995; Pitkin 1967; Young 2000).

Pressley's campaign answers practical questions for researchers and practitioners alike: How do race *and* gender affect who gets elected, as well as who is voting? What issues do historic-first candidates prioritize? Does diversity in electorates make a difference? While partisanship has long been a prominent feature in campaigns and elections, understanding how race and gender interact to influence voter turnout will matter increasingly more in diverse electoral contexts. Unlike her opponent, Pressley demonstrated the need for a preferable descriptive representative like herself (Dovi 2002). Pressley was 19 when she was raped on the campus of Boston University, but prior to that she had endured years of childhood sexual abuse (Levenson and Ebbert 2018). Her father's struggle with a heroin addiction and his incarceration for 16 years intermittently placed her in a unique position to understand certain policy implications for the school to prison pipeline, community policing, and child welfare. These personal challenges made her relatable to constituents, connecting lived experience, political representation, and legislative issues to multiple axes of identity. Pressley faced an American electorate that was especially appreciative of what it perceived to be her unique authenticity and emotional intelligence derived from these formative life experiences, dating back to childhood and early adulthood. Her personal narrative, however, cannot be treated as an isolated biography when it provides guidance for understanding how the political context and demographic makeup of Boston shaped the impact of such an intersectional actor. Once she emerged onto the political scene as a historic-first candidate, Pressley prioritized her policy preferences while holding party identification constant and reconciling the limits of her presence opposite an opponent with more seniority and an incumbency advantage with her call for descriptive and symbolic representation.

Data and evidence for use (the role of case study analysis)

This essay is informed by a rich array of sources from campaign materials and newspaper accounts to public opinion and census data, voter turnout reports, stump speeches, and social media content as well as interviews. Still, this research is exploratory in nature rather than definitive. The underlying justification for said approach is to amass qualitative data and evidence for future use. The case study helps inform the knowledge production process, providing a baseline against which other historic firsts might fit categorically to achieve broader knowledge through the analysis of a wider range of cases based on a set of commonalties deemed important for comparison. It lays the groundwork for future researchers to observe sufficiently similar patterns to evaluate additional cases based on real world conditions, with the most ambitious goal being the creation of a large-N data set, with cases that vary by gender, race, ethnicity, and time so commonalities and differences can be systematically coded and problematized, but *without* distorting the symbolic empowerment framework. Such a data set might yield secondary categories that differentiate between winners and losers, establish a pioneer cohort in relation to contemporaries, or identify some partial cases that fail to symbolically empower. Indeed, for every Ayanna Pressley, there are surely other candidates who achieved identity alignment with segments of the mass public but failed to win election.

Adding new cases to make credible claims about both the complexity and importance of historic first candidates at the level of state, local, and national government can only enhance our current understanding of symbolic empowerment. Whether variations in application or meaning as well as categorization are accepted or contested will be an abiding issue for future research. For now, I jumpstart this line of scholarly inquiry with an in-depth, multi-faceted case study analysis that paves the way for knowledge production and provides evidence for causal claims – that is, if one is seeking to understand what variables are relevant on the ground and in particular contexts, the crucial information this case study provides will bear on the applicability of causal generalizations to be empirically tested through statistical and quantitative means in future studies (Crasnow 2011). Now we turn to the plan of this study and a brief roadmap of what follows.

The plan of this case study: a roadmap in brief

This essay situates the main subject – historic-first candidate Ayanna Pressley – strategically in terms of identity, geography, and temporality. Starting with an overview of Pressley's childhood and early adulthood, I segue into an analysis of state and local politics in Boston, including the historical context and political landscape leading up to Pressley's bid for the US House of Representatives. An introduction to Pressley's opponent, Congressman Michael Capuano, is provided and especially important when considering the complexities of her campaign. I cover Pressley's ground game, demonstrating how she strategically connected with voters and secured her win.

Ayanna Pressley and her formative experiences

Ayanna Pressley was born in Cincinnati, Ohio in 1974. She was raised in Chicago, Illinois by her mother, Sandy Pressley. As a single mother and tenant rights organizer, Sandy lived paycheck to paycheck (Levenson and Ebbert 2018). At an early age, Ayanna's mother exposed her to community organizing. Her mother also taught Ayanna to use her voice, and to be unapologetic when standing up for issues that mattered to her and their local community. Pressley's ambition was fueled by her religious upbringing, socioeconomic background, community activism and local politics, as well as historic events. She accompanied her mother to tenant rights meetings, protests, marches, and political rallies, which cultivated a relationship with local government. At 10 years old, Ayanna joined her mother at the victory celebration of Harold Washington who was elected mayor of Chicago. He became the city's first Black mayor in the early 1980s (Levenson and Ebbert 2018). Despite numerous challenges during her youth, Pressley thrived at an elite college prep private school – the Francis W. Parker School – located in Chicago. She was president of student government, a cheerleader, a competitive debater, and voted "Most Likely to Become Mayor" of Chicago. Pressley was also the commencement speaker in her senior year (Levenson and Ebbert 2018).

Upon graduation, Pressley moved to Massachusetts to attend Boston University and her mother moved to New York City (Levenson and Ebbert 2018). As a freshman, Pressley served as student president of her college within the university and student senator (Levenson and Ebbert 2018). Pressley also organized a student event to honor Reverend Dr. Martin Luther King Jr.'s birthday and invited then-US Representative Joe Kennedy II as a guest speaker (Levenson and Ebbert 2018). Per this introduction, Pressley pursued an internship in the office of Congressman Joe Kennedy as a freshman (Levenson and Ebbert 2018). Despite a successful first year at Boston University, Pressley's college experience was disrupted when she was raped on campus by someone she knew while working as a resident assistant the summer between her freshman and sophomore year (Levenson and Ebbert 2018). At the time, she felt too ashamed to report the incident; however, Pressley began sharing her story publicly years later (Levenson and Ebbert 2018). In her sophomore year, college came to a halt when Pressley's mother lost her job in New York City (Levenson and Ebbert 2018). To help support her mother, Pressley withdrew from college and worked full-time (Levenson and Ebbert 2018).

Once hired as a volunteer coordinator for then-US Senator John Kerry's 1996 reelection campaign against Massachusetts Governor William Weld, Pressley found herself weighing in on team decisions within a year and after Kerry's reelection, she landed a full-time job as a scheduler in his Washington, DC office. After 13 years of working in a variety of roles, including Constituent Services Director and Political Director, for US Senator John Kerry of Massachusetts, Pressley returned to Boston to launch her first city councilor at-large campaign. Despite her experience working in politics, it was not typical in 2009 to have a native from Chicago, let alone an outspoken woman of color, jump into a political race in Boston. That said, it is important that we discuss the demographics of this major metropolitan city and its political history along with other historic first candidates as having paved the way and set the stage for Pressley's inaugural campaign and reelection campaigns as city councilor.

How might context matter? History and political landscape of Boston, Massachusetts

Boston represents the capital of Massachusetts, and the economic engine of the state. While Boston is among the most diverse cities in the country, many of its neighborhoods remain segregated by race and ethnicity (Schuster and Ciurczak 2018). The Hispanic/Latino population in the East Boston neighborhood accounts for 58% of the population compared to only 19% citywide; the Black/African American population in Dorchester makes up 44% of the neighborhood's population yet 23% citywide; and 76% of Back Bay residents are non-Hispanic/White, much greater than the 45% share of non-Hispanic/White residents citywide.[1] Most Black residents live in such predominately Black neighborhoods as Hyde Park, Mattapan, Roxbury, and parts of Dorchester (Austin 2018). They, who are non-immigrant and African American, are the most marginalized both economically and politically of all minority groups in Boston – for example, the median net worth for a white household in Greater Boston is 247,500 USD yet the median net worth of a non-immigrant African American household is only 8 USD (Muñoz et al. 2015).

The root cause of these disparities dates to school desegregation. While the desegregation of public schools became a nationally charged issue following the US Supreme Court's 1954 ruling of *Brown v. Board of Education*, it took 20-plus years for Boston public schools to desegregate and only after a court order mandate issued by US District Judge W. Arthur Garrity (Irons, Murphy, and Russell 2014). Following this ruling and its implementation, racial protests and riots ensued across Boston (Irons, Murphy, and Russell 2014). Over the next decade, it took more than 400 court orders to implement the city's busing plan between mainly Black and white neighborhoods (Irons, Murphy, and Russell 2014). During this transformational period for Boston and the Boston public schools, white student enrollment significantly declined; today, minority populations represent 76% of the Boston public school student body (BPS Communications Office 2019). During school desegregation, other areas of local policy underwent change. In 1975, the city's at-large system for political representation was challenged by a group of African American plaintiffs. They filed a federal class-action lawsuit claiming the at-large voting system prevented Black candidates from winning seats on the city council and the five-member school board (Austin 2018). Even though the US District Court determined the at-large system was legal, voters approved a city referendum to replace the at-large system (Austin 2018). As a result, a new city council in Boston was designed to include the seven-district plus four at-large, elected offices, rather than nine at-large offices (Austin 2018).

By the turn of the 21st century, political leadership remained sparse among Black state legislators, and entirely absent among Massachusetts constitutional offices and local elected offices in Boston. Yet, there was a rise of Black political newcomers. Hailing from the Boston area, Marie St. Fleur and Linda Dorcena Forry – two Haitian women – were elected to the Massachusetts State House of Representatives from districts that included such parts of Boston as Dorchester, Mattapan, and Roxbury (Austin 2018). In 2006, Governor Deval L. Patrick, a business leader turned elected official from Milton – a town adjacent to Boston – became the state's first Black governor and the nation's second.

By 2009, Ayanna Pressley returned to Boston after working as an aide for US Senator John Kerry in Washington, DC and launched her first campaign for office. Pressley kicked off her campaign by raising awareness of issues that resonated with her personally, including women's health and criminal justice reform; however, she was advised not to focus on such issues that would pigeon-hole the campaign and cost her votes. Pressley disregarded this advice, sharing her lived experience and vision for the city. She saw firsthand a city still scarred by the era of school desegregation. Her personal life story was all too familiar and resonated with residents who similarly had experienced trauma that did not discriminate by race, gender, or socio-economic status across generations. She emerged as a relatable, public figure with whom voters could engage and feel good about, stoking their desire to get involved in the electoral process – for example, Pressley implemented a "100 Club" campaign strategy, asking her supporters to recruit ten more registered voters to cast a ballot in her favor (Austin 2018). She also gained endorsements from women advocacy groups – namely, the Massachusetts Women's Political Caucus, and the University of Massachusetts-Boston's Center for Women in Politics and Public Policy (Austin 2018). Her experience in serving as the Political Director for Senator Kerry also attracted support from local, state, and federal elected officials (Austin 2018).

In Boston, mayoral elections are every four years and city council elections are every two years including the election for four at-large city councilors to represent the entire city and seven additional city councilors to represent districts within the city. For the at-large city council general election, the top four candidates to receive the most votes are elected. Despite a crowded field including eight candidates in the general election and even more in the primary election, Pressley scored 41,879 votes and ranked 4th among eight City Councilor At-Large candidates in the general election to become one of the city's four City Councilors At-Large (Seelye and Herndon 2018). In her first political race, Pressley achieved a historic first by becoming the first woman of color to be elected to the Boston City Council.

As City Councilor At-Large, Pressley swiftly transitioned from campaigning to governing. She established and chaired the City Council's Committee on Healthy Women, Families, and Communities, a committee focused on the issues she promised to pursue as a candidate: stabilizing families and communities, preventing violence and trauma, combatting poverty, promoting career advancement, addressing teenage pregnancy and health education, as well as abortion rights. Pressley led with issues she believed mattered to voters and correspondingly increased her likability among constituents. As a result, she garnered the most votes for reelection in 2011, 2013, and 2015; and the second highest votes in 2017. This feat marked the first time in Boston's history that a person of color and a woman achieved such an outstanding record of support as a member of the Boston City Council (Seelye and Herndon 2018). It was no easy accomplishment especially in her second reelection campaign. In the summer prior to the 2013 primary election, Pressley's mother passed away from leukemia. As her mother became increasingly ill, she became less present in city council meetings and on the campaign trail. Still, voters showed their support at the polls. Pressley came in first among candidates in more than half of Boston's 22 wards. She garnered 85% of the votes by Black/African Americans in the neighborhoods of Roxbury, Jamaica Plain, and Roslindale, and even came in second among candidates in the mostly white neighborhood of West Roxbury (Austin 2018). See Figure 1 for total votes received by Pressley for city council.

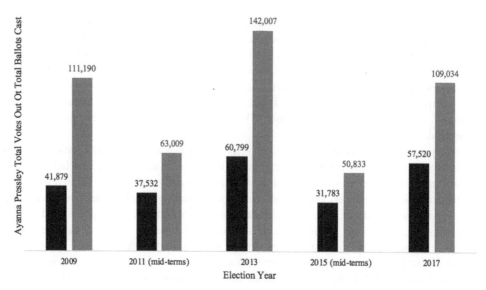

Figure 1. Ayanna Pressley Total Votes Received Out of Total Ballots Cast for Boston City Councilor At-Large (2009–2017). City of Boston, Elections Department, 2009–2017, https://www.boston.gov/departments/elections/state-and-city-election-results

Despite Pressley's historic firsts and that of Governor Patrick among others, people of color as well as women remain grossly underrepresented in Massachusetts state and local government. According to a 2019 MassINC study, white residents are overrepresented in the State Legislature by approximately 16%, with 31 additional members of color needing to be elected to properly represent Asian, African American, and Latino residents (Levine, Foreman, and Bliss 2019). Similar disparities exist among women in state politics. While 52% of adult residents are women, the Massachusetts State Legislature is comprised of less than 29% women (Levine, Foreman, and Bliss 2019). The Massachusetts State Legislature led a statewide redistricting plan after the 2010 US Census and shifted from 11 to 10 congressional seats (Thys 2010). Redistricting resulted in the first majority-minority district in Massachusetts, the 7th Congressional District (Koczela 2018). Formerly considered the Massachusetts 8th Congressional District, this newly created district was comprised of 40.8% white residents compared to the 70.7% white residents across the state. As such, it left advocates hopeful that it would increase diversity among state elected officials and spark greater influence within neighborhoods of color (Salsberg 2016).

The Massachusetts 7th Congressional District is comprised mostly of Boston along with parts of Cambridge and the town of Milton as well as the cities of Chelsea, Everett and Somerville and the town of Randolph. Leading up to its first election in 2012, this metropolitan electorate was more diverse and less clearly defined than in the past by people of color – including Black, Latino, and Asian residents – who comprised 56% of residents from the cities of Somerville, Chelsea, and Everett, a third of the town of Milton, half of the city of Cambridge, and much of the city of Boston (Miller 2018b). In Boston, alone, 28.9% of residents are foreign born with significant representation from China, Dominican Republic, Haiti, Vietnam, El Salvador, Cape Verde among other Latin, Asian, and European countries, and of the foreign-born residents, 46% are naturalized citizens (Lima 2018).

Pressley's opposition: Congressman Michael Capuano

By 2018, the 7th Congressional District (and its former, the 8th Congressional District) had been served by Congressman Michael Capuano for 10 consecutive terms. Before serving in Congress for nearly 20 years, Capuano was first an alderman, then mayor for almost ten years in the city of Somerville – a 4.1 square mile municipality that is a part of the 7th Congressional District and abuts the cities of Boston and Cambridge. Capuano was born to first-generation Irish and Italian immigrants in Somerville in 1952, over two decades before Pressley was born (DeCosta-Klipa 2018). Capuano graduated from Dartmouth College in New Hampshire before returning to Boston to earn his law degree at Boston College Law School (DeCosta-Klipa 2018). He first entered local politics by serving on his hometown's Board of Alderman. Capuano attempted three times to run for mayor of the city of Somerville, finally winning with his third campaign in 1989 (DeCosta-Klipa 2018). As mayor, he continued to pursue higher office. By 1998, Congressman Joe Kennedy II's seat opened, and Capuano entered a crowded race with ten candidates; he successfully won his inaugural congressional race to represent his hometown and surrounding communities in the US House of Representatives (DeCosta-Klipa 2018). As a US Congressman, Capuano was an active member of the Congressional Progressive Caucus (DeCosta-Klipa 2018).

During his 20 years representing the district, Capuano was outspoken against Wall Street during the Great Recession, the Iraq War, and the No Child Left Behind education bill (DeCosta-Klipa 2018). He even sued the administrations of President George W. Bush and President Barack Obama, standing opposed to the presidents' executive war powers (DeCosta-Klipa 2018). As a bold, progressive leader in Congress, Capuano maintained likability within the district evidenced by the fact he never faced opposition within the Democratic party in any of his reelections prior to 2018 (Massachusetts Election Statistics). According to nonpartisan studies of his voting record, Capuano was true to his progressive values (Pindell 2018). His 2018 reelection campaign press secretary described Capuano as "an unwavering fighter for progressive values who is taking on Donald Trump at every turn and working hard for the people he represents" (Pindell 2018).

Pressley versus Capuano

In Massachusetts, opponents from each political party square off in primary elections, then the winning candidate from each party competes against each other in the general election on the first Tuesday in November of the election year. For the Massachusetts 7th Congressional District, the only candidates in the race were Capuano and Pressley, both Democrats; therefore, whoever won the primary would be the presumptive winner to represent the district in the US House of Representatives. The head-to-head campaign between Pressley and Capuano spanned roughly eight months, leading up to the primary election on September 4, 2018. With the Massachusetts primary election serving as the standoff between the only two candidates for the 7th Congressional District, all eyes were waiting for the results the evening of the primary election not only locally but nationally, too. Soon after polls closed, it was confirmed that Pressley defeated Capuano by a landslide, beating the long-term incumbent by 17.2 percentage points (Massachusetts Election Statistics). Pressley successfully earned 58.5% of the votes compared to Capuano who only secured 41.3% of the 106,556 total ballots cast (Massachusetts Election Statistics). After her primary win and a general election without opposition, Pressley went on to become the first Black woman from Massachusetts elected to the US Congress and the first person of color to represent the Massachusetts 7th Congressional District. See Table 1 for primary results.

Table 1. 2018 U.S. House Democratic Primary: Massachusetts 7th Congressional District.

City/Town	Pressley	Capuano	All Others	Blanks	Total Votes Cast
Boston	40,615	22,914	127	2,800	66,456
Cambridge	6,029	4,655	7	185	10,876
Chelsea	968	1,139	0	128	2,235
Everett	1,498	2,804	11	471	4,784
Milton	815	606	1	33	1,455
Randolph	1,835	1,889	4	93	3,821
Somerville	8,286	8,423	22	198	16,929
TOTAL	60,046	42,430	172	3,908	106,556

Source: Massachusetts Election Statistics, Secretary of the Commonwealth, https://electionstats.state.ma.us/elections/search/year_from:2018/year_to:2018/office_id:5/district_id:58690

How did Pressley's campaign secure her victory? By way of background, there was a political outcry that had swarmed the nation by 2018. It was apparent not only in Boston but districts across the country that there was a lack of Black and women political leaders. Several successful campaigns emerged in 2018 – locally, Massachusetts District Attorney Rachel Rollins of Suffolk County, and nationally, Alexandria Ocasio-Cortez, who ran for the US House of Representatives against an incumbent in the New York Democratic primary, and Ilhan Omar, who launched a congressional campaign after the Democratic incumbent representing her district in Minnesota chose not to seek reelection. Additionally, "Time's Up" and "#MeToo" national movements were widespread. By 2018, protests had become commonplace in Boston and across the country, rallying to protect the rights of women, Black lives, immigrants, LGBTQ communities and more. In Massachusetts, City Councilor Pressley and Congressman Capuano were among the most vocal leaders that joined rallies and demonstrations in support of these communities.

According to Pressley, she was motivated to address the systemic inequalities and disparities she had long talked about in Boston. Neither the national political climate nor the presidential election of Donald Trump mattered as much (Seelye and Herndon 2018). Pressley announced her campaign to run against incumbent Congressman Capuano in January 2018. Within days of her announcement, race and gender became a focal point of the campaign. Capuano and Pressley were interviewed separately by WBUR, Boston's NPR station. During this radio interview, Capuano admitted that identity can influence a voter's choice though there are many other deciding factors and quipped: "I cannot be a woman of color" (Miller 2018b). While Capuano stated the obvious, he goes onto acknowledge the implicit, unspoken role race and gender can play in the campaign environment. Capuano expressed that he did not think voters would weigh their decision to vote or not vote for him because he was white and male (Miller 2018b). Still, Pressley was his first opponent in a Democratic primary since becoming a congressman in 1998 and he was quick to point out her race and gender. His remarks could have easily been received negatively and labeled offensive by listeners.

Given the degree of uncertainty associated with this electoral contest, media messaging took on additional importance in terms of content. As in most biracial electoral contests, the media as well as white opponent could inject race and gender in extraordinary ways (Terkildsen and Damore 1999). Capuano's remarks could be thought of, in a most general sense, as an effort to minimize perceived political risk when considering the demographic makeup of the district. In response, Pressley employed identity-based appeals and her multiple group identity became a strategic resource from which she could reap votes.

In a separate interview with the same WBUR reporter, Pressley acknowledged she and Capuano shared progressive values but asserted that she would bring a different lens to the same political issues (Miller 2018b). Acknowledging that everyone has their own perspective in life, she astutely shared "when you have issues that are being developed through a completely monolithic and homogenized prism, everyone suffers for that" (Miller 2018b). Pressley continued to drive this message home to members of Massachusetts' only majority-minority congressional district through the control of campaign communications from broad and narrow-cast messages to sociocultural cues as well as language. Both her race (Blackness) and gender (female) became deployable, reputational assets that provided certain tangible and intangible benefits not available her opponent on account of his whiteness and maleness. Pressley's race and gender went from passive attributes to elevated resources when emphasized on the campaign trail. Pressley could do so based on a set of assumptions regarding political representation used to critique her opponent and assume the upper hand.

Notably, Pressley held her campaign launch in Cambridge, outside of her home turf of Boston, at a restaurant filled with over 300 people in early February (Bay State Banner 2018). As she engaged with supporters, Pressley vowed to work on issues, such as increasing health-care costs, the gap of income inequality, access to capital for small businesses, and the lack of affordable housing (Bay State Banner 2018). Despite being in her fifth term as city councilor and one of the most popular of the city councilors in Boston, Pressley still had to formally introduce herself as a congressional candidate to the majority of Boston as well as half of the city of Cambridge, one-third of the town of Milton, and the cities of Somerville, Chelsea, and Everett, and the town of Randolph – all comprising the 7th Congressional District and all-too familiar for Capuano's campaign. Though they shared similar progressive values, Pressley had to distinguish herself from Capuano and tailor her message to appeal to white and minority constituencies alike using a toggling approach (Collet 2008). Stressing that voting as a progressive would not lead to progress, Pressley alleged that she could lead in new ways on account of her personal biography and unique angle of vision as a Black woman with a multi-track strategy whereby race and gender could be at once emphasized and de-emphasized by this historic-first candidate to mobilize any given constituency (Catanese 2018; Collet 2008).

By the time of her campaign launch event, WBUR released a poll that surveyed likely Democrats and showed Capuano with a 12 percentage point lead over Pressley districtwide (Bay State Banner 2018). However, this same poll indicated Pressley held an 11-point lead over Capuano in Boston (Bay State Banner 2018). But, six months into the campaign, Pressley faced the same question repeatedly: what sets her apart from Capuano? Capuano, a 66-year-old white man who had served the district for nearly 20 years, had the advantage of always referring to his congressional voting record, advocacy on progressive policies, and seniority in the US House of Representatives (Levenson 2018). When it came to policies and values, Pressley and Capuano arguably shared too similar of positions to strike a contrast that resonated with voters (Levenson 2018).

Both campaigns could debate the impact of votes versus advocacy, and small differences on positions like abortion and gun control; yet these differences were quite miniscule for the average voter to differentiate between two liberal, progressive candidates. Pressley, for example, explained on the campaign trail that she would advocate even more than Capuano had done to repeal the Hyde Amendment, which bans federal funding of most abortions (Levenson 2018). Capuano, however, quickly defended his record in opposition of this amendment and the long-time effort by Congress in attempt to repeal it, coupled by a supportive statement from a Connecticut congresswoman who underscored Capuano's leadership in protecting and advocating for women's rights (Levenson 2018). Since policy differences would not be the game changer in this campaign, it made it difficult for the average voter to distinguish between the two candidates based on policy preferences alone (Levenson 2018). So much so that on the eve of the September primary, *The New York Times* declared that the primary results will be a testament to political organizing and "whether voters in the racially diverse district prefer a black woman to the white male incumbent" (Herndon 2018).

So how did Pressley transition from lagging in the polls to a landslide victory in the primary election? Pressley worked hard at identifying with voters, emphasizing her personal biography as much as her policy stands. She had the instinctive ability to establish trust across racial and ethnic constituencies by virtue of her experiences with these communities, knowledge of their norms, languages, and cultural practices, including deep connections with key political actors (Collet 2008).

Over the course of her eight-month campaign, Pressley positioned herself as a change agent, reiterating her campaign slogan time and again – change can't wait – in reference to issues that not only women or people of color could relate to, but issues that impacted approximately 800,000 residents of the district regardless of gender or race. From underscoring this message in stump speeches to creating trending hashtags, the mantra "change can't wait" began to take hold and resonate with a new generation of supporters on social media platforms like twitter and made the campaign more accessible to wider audiences. While Capuano had the incumbency advantage, Pressley took the position that "a young and majority-minority district needed a fresh voice in Washington" (Scott 2018) and her personal life story afforded her credibility with the very demographic she aimed to represent. She shored up her commitment to fight for the underdog, declaring "I fundamentally believe that the people closest to the pain should be closest to the power" on the campaign trail (Scott 2018). Pressley's public visibility and social media presence raised the salience of multiple group identities – age, race, ethnicity, and gender – shared by the demographic majority in Boston. For this district, 20.8% were Black or African American residents and another 20.2% were Hispanic or Latino residents (U.S. Census Bureau 2018). Besides this, women were 52% of the district's population and a younger cohort between the ages of 20 and 49 (like Pressley) constituted 54% of all residents, and another 25% of all residents between the ages of 20 and 29 years old, were not of voting age or even born when Capuano first took office (Census Reporter).

Nevertheless, with Capuano's seniority and favorability in Congress, he secured several key endorsements from local leaders like Mayor Marty Walsh of Boston and former Massachusetts Governor Deval Patrick as well as such public figures as US House Representatives John Lewis of Georgia, and Maxine Waters of California plus the Congressional Black Caucus PAC (Herndon 2018; Seelye and Dezenski 2018). In March, Congressman Lewis described Capuano as a "champion" and "fierce advocate for those who have often been forgotten or left behind," crediting Capuano for his track record on issues including income inequality, civil rights, gun control, health care, affordable housing, gender pay equity, immigration, or transportation (Miller 2018a).

Even though Pressley did not have the Boston-bred pedigree, she did not let that become a disadvantage when enlisting endorsements. In fact, there had been a yearning for change in the city and the state of Massachusetts. It helped that the state's Attorney General Maura Healey recognized that shift in perspectives. Upon endorsing Pressley, Attorney General Healey described Pressley as someone who "really can speak to people and speak to issues that are real to people" (Catanese 2018). While many elected officials in the Massachusetts congressional delegation remained neutral during the race, like Senator Elizabeth Warren, Pressley did earn the endorsement from her city council peers including Councilors Annissa Essaibi George, Michelle Wu, and Kim Janey along with a contingent of state and local legislators in the Greater Boston region (DeCosta-Klipa 2018). Pressley received endorsements on the national level from Indivisible, an anti-Trump grassroots organization, and the National Women's Political Caucus (DeCosta-Klipa 2018). *The Boston Globe* and *The Boston Herald* typically share editorial board endorsements approximately a week prior to an election, and just before the primary, both outlets endorsed Pressley (DeCosta-Klipa 2018). *The Boston Globe* touted Pressley's "creative approach to reducing inequality is the mindset the district needs" as well as her ability to be "an advocate in touch with the everyday experiences of the district's residents, including the most vulnerable" (The Boston Globe Editorial Board 2018).

Roughly one month prior to the September primary election, Capuano maintained a 13-point lead based on a poll conducted by WBUR of 403 likely voters in the district over three days in late July (Seelye and Herndon 2018). Pollsters suggested Pressley could take the lead if she secured an increase in voter turnout among nonwhite as well as young voters (Thys 2018). Why was this important? The WBUR poll reported that while most likely voters did not think gender would impact vote choice, most registered voters believed race was a major or at least minor consideration that may influence vote choice (Thys 2018). While the 7th Congressional District is comprised of mostly nonwhite residents, this majority were not registered voters or among those who habitually turnout. The same WBUR poll reporting Capuano's lead also showed Pressley with a 23-point lead against Capuano among African American registered voters (Thys 2018). These poll results were significant. Upon reviewing voter turnout in 2014 – the immediate past mid-term election cycle – 65% of votes were cast by white voters despite white residents only accounting for 42% of the population (Koczela 2018). This known disparity between the demographic makeup of residents who were registered voters or voting eligible and those registered who cast votes afforded Pressley an opportunity. She would engage previously inactive voters or residents who had not yet registered but who were eligible to vote in the primary election. Pressley seized upon this opportunity as a veteran campaigner. She capitalized on her past experiences, connecting with voters as a candidate for city council and campaign volunteer working on US Senator John Kerry's reelection bid.

Building off her successful "100 Club" campaign strategy as a candidate for city council, she tapped other respected leaders to attract new voters, mobilize existing voters, and get out the vote across the district. By April, the campaign had activated more than 300 volunteers throughout the district (Daniel 2018). Among campaign volunteers included City Council President Damali Vidot of Chelsea, who also endorsed Pressley and hit the trail with over 40 volunteers on the campaign's first "Day of Action" in the early spring (Daniel 2018). She opined that "leadership like Ayanna's is what our country is missing at this critical moment in history" and called for "representatives that will lead with us, for us, and alongside us to help build the communities we deserve" (Daniel 2018). In addition to coalition building municipality by municipality within the district, Pressley also organized support among ethnic groups in the community. Recognizing the significant Haitian community in Boston, Pressley tapped Marie St. Fleur, a former Massachusetts State Representative and Haitian from the Boston neighborhood of Dorchester, to rally support among the Boston area Haitian community (Catanese 2018), a task St. Fleur had also done during Senator Kerry's campaign (Austin 2018). Given St. Fleur's credibility with Haitians, there was an ease in putting out a call to action within this group. During a weekend campaign stop, Pressley joined St. Fleur for a community event in which St. Fleur said: "When you leave here today, I ask for you to take [Pressley's] energy" (Catanese 2018). Events like this one and others energized racial and ethnic groups from neighborhoods, and communities that had traditionally or previously been overlooked by political actors.

Both the courtship, and active use, of free and paid ethnic media was a vitally important campaign resource. It tied those who otherwise may have remained out of reach due to language barriers to the campaign with minimal risk of alienating out-group voters (read: white) – for example, 37% of Boston residents speak a second language other than English at home. Pressley introduced herself to these prospective voters by expanding her campaign communications to include Spanish, Haitian, Chinese and African American media outlets – for example, the campaign ran media advertisements in Spanish on Telemundo and Univision that featured local Latino community members who voiced their support (Martinez 2018). Such a campaign communications strategy was clever, with Spanish being the most common language other than English spoken by Boston residents (Lima 2018). Josiane Martinez (2018), architect of the campaign's multilingual communications strategy, credits this campaign strategy with drawing "tens of thousands of new voters" to the primary election.

The breakdown of election results

The election attracted 73% more voters compared to the immediate past mid-term Congressional election for Massachusetts's 7th Congressional district seat in the US House of Representatives. When Capuano ran unopposed in 2014 only 61,725 votes were counted compared to 106,556 ballots cast in 2018 (Massachusetts Election Statistics). Consistent with national trends, the district experienced a major spike in turnout among Black voters, representing 23% of district turnout compared to only 4% of turnout in all other Massachusetts primaries, which also have significantly less Black residents and voters (Duggan 2019). Still, white voters constituted most voters in this diverse congressional district – specifically, 55% of first-time voters and 63% of habitual voters in the district were white in this election (Duggan 2019). While 50% of voters were first-time voters in the 7th Congressional District primary election, 24% of voters had not voted previously in any of the past five presidential primaries (Duggan 2019). According to analysis provided by WBUR, the 24% of first-time voters included 55% women and 66% between the ages of 18 to 44 years. Of the 66% between 18 and 44 years old, 34% were between the ages of 18–29 years old. Of this younger cohort, 20% were women, representing the most significant population among these new voters.

Conclusion

Ayanna Pressley has been making history ever since her first city council race in 2009. Pressley's win in 2018 broke yet another glass ceiling as she became the first Black woman from Massachusetts elected to the US Congress, and the first woman and person of color to represent 7th Congressional District. Pressley's win symbolizes another step forward for women and people of color in Massachusetts. While the way in which Pressley's public visibility raised the salience of group identities – age, race, ethnicity, and gender – is significant and meaningful, it is equally important to recognize that historic first candidates like herself want members of their home district to recognize them as one of them based on policy interests, not simply their physical characteristics.

Recalling the WBUR interview at the start of the campaign when Capuano said he could not be a woman of color, Pressley made it clear to potential voters sitting in pews at the Old South Meeting House in Boston, "I am Black, and I am a woman. And I embrace both of those facts. But to suggest that the only difference is my race, and my gender is wrong and toxic. And the voters of the 7th Congressional District aren't buying it. The issues I have worked on my entire life transcend my identity" (Dezenski and Griffiths 2018). In another interview during the campaign, Pressley shared: "I've never asked anyone to vote for me because I'm black and a woman. I'm asking people to consider me because I'm pledging to be a vote, a voice, and a partner. I'm asking people to vote for me because I'm an activist leader and a problem solver" (Feller 2018). Though Pressley did not base her campaign solely on identity politics, it was a visible contrast between her and her opponent, allowing residents especially women, young adults, and Black residents to see someone for the first time "stand for" them on the campaign trail. Pressley reminded voters that "change can't wait" and this slogan should not be overlooked or forgotten.

As the chant "change can't wait" roared through the crowd the night of the general election on November 6, 2018, Pressley stood with poise and ease at the podium. In her acceptance speech, Pressley reflected on the evening – a historic victory not only for herself but women candidates across Massachusetts and the country. As she addressed what she described as her "broad and diverse coalition of voters, disrupters, believers, resisters, persisters, activists, and agitators" she emphatically stated she knew "for a fact none of us ran to make history. We ran to make change." Pressley joins women of color elected to the US House of Representatives in 2018 who have promised to uphold an agenda to fight for social and economic justice (Perry 2019). This landmark victory demonstrates that historic-first candidates can achieve representation under conditions that may otherwise discourage their candidacy (read: incumbency advantage).

By focusing on identity, making gender and race salient considerations, Pressley increased the likelihood that such categories of difference would become important references for electoral judgments. But is that all that led to a successful campaign? The short answer is no. Analyzing this candidate-centered campaign through an intersectional lens ensures a more complete picture of the myriad of dynamics and electioneering at play, including but not limited to, identity-based appeals and a meld of mobilization with coalition-building. Looking critically and with complexity at the role of race and gender in the electoral process is necessary to explore alternative ways of thinking about strategy for candidates, voters, and campaigns in cities like Boston that have become incredibly diverse. So, how did she achieve such a historic victory? Like her campaign strategy since becoming a Boston city councilor in 2009, Pressley forged a multiracial grassroots coalition that should remind readers of Shirley Chisholm's historic-first candidacies – specifically, her becoming the first Black woman elected to the US Congress in 1968 from New York.

Chisholm brought formerly inactive people (those who previously saw no connection between campaigns and their own lives) into the electoral process (Simien 2015). She established a strong mutual relationship with dispossessed subgroups from historically disadvantaged populations located within her district, as did Pressley, who similarly reached vulnerable populations who had been unjustly excluded from and stigmatized by the political process (Simien 2015). Growing up, Pressley witnessed the leadership of US Congresswoman Chisholm and felt inspired by her commitment to fighting injustice while lifting the voices of historically marginalized Americans. Little did Pressley know that years later she, too, would successfully become a member of the US Congress and, in fact, work from the same office once occupied by Chisholm (Ruiz-Grossman 2018).

Fortunately for Pressley, descriptive and symbolic representation mattered as much as substantive representation for her constituents. Pressley like Capuano could claim that in addition to exemplary public service on issues that disproportionately affect women and racial minorities – abortion and gun control – she offered an alternative public image of political leadership. Context mattered insofar as

Pressley's own perception of her constituency and the votes she'd likely secure offered her a strategic advantage and influenced her ground game. The demographic majority's interest in such domestic policy issues – substance abuse disorders, mass incarceration, and sexual assault – made it possible for Pressley to establish a strong mutual relationship with dispossessed subgroup members of her home district, revitalize democracy, and strengthen its legitimacy by moving beyond party and ideology to highlight differences between her and her opponent, Capuano, with a key contextual factor being the demographic makeup of the district (Collet 2008; Dovi 2002).

Holding true to her policy preferences, she was able to complicate what was thought to be their "limited policy differences" as both progressive members of the same political party by focusing on her identity as a woman of color. Her cumulative life experiences differed remarkably from her opponent, and more closely resembled that of local constituents. From a policy perspective, she stood to give prominence to issues that otherwise would have either been overlooked or ignored by a progressive white, male incumbent of the same political party. Such identity markers as age, race, and gender alongside lived experience informed her policy perspective, and signaled differences between her and the incumbent. On this basis, Pressley could win election.

Although it has sparked much debate, intersectionality research has, to its credit, brought to the fore intersectional actors and generated a deeper appreciation for historic-first candidates like Pressley and how their identities inform campaigns. The role that race and gender play in mobilizing diverse electorates is an understudied facet of American elections (as are historic-first candidacies). A more comprehensive study of American political behavior would include support for historic firsts. The utility of such an approach cannot be overstated, given that it affords those who study campaigns and elections a remarkable opportunity to expand the theoretical capacity of intersectionality research by studying the role of identities (plural) in determining political behaviors, and electoral outcomes as shown here.

Note

1. This 2015 data comes from the Boston Planning and Development Agency.

Disclosure statement

No potential conflict of interest was reported by the author(s).

ORCID

Evelyn M. Simien http://orcid.org/0000-0003-3101-5654

References

Austin, Sharon D. Wright. 2018. *The Caribbeanization of Black Politics*. Albany: SUNY Press.

Bay State Banner. 2018. "Pressley Launches Bid for Congressional Seat." February 21. https://www.baystatebanner.com/2018/02/21/pressley-launches-bid-for-congressional-seat/

Beth Reingold, ed. 2008. *Legislative Women: Getting Elected, Getting Ahead*. Boulder, CO: Lynne Rienner.

Beth, Reingold, Kerry L Haynie, and Kirsten Widner. 2021. *Race, Gender, and Political Representation: Toward a More Intersectional Approach*. New York, NY: Oxford University Press.

The Boston Globe Editorial Board. 2018. "Endorsement: Democrats Should Choose Ayanna Pressley for the Seventh District." *The Boston Globe*, August 26. https://www.bostonglobe.com/opinion/editorials/2018/08/25/endorsement-democrats-should-choose-ayanna-pressley-for-seventhdistrict/E5YhYoFCXesjJU2ThByDaK/story.html

BPS Communications Office. 2019. "Boston Public Schools at a Glance." www.bostonpublicschools.org

Brian, Parkinson, Agneta H Fischer, and Antony SR. Manstead. 2005. *Emotion in Social Relations: Cultural, Group, and Interpersonal Processes*. New York: Psychology Press.

Brown, Nadia E. 2014. *Sisters in the Statehouse*. New York: Oxford University Press.

Brown, Nadia E., and Erin C. Cassesse. 2020. "The Role of Gender in the 2018 Midterm Elections." *Political Research Quarterly* 73 (4):923–25. doi:10.1177/1065912920948638.

Brown, Nadia E., and Danielle Casarez Lemi. 2021. *Sister Style: The Politics of Appearance for Black Women Political Elites*. New York: Oxford University Press.

Burge, Camille D. 2020. "Introduction to Dialogues: Black Affective Experiences in Politics." *Politics, Groups, and Identities* 8 (2):390–95. doi:10.1080/21565503.2020.1757804.

Cartwright, Nancy. 2006. "Well-Ordered Science: Evidence for Use." *Philosophy of Science* 73 (5):981–90. December doi:10.1086/518803.

Castle, Jeremiah J. Shannon Jenkins, Candice D Ortbals, Lori Poloni-Staudinger, and J Cherie Strachan. 2020. "The Effect of the #metoo Movement on Political Engagement and Ambition in 2018." *Political Research Quarterly* 73 (4): 926–41.

Catanese, David. 2018. "Ayanna Pressley's Fierce Urgency of Now." *U.S News & World Report*, August 10. https://www.usnews.com/news/the-report/articles/2018-08-10/ayanna-pressleys-fierce-urgency-of-now

Collet, Christian. 2008. "Minority Candidates, Alternative Media, and Multiethnic America: Deracialization or Toggling?" *Perspectives on Politics* 6 (4):707–28. doi:10.1017/S1537592708081875.

Crasnow, Sharon. 2011. "Evidence for Use: Causal Pluralism and the Role of Case Studies in Political Science Research." *Philosophy of Social Science* 41 (1):26–49. doi:10.1177/0048393110387884.

Daniel, Seth. 2018. "Council President Endorses Pressley, Capuano Touts Fundraising." *Chelsea Record*, April 6. http://chelsearecord.com/2018/04/06/council-president-endorses-pressleycapuano-touts-fundraising/

DeCosta-Klipa, Nik. 2018. "Everything You Need to Know about Ayanna Pressley." August 31. Boston.com. https://www.boston.com/news/politics/2018/08/31/ayanna-pressley-massachusetts-primary

Dezenski, Lauren. 2018. "CBC Endorses Capuano in Massachusetts Democratic Primary." *Politico*, May 18. https://www.politico.com/story/2018/05/18/michael-capuano-endorsed-cbc-597659

Dezenski, Lauren, and Brett D. Griffiths. 2018. "Pressley's Counterpoint- UMass Boston Shakeup." *Politico*, May 22.

Dittmar, Kelly 2017. "Finding Gender in Election 2016: Lessons from Presidential Gender Watch." New Brunswick: Center for American Women and Politics, Eagleton Institute of Politics, Rutgers, the State University of New Jersey, with the Barbara Lee Family Foundation.

Dovi, Suzanne. 2002. "Preferable Descriptive Representatives: Will Just Any Woman, Black, or Latino Do?." *The American Political Science Review* 96 (December): 745–54.

Duggan, Maeve. 2019. "24 Percent of 7th District Primary Voters Had Not Voted in Previous 5 Primaries." WBUR, January 4. https://www.wbur.org/news/2019/01/04/ayanna-pressley-first-time-voter-file-analysis

Feller, Madison. 2018. "Ayanna Pressley Already Broke a Double Glass Ceiling. Now, She's Running for Congress." *Elle*, August 29. https://www.elle.com/culture/career-politics/a22854225/ayanna-pressley-massachusetts-congress-city-council-interview/

Finn, Christopher, and Jack Glaser. 2010. "Voter Affect and the 2008 Presidential Election: Hope and Race Mattered." *Analyses of Social Issues and Public Policy* 10 (1): 263–75.

Gavin Brent Sullivan, ed. 2014. *Understanding Collective Pride and Group Identity*. New York: Routledge.

Herndon, Astead W. 2018. "Mike Capuano Is in the Political Fight of His Life." *The New York Times*, September 3. https://www.nytimes.com/2018/09/03/us/politics/capuano-massachusetts-primary.html

Irons, Meghan E., Shelley Murphy, and Jenna Russell. 2014. "History Rolled in on a Yellow School Bus." *The Boston Globe*, September 6. https://www.bostonglobe.com/metro/2014/09/06/boston-busing-crisis-years-later/DS35nsuqp0yh8f1q9aRQUL/story.html

Koczela, Steve. 2018. "Though the 7th District Is Minority-Majority, Most of Its Voters are White." WBUR, February 9. https://www.wbur.org/news/2018/02/09/capuano-pressley-demographics&xid=17259,15700022,15700186,15700191,15700248,15700253

Lazarus, Richard S. 1991. *Emotion and Adaptation*. New York: Oxford University Press.

Levenson, Michael, and Stephanie Ebbert. 2018. "The Life and Rise of Ayanna Pressley." *The Boston Globe*, September 8. https://www.bostonglobe.com/metro/2018/09/08/the-life-and-rise-ayanna-pressley/pqdppGFPoZPSEwo3Ko23BJ/story.html?event=event12

Levenson, Michael. 2018. "Michael Capuano and Ayanna Pressley: What's the Difference?" *The Boston Globe*, July 22. https://www.bostonglobe.com/metro/2018/07/22/capuano-pressley-grapple-with-same-question-what-makes-you-different/64Uffu4cVVpWZVMYwH4jwL/story.html

Levine, Peter, Benjamin Foreman, and Laura Bliss. 2019. "MassForward: Advancing Democratic Innovation and Electoral Reform in Massachusetts." MassINC, November. https://www.tbf.org/-/media/tbf/reports-and-covers/2019/massforward-report-20191113.pdf?la=en

Lima, Alvaro. 2018. "Boston by the Numbers 2018." Boston Planning and Development Agency. September. http://www.bostonplans.org/getattachment/3e8bfacf-27c1-4b55-adee-29c5d79f4a38

López, Ian Haney. 2015. *Dog Whistle Politics*. New York: Oxford University Press.

Mansbridge, Jane. 1999. "Should Blacks Represent Blacks and Women Represent Women? a Contingent "Yes." *The Journal of Politics* 61 (3): 628–57.

Marcus, George E, W Russell Neuman, and Michael MacKuen. 2000. *Affective Intelligence and Political Judgment*. Chicago: University of Chicago Press.

Martinez, Josiane. 2018. "How Ayanna Pressley Won." WBUR, September 7. https://www.wbur.org/cognoscenti/2018/09/07/ayanna-pressley-campaign-strategy-josiane-martinez

McDonald, Maura, Rachel Porter, and Sarah A. Treul. 2020. "Running as a Woman? Candidate Presentation in the 2018 Midterms." *Political Research Quarterly* 73 (4):967–87. doi:10.1177/1065912920915787.

Medenica, Vladimir E., and Matthew Fowler. 2020. "The Intersectional Effects of Diverse Elections on Validated Turnout in the 2018 Midterm Elections." *Political Research Quarterly* 73 (4):988–1003. doi:10.1177/1065912920945781.

Miller, Joshua. 2018a. "Civil Rights Hero John Lewis Endorses Mike Capuano." *The Boston Globe*, March 6. https://www.bostonglobe.com/metro/2018/03/06/civil-rights-hero-john-lewis-endorses-mike-capuano/ksHpI49c8O5IR7FvY02PyL/story.html

Miller, Joshua. 2018b. "Race, Gender Put Forward as Key Issues in Boston Congressional Race." *The Boston Globe*, February 1. https://www.bostonglobe.com/metro/2018/02/01/race-gender-put-forward-key-issues-boston-congressional-race/v6hbmp1cWXFJkgXu3nnj0J/story.html

Muñoz, Ana Patricia, Marlene Kim, Mariko Chang, Regine O. Jackson, Darrick Hamilton, and William A. Darity Jr. 2015. "The Color of Wealth in Boston: A Joint Publication with Duke University and the New School." Boston, MA: Federal Reserve Bank of Boston.

Nunnally, Shayla C. 2012. *Trust in Black America: Race, Discrimination, and Politics*. New York: New York University Press.

Perry, Andre M. 2019. "Black Women are Looking Forward to the 2020 Elections." Brookings Institute, January 10. https://www.brookings.edu/research/black-women-are-looking-forward-to-the-2020-elections/

Phillips, Anne. 1995. *The Politics of Presence*. New York: Clarendon Press.

Phoenix, Davin L. 2020. *The Anger Gap: How Race Shapes Emotion in Politics*. Cambridge, MA: Cambridge University Press.

Pindell, James. 2018. "Should Ocasio-Cortez's Upset Have Michael Capuano Worried?" *The Boston Globe*, June 27. http://www.bostonglobe.com/metro/2018/06/27/after-alexandria-ocasio-cortez-victory-should-mike-capuanoworried/7XlVek7aU2qeuguJZxNfPL/story.html?p1=Article_Related_Box_Article

Pitkin, Hanna Fenichel. 1967. *The Concept of Representation*. Berkeley and Los Angeles, CA: University of California Press.

Ruiz-Grossman, Sarah. 2018. "Ayanna Pressley Will Get the Old Office of Shirley Chisholm, First Black Congresswoman." *Huffington Post*, December 24. https://www.huffpost.com/entry/ayanna-pressley-same-office-shirley-chisholm_n_5c1a94a4e4b0ce5184b9c243?guccounter=1

Salsberg, Bob. 2016. "Gains in Diversity Slow in Massachusetts Politics." *Metrowest Daily News*, June 19. https://www.metrowestdailynews.com/news/20160619/gains-in-diversity-slow-in-massachusetts-politics.

Schuster, Luc, and Peter Ciurczak. 2018. "Boston's More Diverse Than You May Realize." *Boston Indicators*, September 28. https://www.bostonindicators.org/article-pages/2018/september/boston-diversity

Scott, Eugene. 2018. "Ayanna Pressley's Victory Proves It Matters to Democratic Primary Voters 'Who Those Democrats Are." *The Washington Post*, September 5. https://www.washingtonpost.com/politics/2018/09/05/ayanna-pressleys-victory-proves-it-matters-democratic-primary-voters-who-those-democrats-are/

Seelye, Katharine Q. and Astead W. Herndon. 2018. "Ayanna Pressley Seeks Her Political Moment in a Changing Boston." *The New York Times*, September 1. https://www.nytimes.com/2018/09/01/us/politics/ayanna-pressley-massachusetts.html

Simien, Evelyn M. 2015. *Historic Firsts: How Symbolic Empowerment Changes U.S. Politics*. New York: Oxford University Press.

Simien, Evelyn M., and Sarah Cote Hampson. 2017. "Hillary Clinton and the Women Who Supported Her: Emotional Attachments and the 2008 Democratic Presidential Primary." *DuBois Review: Social Science Research on Race* 14 (1): 93–116.

Simien, Evelyn M., and Sarah Cote Hampson. 2020. "Black Votes Count, but Do They Matter? Symbolic Empowerment and the Jackson-Obama Mobilizing Effect on Gender and Age Cohorts." *American Politics Research* 48 (6):725–37. doi:10.1177/1532673X19898665.

Simien, Evelyn M., ed. 2022. *Historic Firsts in U.S. Elections.* New York: Routledge.

Tate, Katherine. 2001. "The Political Representation of Black in Congress: Does Race Matter?" *Legislative Studies Quarterly* 26 (4):623–38. doi:10.2307/440272.

Tate, Katherine. 2003. *Black Faces in the Mirror: African Americans and Their Representatives in the U.S. Congress.* Princeton, NJ: Princeton University Press.

Terkildsen, Nayda, and David F. Damore. 1999. "The Dynamics of Racialized Media Coverage in Congressional Elections." *Journal of Politics* 61 (3):680–99. doi:10.2307/2647823.

Thys, Fred. 2010. "After Losing a House Seat, Someone Must Go." WBUR. December 22. https://www.wbur.org/news/2010/12/22/ma-loses-a-seat

Thys, Fred. 2018. "WBUR Poll: Capuano Maintains 13-Point Lead Over Pressley." WBUR, August 2. https://www.wbur.org/news/2018/08/02/wbur-poll-capuano-pressley-7th-district

U.S. Census Bureau. 2018. "Hispanic or Latino Origin by Race American Community Survey 1-year estimates." https://censusreporter.org

Young, Iris Marion. 2000. *Inclusion and Democracy.* New York: Oxford University Press.

Legislating as Your Full Self: Queer Women of Color in US State Legislatures

Hanna K. Brant and Jordan Butcher

ABSTRACT

While recent gains in diversity in US state legislatures are notable, state legislatures remain disproportionately white and male. In this critical perspective piece, we examine the gains in representation and entrance to office of a group legislators who comprise an important intersection of identity in American politics: queer women of color. We find that the 30 Democratic queer women of color currently in office replaced fellow Democrats in all but four instances and defeated an incumbent in 13 elections. By providing an overview of these legislators, this piece contributes toward advancing a more representative understanding of the diversity of women in elective office. In doing so, we strive to pivot the center on queer women of color political elites and note several avenues for future research.

"Representation matters. I understand that when you show up as your full self in all the identities that you embody, you're able to legislate from a place that's more fully representative of all people."

- Florida State Representative Michele Rayner (Ogles 2021)

"I'm always conscious of the fact that I am intersectional. I'm Black, I'm a woman and I'm a same gender-loving woman, I have to look at it through all of those lenses because that's who I am."

- Nevada State Senator Pat Spearman (Mueller and Carlderon 2021)

"Part of what I realize that my responsibility is not just legislating for the moment but also making sure I'm opening a door and I'm holding that door open for the next trans woman of color to step into office."

-Kansas State Representative Stephanie Byers (McShane 2021)

"I'm going to be unapologetically Black, I'm going to be unapologetically queer, and I'm going to be unapologetically young."

- Rhode Island State Senator Tiara Mack (Compton 2020)

Representative Rayner and Senator Mack were first elected in November 2020 and are currently the only out lesbian Black women serving in their state's legislature. Senator Spearman has been in her current position since 2012 and is one of three queer women of color currently serving in Nevada. Upon assuming office in January 2021, Representative Byers became the first out transgender Indigenous elected official in the United States. Taken together, the words of these legislators embody the experience of queer women of color and how intersecting identities can influence elected officials' behavior and experience in office (Bratton, Haynie, and Reingold 2007; Brown 2014).

At the beginning of the 2022 legislative session there were 30 queer women of color serving across 19 state legislatures. In this piece, we use "queer" as an umbrella term for the LGBTQ+ community and "women of color" to refer to Latinas, Black women, Asian women, and Indigenous women (Bejarano and Smooth 2022; Matos, Greene, and Sanbonmatsu 2021).[1] Fifteen legislators are Black/African American, 11 are Latinx/Hispanic, two are multiracial, and two legislators are Indigenous/Native American (see Table 1 for more information). A majority of the legislators identify as lesbian (18), while eight identify as queer, three as bisexual, and one legislator identifies as pansexual.

Of these 30 legislators, half have assumed office since 2020. This increase in representation is no small feat: queer women of color now comprise nearly 16% of the 186 LGBTQ+ state legislators (Victory Institute) and 5% of the 624 women of color state legislators currently in office (Center for American Women and Politics).[2] For comparison, there are only 2,308 female state legislators out of the 7,383 legislators nationwide. Several of these women are historical firsts in their position. While many are planning to seek reelection, a few have recently announced candidacies for other offices.

Queer women of color are making greater strides in state legislatures compared to other elected offices (Carroll and Sanbonmatsu 2013; Shah, Scott, and Juenke 2019).[3] To put the current state of representation into perspective: there are no queer women of color in governorships or other statewide positions (e.g. attorney general, lieutenant governor), there is one queer women of color in Congress (Democratic Representative Sharice Davids of Kansas), two queer women of color currently serve as mayors (Lori Lightfoot of Chicago, IL and Liz Ordiales of Hiawassee, GA), and 12 queer women of color occupy judicial seats (Victory Institute). The next comparable level of office in the United States that queer women of color are making strides in are local positions (Crowder-Meyer, Gadarian, and Trounstine 2015), such as city council and school board, with the Victory Institute identifying 44 queer women of color in these positions across the country.[4]

Queer women of color comprise an important intersection of identity in American politics due to race, ethnicity, sex, sexual orientation, and gender identity (Crenshaw 1991). Previous research has explored the influence of identity by analyzing candidate emergence (Pettey 2018; Pyeatt and Yanus 2021; Sanbonmatsu 2015a; Shah, Scott, and Juenke 2019; Silva and Skully 2019), the legislative behavior of women (Hogan 2008; Osborn 2012; Schmitt and Brant 2019; Swift and VanderMolen 2021; Thomas and Welch 1991), the intersection of race and gender for candidate emergence and legislative behavior (Bejarano and Smooth 2022; Bratton and Haynie 1999; Brown 2014; Fraga et al. 2007; Orey et al. 2007; Reingold, Widner, and Harmon 2020; Smooth 2011), and LGBTQ+ state legislators (Haider-Markel 2010, 2007; Herrick 2009; Perry, Manley, and Burgess 2017). Yet, a dearth of studies center queer women of color through an intersectional lens, perhaps in large part, due to queer women's underrepresentation in elective office more broadly.

However, "pivoting the center" (Aptheker 1989; Brown 1989) on women in politics to queer women of color contributes a more representative understanding of the diversity and experiences of women in elective office and has important implications for the intersectional role of descriptive representation in American politics (Uhlaner and Scola 2016; Mansbridge 1999; Montoya et al. 2021). As noted above, compared to other elected positions, the number of queer women of color is increasing in state legislatures. In the broader context of elective office, an analysis of state legislatures is important because state legislatures serve as a pipeline to higher office (Sanbonmatsu, Carroll, and Walsh 2009; Sanbonmatsu 2015b). Put another way, those who serve in the state legislature often use their position as a stepping-stone for serving in Congress or a statewide position. Therefore, an analysis of the representation of queer women of color in state legislatures may provide a glimpse into the future of women's representation in higher office.

To contribute to an intersectional understanding of women's representation in American politics, we provide a descriptive overview of the entrance of queer women of color to state legislative office and note several avenues for future research. In addition to discussing the states that these women are from, we share information on the women who serve and their path to office. Specifically, we provide an overview of their backgrounds, occupation, and how their experiences led them to running for state office.

Table 1. Queer Women of Color in State Legislatures, 2022.

State	Legislator (District)	Race and Sexual Orientation	Lower Chamber	Year Elected	Defeated Incumbent	Previous Elected Experience
California	Sabrina Cervantes (60)	Latinx/Hispanic; lesbian	✓	2016	✓	
California	Susan Talamantes Eggman[b, d] (5)	Latinx/Hispanic; lesbian		2020		✓
Colorado	Leslie Herod [d] (8)	Black; lesbian	✓	2017		✓
Colorado	Sonya Jacquez Lewis (17)	Latinx/Hispanic; lesbian		2020		
Delaware	Marie Pinkney (13)	Black; lesbian	✓	2020	✓*	
Florida	Michele Rayner [c] (70)	Black; lesbian		2020		
Georgia	Kim Jackson (41)	Black; lesbian	✓	2020		
Georgia	Park Cannon [b, c, d, e] (58)	Black; queer	✓	2015		
Georgia	Renitta Shannon [c] (84)	Black; bisexual	✓	2016	✓*	
Kansas	Susan Ruiz [d] (23)	Latinx/Hispanic; lesbian	✓	2019	✓	
Kansas	Stephanie Byers (86)[f]	Indigenous/Native American; lesbian	✓	2020		
Kentucky	Keturah Herron [c, d, e] (42)	Black; queer		2022		
Maryland	Mary Washington [c, d, e] (43)	Black; lesbian	✓	2019	✓*	✓
Minnesota	Athena Hollins (66B)	Multiracial; queer	✓	2020	✓*	
Minnesota	Heather Keeler (4A)	Indigenous/Native American; lesbian	✓	2020		
Missouri	Ashley Manlove [c, d, e] (26)	Black; lesbian	✓	2018		
Nevada	Cecelia González [d] (16)	Multiracial; bisexual		2020		
Nevada	Dallas Harris[a, c] (11)	Black; lesbian		2018		
Nevada	Pat Spearman (1)	Black; lesbian		2012	✓*	
New Mexico	Brittney Barreras [c] (12)	Latinx/Hispanic; queer	✓	2021	✓*	
New York	Jessica González-Rojas (34)	Latinx/Hispanic; queer	✓	2020	✓*	
North Carolina	Vernetta Alston [a, c, d, e] (29)	Black; lesbian	✓	2020		✓
Rhode Island	Tiara Mack [c] (6)	Black; lesbian		2021	✓*	
Texas	Celia Israel [c] (50)	Latinx/Hispanic; lesbian	✓	2015		
Texas	Jessica González [c] (104)	Latinx/Hispanic; lesbian	✓	2019	✓*	
Texas	Mary González [c] (75)	Latinx/Hispanic; pansexual	✓	2012		
Washington	Emily Randall [d] (26)	Latinx/Hispanic; queer		2018		
Washington	Kirsten Harris-Talley [c] (37-2)	Black; queer	✓	2020	✓	✓
West Virginia	Danielle Walker [d] (51)	Black; queer	✓	2018		
Wisconsin	Marisabel Cabrera (9)	Latinx/Hispanic; bisexual	✓	2018	✓*	

Information on legislators derived from the Victory Institute, Ballotpedia, and personal websites.
[a] Originally appointed to seat and then successfully ran for full term (Dallas Harris NV-11; Vernetta Alston NC-29).
[b] Predecessor was also a queer woman. Two instances: Susan Talamantes Eggman replaced Cathleen Galgiani, a white lesbian. Park Cannon replaced Simone Bell, a Black lesbian.
[c] Predecessor was also a legislator of color (14 instances).
[d] Predecessor was also a woman (10 instances).
[e] Predecessor was also woman of color (4 instances).
[f] Legislator identifies as a transgender woman. One legislator: Stephanie Byers.
✓*: Defeated co-partisan incumbent. With the exception of Brittney Barreras (NM-12), who defeated her co-partisan incumbent in the general election who ran as a write-in candidate, all other incumbent co-partisans defeated in primary elections. Legislators without ✓ ran for current position in an open-seat race. Legislators with only ✓ and no * defeated an incumbent of the opposing party.

Increasing representation

We utilize information from the Victory Institute to identify queer women of color serving in state legislatures in 2022. The Victory Institute relies on the public, self-identification by individuals as part of the LGBTQ+ community to categorize candidates and officials.[5] The Victory Institute notes individuals' sexual orientation (e.g., gay, lesbian, bisexual, queer, asexual), gender identity (e.g., cisgender man or woman, transgender man or woman, genderqueer, nonbinary), race, and partisan affiliation. To the best of our knowledge, the Victory Institute provides the most comprehensive data available on LGBTQ+ candidates and elected officials across multiple levels of government in the United States. We utilize legislators' Ballotpedia pages, official legislative profiles, and personal websites to collect information on their background, including occupation, previous political experience, and election results.

Table 1 presents an overview of the current queer women of color who are serving, their political experience, and whether they challenged an incumbent. Most of these legislators represent urban districts including, at least in part, a major city.[6] Additionally, most represent a majority-minority district (22), while eight represent a district with a majority of white voters (Phillips 2021; Shah, Scott, and Juenke 2019).[7] Of the 19 states queer women of color represent, only five have term limits, which constitutes eight of the 30 legislators (Pettey 2018).[8]

The 30 queer women of color make up only a small percentage of the 7,383 state legislators and come from a select number of states. Texas, Georgia, and Nevada each have three queer women of color currently in office, while California, Colorado, Kansas, Minnesota, and Washington each have two. There are 11 additional states with only one queer woman of color serving. All of the women currently serving are members of the Democratic Party, and in all but four instances, replaced co-partisans. Additionally, there is a great deal of overlap in the race of new legislators and their predecessors (Clark 2019; Hamm and Martorano Miller 2018).

In 14 instances the predecessor was a legislator of color, in 10 the predecessor was also a woman, and in four cases the predecessor was also a woman of color. In two instances the predecessor was also a queer woman: Susan Talamantes Eggman replaced Cathleen Galgiani, a white lesbian, and Park Cannon replaced Simone Bell, a Black lesbian. Five legislators have prior political experience; however, many have experience in community advocacy organizations related to the LGBTQ+ community and/or their racial or ethnic identity (Bejarano and Smooth 2022). Thirteen defeated an incumbent during either the primary or general election (Pettey 2018; Pyeatt and Yanus 2021). In the 2020 election, eight women did not have a general election challenger and 20 won election with more than 65% of the vote. Only two of the women currently in office were originally appointed, but later won election for a full term.[9] In the proceeding sections, we provide a more descriptive overview of the legislators' backgrounds and entrance to office by state.

States driving change

Nevada, Texas, and Georgia have the most queer women of color currently serving at three members in each state.[10] These states also have higher minority populations, and, in fact, Texas and Nevada are among the top ten states with the most minority lawmakers (National Conference of State Legislatures).[11] Furthermore, Nevada is the only legislature where women hold the majority of seats, making up 60% of the legislature as of 2021 (Haynes and Butcher 2021). Not only do these three states have multiple queer women of color in office, but also the longest serving queer women of color: in 2012, Mary González was elected to the Texas House and Pat Spearman to the Nevada Senate.

Nevada

There are five LGBTQ+ legislators in Nevada. The three queer women of color we highlight below make up 60% of the LGBTQ+ Nevada legislators while the remaining two are white cisgender women. Elected in 2012, Pat Spearman was the first out lesbian to serve in the Nevada legislature. Spearman is a decorated Army veteran and former pastor. She has served multiple leadership roles during her time in the state Senate, including Chair of Commerce and Labor Committee, Vice-Chair of Health and Human Services, and Chief Majority Whip. Facing term limits in Nevada, Spearman is currently in her final term in the Senate and is running for the Mayor of Las Vegas.

In 2018, Dallas Harris was appointed to the Nevada State Senate. Following her appointment, she secured her seat in 2020 with 58% of the vote. When she entered office, Harris was one of four openly LGBTQ+ members in the legislature. Harris, who is an attorney, has worked at a number of government and nonprofit organizations.

The most recent addition to the Nevada legislature is Representative Cecelia González, who in 2020 became the first openly LBGTQ+ Asian legislator. As a candidate, González centered her campaign around her Thai-Mexican American heritage. She beat her Republican challenger with 65% of the vote. Prior to becoming a lawmaker, she was an educator and activist who focused heavily on issues relating to women, education, and criminal justice.

Texas

Similar to Nevada, all six LGBTQ+ legislators in Texas are women: three legislators are queer women of color and three are white cisgender women. Mary González, who is pansexual, is one of the longest serving members currently in office, having first been elected to the Texas House of Representatives in 2012. Representative González serves as the chair of the Texas House LGBTQ+ Caucus. González is currently planning to seek reelection, and if reelected, would become the longest serving queer woman of color state legislator.[12]

Representative Celia Israel was first elected in 2014 during a special election but will not be seeking reelection in 2022. Instead, Israel is running for the mayor of Austin because the incumbent is terming out of office.[13] Prior to serving in elected office, Israel worked for former Governor Ann Richards.

The most recently elected queer woman of color from Texas is attorney Jessica González, who in 2018 defeated the incumbent, Roberto Alonzo, in the Democratic primary election. González was a former staffer in the US House of Representatives and clerk with the Department of Justice. González serves as the Vice-Chair of the LGBTQ+ Caucus and the Elections Committee.

Georgia

Kim Jackson, Renitta Shannon, and Park Cannon all represent the state of Georgia. What is of interest is the electoral success of these women. In the 2020 election, incumbents in the lower chamber, Shannon and Cannon, won with 100% of the vote as they faced no challengers. Newcomer, Senator Kim Jackson, won with nearly 80% of the vote as a first-time candidate. Together, these legislators account for three of the seven out LGBTQ+ legislators in Georgia. The remaining four legislators include two cisgender men of color, one white cisgender man, and one white cisgender woman.

Cannon, who was elected in a 2015 special election, has been in office the longest. Being Black and fluent in Spanish, Representative Cannon has long focused on social issues and advocacy. Cannon's history of advocacy brought her to work closely with former Representative Simone Bell, who personally asked Cannon to pursue the seat that Bell would be vacating (Crowder-Meyer 2013; Dittmar 2015a). It is worth noting that both Bell and Cannon are queer women of color, which suggests the potential for district-specific effects (see Clark 2019).

Renitta Shannon, who represents Assembly District 84, has been in office since 2016 and recently announced her candidacy for Lieutenant Governor of Georgia. The newest member from Georgia is Senator Kim Jackson, who was the first openly queer senator in the state. Jackson, who is an ordained minister, has focused her agenda on social justice and social welfare.

There are five states that each have two queer women of color serving: California, Colorado, Kansas, Minnesota, and Washington. There are more Democratic elected lawmakers in each of these states, as well as higher numbers of women and minorities. Washington and Colorado both make the top ten list for most female lawmakers (National Conference of State Legislatures). Interestingly, California, Colorado, and Washington each currently have eight out lawmakers serving in the state legislature (Victory Institute). While Kansas does not have a high number of women or minority lawmakers, it is the only state represented by a queer woman of color in Congress, Sharice Davids (D-03). Minnesota also does not rank among the top states for women and minorities members but is one of a handful of states with a female Speaker of the House.

California

Currently, two queer women of color serve in the California legislature. Senator Susan Talamantes Eggman, an Army veteran and former social work professor, has centered her policy agenda on healthcare, veterans, and benefitting her local community. Prior to serving in the state legislature, Eggman served as the only openly queer member of the City Council of Stockton. She then secured a seat in the state Assembly in 2012, where she served until her Senate election in 2020. As noted above, Eggman's predecessor was Cathleen Galgiani, who is also a queer woman.

Elected in 2016, Sabrina Cervantes is currently serving her second term in the General Assembly. Prior to becoming a representative, Cervantes worked to increase voter turnout as the Director of the California Voter Registration Project. She currently serves as the chair of the Jobs, Economic Development, and Economy Committee. Cervantes is also the first Latina millennial representative in the California Assembly.

Colorado

State Representative Leslie Herod won the 2020 election with 100% of the vote and no challengers. In the 2016 election, Herod did face a challenger and won with more than 80% of the vote. Before serving in the legislature Herod worked in government and community advocacy, including serving as the President of the Colorado Black Women for Political Action organization (Bejarano and Smooth 2022). Representative Herod was the first Black LGBTQ+ member to serve in the Colorado Assembly.

In 2020, Sonya Jacquez Lewis was elected to the Colorado State Senate with nearly 70% of the vote. Even though Lewis is a first-time lawmaker she has a history in public service, first serving on the Boulder County Board of Health. She also served as president of the group formerly known as Boulder Pride.

Kansas

Representative Stephanie Byers, elected in 2020, is the first elected transgender Indigenous lawmaker in the United States. As one of only seven transgender lawmakers in the country, she was inspired to seek office by the national efforts to block transgender rights (Bernard 2021). Byers is a retired teacher and has focused her first year in office on advocating for transgender students. Even though she had no prior political experience, Byers had long been an advocate of the LGBTQ+ community and was even named Educator of the Year by an "LGBTQ youth advocacy group" (McShane 2021).

Representative Susan Ruiz was elected in 2018, becoming one of the first two openly LGBTQ+ Kansas state legislators. In both 2018 and 2020 Ruiz had Republican opposition in the general election. In 2018, Ruiz won with 52% of the vote beating Republican incumbent, Linda Gallagher. In 2020, Ruiz secured reelection with 55% of the vote. Unlike members from other states discussed earlier, Byers and Ruiz are in a primarily Republican state, yet comprise 50% of the LGTBQ+ legislators in Kansas, with the other two legislators including a white cisgender man and woman.

Minnesota

Minnesota Representative Athena Hollins was elected in 2020. In the Democratic primary Hollins defeated 18-year incumbent, John Lesch with 50.7% of the vote, and went on to win the general election with nearly 80% of the vote. Hollins is an attorney and previously served on her local community council.

Representative Heather Keeler, who won a seat in the Minnesota House of Representatives in 2020, describes herself not as a politician, but as an activist. Her position in the legislature is simply a continuation of her long-held activism. As part of her platform, she discussed her LGBTQ+ and Indigenous identities and the importance of having people like her represented. While in office Keeler has focused particular attention to recognizing Indigenous Peoples' Day in her community. Hollins and Keeler are two-thirds of the LGBTQ+ Minnesotan legislators, with their colleague being a white cisgender man.

Washington

The state of Washington also has two queer women of color currently serving in office and eight LGBTQ+ legislators total. Emily Randall was first elected to an open seat in the Senate in 2018 and won with 50.1% of the vote, narrowly beating her Republican challenger. Senator Randall has focused her agenda on affordable and accessible healthcare for women, children, and members of the LBGTQ+ community.

Kirsten Harris-Talley was elected to the Washington House of Representatives in 2020. Harris-Talley has a history of involvement in political activities, serving as Executive Director of NARAL Pro-Choice Washington and SURGE Reproductive Justice (a BIPOC, queer, and trans- led organization). In her run for an open seat, Harris-Talley won with 65.5% of the vote over a male Democratic challenger.

Ground breaking women

There are 11 states with one queer woman of color currently serving in office. These 11 states can be divided into two groups: those with greater proportions of women and minorities in office and those without (National Conference of State Legislatures).

Single states with more minority lawmakers

Maryland and Rhode Island are both in the top 10 for the highest percentage of female legislators, while Florida, Maryland, and New Mexico are all in the top 10 states for the highest number of minority lawmakers. Maryland (1), North Carolina (7), and Florida (8) have some of the highest proportions of Black lawmakers (National Conference of State Legislatures). New Mexico ranks first for the number of Hispanic/Latinx lawmakers and New York ranks ninth. Maryland, the only state that ranks in the top 10 for both female and minority lawmakers, is home to the current longest-serving LGBTQ+ Black lawmaker, Mary Washington. Of these states, four out of the five have five or more LGBTQ+ lawmakers.

Mary Washington of Maryland was elected to the House of Delegates in 2010 and became the first openly LGBTQ+ and Black candidate elected to office in the state and the second in the nation. Following her career in the lower chamber, Washington was elected to the state Senate in 2018 with over 98% of the vote. Prior to serving, she was the Director of the Housing Authority in Baltimore. With her tenure in both chambers, Washington holds the title of longest serving legislator who is a queer woman of color.

Michele Rayner from Florida became the first openly queer Black woman to serve in the state legislature. Representative Rayner previously worked as a public defender, as well as a civil rights attorney. Facing three challengers during the primary election and no general election challenger, Rayner secured election with only 31% of the vote. Rayner was first elected in 2020 but already has her sights set on a congressional seat.

A lifelong advocate and former member of the New York State Committee, Jessica González-Rojas was elected to the New York Assembly in 2020. During the primary election she beat the Democratic incumbent and won the general election with nearly 80% of the vote. González-Rojas has long pursued areas of social justice and rights for Latina women and the LGBTQ+ community. González-Rojas has a long history invested in community advocacy organizations and an educational background in public policy.

Former Durham City Council Member, Vernetta Alston, was appointed to the North Carolina Legislature in 2020. Later that year she was elected to a full term with 100% of the vote. In her role as a parent and lawmaker, Representative Alston recently helped organize the very first "Gender Expansive Parents Day" in Durham. As of December 2021, Alston has filed for reelection.

Different from many of the other legislators that we discuss, Brittney Barreras of New Mexico won her seat without choosing a party affiliation and had no prior political experience. Which, according to Barreras, was simply an accident as part of her voter registration was left blank.[14] Interestingly, the incumbent, Art De La Cruz, did not file for the seat because he was not appointed until September, and instead, was a write-in candidate but lost with 26% of the vote. While Barreras ran as an Independent she noted she leaned Democratic but wanted to work with members from both parties.[15] Following her election to the New Mexico House of Representatives she changed her affiliation to the Democratic Party out of fear of running against a Democrat in future elections.

Tiara Mack from Rhode Island is one of the youngest lawmakers and was elected at only 26 years old. Mack unseated an incumbent, Harold Metts, in the Democratic primary election who had been serving longer than she has been alive. During her campaign, Representative Mack focused on the intersectionality of her identity to build relationships with voters and would introduce herself as, "Tiara Mack, a queer, Black, formerly low-income educator and activist" (Compton 2020; see also Bejarano 2013; Dittmar 2015b; Fraga et al. 2008; Greene, Matos, and Sanbonmatsu 2022).

Single states with fewer minority lawmakers

There are a handful of states that do not have large populations of women or minorities in office but currently have one queer woman of color in office. Of these states, Wisconsin has the most LGBTQ+ lawmakers with five. Even though Delaware, Missouri, West Virginia, and Wisconsin have fewer minorities serving, it may be the unique intersection of identities that have helped queer women of color secure a seat in these states (Fraga et al. 2008).

Senator Marie Pinkney, a former social worker, was the first Black LBGTQ+ candidate to win a seat in the Delaware legislature. Pinkney won the 2020 general election with 75% of the vote but had narrowly beat the 20-year incumbent in the Democratic primary election. In the spring of 2021, Pinkney, along with her two LGTBQ+ colleagues, were inspired by the recently formed Legislative Black Caucus and organized the very first LGBTQ+ Caucus in Delaware (Holman and Mahoney 2019).[16]

Ashley Manlove of Missouri, first won an open seat in 2018 with 100% of the general election vote.[17] In the 2020 election, again facing no general challenger, Manlove won with 100% of the vote. Manlove comes from a Missouri political dynasty of sorts, both her uncle and grandmother have served in the Missouri legislature. With her election, Manlove became the only female and LGBTQ+ legislator of color in the legislature. Her four LGBTQ+ colleagues are white cisgender men, two of which are members of the Republican Party. Prior to becoming a lawmaker, Manlove was an intelligence analyst for the Missouri National Guard and the Army. With her experience in analysis and accounting she currently serves as the Ranking Minority Member on the House Ways and Means Committee. In addition to her legislative responsibilities she serves as the Chairwoman of the Missouri Legislative Black Caucus.

In February of 2022, Kentucky elected its first LGBTQ+ representative, Keturah Herron, who is the third Black female lawmaker to be elected in the state. Herron defeated her Republican opponent, a white female, for an open seat during a special election. Her prior experience includes working on policy with the ACLU in Kentucky (Bejarano and Smooth 2022). Herron is an advocate for racial justice, juvenile justice, and transgender student rights. Herron advocated for a ban of no-knock search warrants after the killing of Breonna Taylor by Louisville police.

The election of Danielle Walker to the West Virginia House of Delegates is unique because she represents the largest multi-member district in the state. With Walker's election in 2018 (and one other new comer) Democrats now hold the entire district.[18] Walker is the only Black woman in the legislature and only the second LGBTQ+ woman. Walker came out during a press conference in 2021 while advocating for the Fairness Act, which would add protections to those in the LGBTQ+ community.

Assembly member Marisabel Cabrera of Wisconsin had a slightly different election process than other legislators. In 2016 Cabrera unsuccessfully ran for office and lost to Democrat Josh Zepnick (first elected in 2002). However, in 2017 Zepnick was accused of sexual harassment and, although he refused to resign, his legislative duties were revoked. Following the scandal, Cabrera successfully defeated Zepnick in 2018. Prior to her term in the legislature she was the chair of the Milwaukee Police and Fire Commission and the Latino Caucus for the Wisconsin Democratic Party.

Future research

There is a great deal of room for expansion on research that centers queer women of color political elites. Building upon traditional research questions might, for example, include an analysis of the content of floor speeches, roll call votes, legislative success and effectiveness, and campaign behavior of queer women of color. Accounting for the intersection of sexuality and gender identity of legislators could expand conventional wisdom about women's legislative behavior.

Our descriptive findings suggest there may be district-specific effects with queer women of color serving in seats previously occupied by a legislator of color and/or a woman (Clark 2019) and a majority of legislators serving in majority-minority districts (Phillips 2021; Shah, Scott, and Juenke 2019). Future analysis should explore these potential district-specific effects through a lens of women-friendly districts as well (Palmer and Simon 2008; Pyeatt and Yanus 2016, 2017). There is also a new wave of research dedicated to queer friendly district effects, an area largely unexplored in the American context (see Kane 2022). As our understanding of district-specific effects continues to develop, this can be applied to our understanding of success for queer women of color.

There is also potential to analyze intra-group comparisons between queer women of color and other women of color (Brown 2014), between queer women and other LGBTQ+ legislators, and collaboration on legislation (Holman and Mahoney 2018; Holman, Mahoney, and Hurler 2021). Furthermore, as the tenure in office for queer women of color increases scholars should explore the leadership roles and higher-office aspirations of queer women of color.

Discussion

In this brief critical perspective piece, we bring to center an understudied and underrepresented group of legislators. Legislatures are raced-gendered institutions in that, "race-specific constructions of masculinity and femininity are intertwined in the daily culture of the institution" (Hawkesworth 2003, 537; see also Dittmar 2021; Brown and Lemi 2021), but they are also cisheteropatriarchal institutions by promoting and normalizing male heterosexuality and cisgender identity as the default (Alim et al. 2020). The intersection of the identity of queer women of color may fundamentally change the institution symbolically and substantively when queer women of color traverse an institution not intended for them to occupy (Mansbridge 1999; Pitkin 1967). Queer women of color legislators must perform multiple acts of representation by representing the interests of all their communities as well as their own interests as queer women of color (Beckwith 2014). LGBTQ+ rights, particularly trans rights, are under threat in many state legislatures across the country. Queer women of color legislators must navigate a workplace in which their colleagues can introduce policies that are a fundamental attack on their existence as a queer person of color. Accounting for the intersection of sexual orientation, race, and gender identity in analyses of legislators' experiences and behavior will provide a fuller understanding of the power of descriptive representation (Mansbridge 1999; Pitkin 1967), particularly at a time when LGTBQ+ youth experience higher rates of bullying and are at a higher risk of suicide compared to their straight, cisgender peers.[19]

We began with a quote by Florida State Representative Michele Rayner and will conclude with one as well, "I show up as a Black, queer, Southern woman ... I think that all of those identities that I embody need to be present because that's what America looks like" (Ogles 2021). Representative Rayner-Goolsby recently announced her candidacy for Florida's 13th congressional district and signifies the future of American women in politics. An understanding of the experiences and legislative behavior of women in elective office must account for queer women of color.

Notes

1. In our discussion, we use "queer" and "women of color" when referring to the collective group of legislators and identify sexual orientation and race/ethnicity when discussing individual legislators.
2. The Victory Institute's database of out LGBTQ+ individuals currently serving in public office the United States can be accessed here: https://outforamerica.org/. Date of last access: February 23, 2022. Information on women in American state legislatures in 2022 is published by the Center for American Women and Politics and can be found here: https://cawpdata.rutgers.edu/. Date of last access: February 8, 2022. To identify a count of women of color only, we utilize CAWP's searchable database and restrict our search to state legislatures and select all but white and unavailable for race/ethnicity. This search resulted in 624 unique individuals.
3. In February 2022, Chantale Wong became the first out lesbian and LGBTQ+ person of color to serve in an ambassador-level position when the Senate confirmed her appointment as Director of the Asian Development Bank. See: https://www.hrc.org/press-releases/chantale-wong-makes-history-as-first-openly-lesbian-senate-confirmed-ambassador.
4. Women serve in local or judicial positions in just 25 states. There are only three states that have five or more queer women of color serving in these positions: California (12), New York (6), and Texas (5). There are 13 states with only one local official and one state (Tennessee) with a queer woman of color in a judicial position.
5. As a supplement to the Victory Institutes identification of out LGBTQ+ officials, the authors also cross-referenced legislators' self-identification as LGBTQ+ through news sources and legislators' websites and social media. Legislators may update the public regarding their identity to better reflect their lived experience. Our information is most recently updated through February 23, 2022.
6. We evaluated using the standard set by the US Census Bureau, which states an urban area as more than 50,000 people. Representative Emily Randall, Heather Keeler, and Danielle Walker are the only women whose district does not encompass at least one city with a large population.
7. The following legislators do not represent a majority-minority district: Sonya Jacquez Lewis, Leslie Herod, Marie Pinkney, Susan Ruiz, Emily Randall, Stephanie Byers, Heather Keeler, Danielle Walker. Information provided by the US Census.
8. The term-limited states represented here are California, Colorado, Florida, Nevada, and Missouri. There are currently 15 states that implement legislative term limits.
9. There is a lack of research about the gendered differences of who fills open seats or wins special elections in state legislative races (Holman 2017; see Brant and Marvin Overby 2020 regarding appointments in the US Senate).
10. However, these states do not have the most LGBTQ+ legislators. Nevada has five LGBTQ+ legislators, while Georgia and Texas have seven and six, respectively. Vermont and New Hampshire are tied for the most LGBTQ+ legislators at 12 each, however, all legislators are white (Victory Institute).
11. Accessed from: https://www.ncsl.org/research/about-state-legislatures/state-legislator-demographics.aspx. Date of last access December 22, 2021.
12. Mary Washington, who since 2010 has served in both chambers of the Maryland legislature, is the current longest serving legislator. Lucia Guzman of Colorado served from 2010–2018 and then termed out. JoCasta Zamarripa served in Wisconsin from 2012–2020. Representative Spearman of Nevada is currently serving but will face term limits and be forced to leave in 2024.

13. For information on Israel's recently announced campaign see: https://www.statesman.com/story/news/2022/01/11/texas-house-member-celia-israel-democrat-run-mayor-austin-tx-2022/9164370002/.
14. https://www.santafenewmexican.com/news/local_news/independents-day-brought-no-fireworks-to-new-mexico/article_153e15f0-236e-11eb-8a03-37ebf876c5ba.html.
15. Local news stories captured the election of Barreras. https://www.krqe.com/news/politics-government/rare-independent-lawmaker-headed-to-roundhouse/.
16. See https://www.delawarepublic.org/politics-government/2021-05-14/state-lawmakers-form-lgbtq-caucus. Date of last access December 22, 2021.
17. The seat was previously occupied by Democrat Gail McCann Beatty, a Black woman, who resigned to take a county job.
18. Danielle Walker represents district 51 in the West Virginia House of Delegates, which contains five seats elected in a free for all election. Walker and Evan Hansen secured enough votes to remove two Republican incumbents Joe Statler and Cindy Finch. Due to serving in a multi-member district Walker won election with roughly 10% of the vote.
19. See a report by the Trevor Project here: https://www.thetrevorproject.org/survey-2021/?section=SuicideMentalHealth.

Acknowledgments

The authors would like to thank the editors and guest editors of this issue, Drs. Nadia E. Brown, Christopher J. Clark, and Anna Mahoney. In addition, we would like to thank Noah Haynes, Cody A. Drolc, Amanda Roth, Amy Braksmajer, Karleen West, Abbey Bowman Rogers, Brandon Beomseob Park, Alice Rutkowski, and the LGBTQ Working Group at SUNY Geneseo for their helpful comments and assistance with this project

Disclosure statement

No potential conflict of interest was reported by the author(s).

References

Alim, H. Samy, Jooyoung Lee, Lauren Mason Carris, and Quentin E. Williams. 2020. "Language, Race, and the (Trans) Formation of Cisheteropatriarchy." In *The Oxford Handbook of Language and Race*, eds. H. Samy Alim, Angela Reyes, and Paul V. Kroskrity. New York: Oxford University Press, 291–314.

Aptheker, Bettina. 1989. *Tapestries of Life: Women's Work, Women's Consciousness and the Meaning of Daily Life*. Amherst, MA: University of Massachusetts Press.

Beckwith, Karen. 2014. "Plotting the Path from One to the Other: Women's Interests and Political Representation." In *Representation: The Case of Women*, eds. Michelle Taylor Robinson and Maria Escobar-Lemmon. New York: Oxford University Press, 19–40.

Bejarano, Christina. 2013. *The Latina Advantage: Gender, Race, and Political Success*. Austin: University of Texas Press.

Bejarano, Christina, and Wendy Smooth. 2022. "Women of Color Mobilizing: Sistahs are Doing It for Themselves from GOTV to Running Candidates for Political Office." *Journal of Women, Politics & Policy* 43 (1):8–24. doi:10.1080/1554477X.2022.2008398.

Bernard, Katie. 2021. "Here's How Kansas' First Transgender Lawmaker Fought for LGBTQ Children and Herself." *The Kansas City Star*, June 21.

Brant, Hanna K., and L. Marvin Overby. 2020. "Female Appointed Successors in the United States Senate." *Journal of Women, Politics & Policy* 41 (4):527–41. doi:10.1080/1554477X.2020.1743121.

Bratton, Kathleen A., and Kerry L. Haynie. 1999. "Agenda Setting and Legislative Success in State Legislatures: The Effects of Gender and Race." *The Journal of Politics* 61 (3):658–79. doi:10.2307/2647822.

Bratton, Kathleen A., Kerry L. Haynie, and Beth Reingold. 2007. "Agenda Setting and African American Women in State Legislatures." *Journal of Women, Politics & Policy* 28 (3–4):71–96. doi:10.1300/J501v28n03_04.

Brown, Elsa Barkley. 1989. "African-American Women's Quilting." *Signs: Journal of Women in Culture and Society* 14 (4):921–29. doi:10.1086/494553.

Brown, Nadia E. 2014. *Sisters in the Statehouse: Black Women and Legislative Decision Making.* New York: Oxford University Press.

Brown, Nadia E., and Danielle Casarez Lemi. 2021. *Sister Style: The Politics of Appearance for Black Women Political Elites.* New York: Oxford University Press.

Carroll, Susan J., and Kira Sanbonmatsu. 2013. *More Women Can Run: Gender and Pathways to the State Legislatures.* New York: Oxford University Press.

Clark, Christopher J. 2019. *Gaining Voice: The Causes and Consequences of Black Representation in the American States.* Oxford University Press.

Compton, Julie. 2020. "'Unapologetically Black and Queer' Tiara Mack Is Headed to the Rhode Island Senate." *NBC News*, November 18.

Crenshaw, Kimberlé. 1991. "Mapping the Margins: Identity Politics, Intersectionality, and Violence against Women." *Stanford Law Review* 43 (6):1241–99. doi:10.2307/1229039.

Crowder-Meyer, Melody. 2013. "Gendered Recruitment without Trying: How Local Party Recruiters Affect Women's Representation." *Politics & Gender* 9 (4):390–413. doi:10.1017/S1743923X13000391.

Crowder-Meyer, Melody, Shana Kushner Gadarian, and Jessica Trounstine. 2015. "Electoral Institutions, Gender Stereotypes, and Women's Local Representation." *Politics, Groups, and Identities* 3 (2):318–34. doi:10.1080/21565503.2015.1031803.

Dittmar, Kelly. 2015a. "Encouragement Is Not Enough: Addressing Social and Structural Barriers to Female Recruitment." *Politics and Gender* 11 (4):759–65. doi:10.1017/S1743923X15000495.

Dittmar, Kelly. 2015b. *Navigating Gendered Terrain: Stereotypes and Strategy in Political Campaigns.* Philadelphia, PA: Temple University Press.

Dittmar, Kelly. 2021. "Invisible Forces: Gender, Race, and Congressional Staff." *Politics, Groups, and Identities*:1–17. doi:10.1080/21565503.2021.1908370.

Fraga, Luis Ricardo, Linda Lopez, Valerie Martinez-Ebers, and Ricardo Ramírez. 2007. "Gender and Ethnicity: Patterns of Electoral Success and Legislative Advocacy among Latina and Latino State Officials in Four States." *Journal of Women, Politics & Policy* 28 (3–4):121–45. doi:10.1300/J501v28n03_06.

Fraga, Luis Ricardo, Valerie Martinez-Ebers, Linda Lopez, and Ramírez Ricardo. 2008. "Representing Gender and Ethnicity: Strategic Intersectionality." In *Legislative Women: Getting Elected, Getting Ahead*, ed. Beth Reingold. Boulder, CO: Lynne Rienner, 157–74.

Greene, Stacey, Yalidy Matos, and Kira Sanbonmatsu. 2022. "Women Voters and the Utility of Campaigning as 'Women of Color.'" *Journal of Women, Politics & Policy* 43 (1):25–41. doi:10.1080/1554477X.2022.2007467.

Haider-Markel, Donald P. 2007. "Representation and Backlash: The Positive and Negative Influence of Descriptive Representation." *Legislative Studies Quarterly* 32 (1):107–33. doi:10.3162/036298007X202001.

Haider-Markel, Donald P. 2010. *Out and Running: Gay and Lesbian Candidates, Elections, and Policy Representation.* Georgetown University Press.

Hamm, Keith E., and Nancy Martorano Miller. 2018. "Legislative Politics in the States." In *Politics of the American States*, eds. Virginia Gray, Russell Hanson, and Thad Kousser. California: CQ Press, 187–234.

Hawkesworth, Mary. 2003. "Congressional Enactments of Race–gender: Toward a Theory of Raced–gendered Institutions." *American Political Science Review* 97 (4):529–50. doi:10.1017/S0003055403000868.

Haynes, Noah, and Jordan Butcher. 2021. "More Women than Men Serve in Nevada's State Legislature. How Did that Happen?" *The Washington Post*, December 23.

Herrick, Rebekah. 2009. "The Effects of Sexual Orientation on State Legislators' Behavior and Priorities." *The Journal of Homosexuality* 56 (8):1117–33. doi:10.1080/00918360903279361.

Hogan, Robert E. 2008. "Sex and the Statehouse: The Effects of Gender on Legislative Roll-call Voting." *Social Science Quarterly* 89 (4):955–68. doi:10.1111/j.1540-6237.2008.00593.x.

Holman, Mirya R. 2017. "Women in Local Government: What We Know and Where We Go from Here." *State and Local Government Review* 49 (4):285–96. doi:10.1177/0160323X17732608.

Holman, Mirya R., and Anna Mahoney. 2018. "Stop, Collaborate, and Listen: Women's Collaboration in US State Legislatures." *Legislative Studies Quarterly* 43 (2):179–206. doi:10.1111/lsq.12199.

Holman, Mirya R., Anna Mahoney, and Emma Hurler. 2021. "Let's Work Together: Bill Success via Women's Cosponsorship in U.S. State Legislatures." *Political Research Quarterly*:106591292110201. doi:10.1177/10659129211020123.

Holman, Mirya R., and Anna Mitchell Mahoney. 2019. "The Choice Is Yours: Caucus Typologies and Collaboration in U.S. State Legislatures." *Representation* 55 (1):47–63. doi:10.1080/00344893.2019.1581079.

Kane, Kellan. 2022. "Queer'ying the Districts: Establishing a Measure of Queer-friendly State Legislative Districts." Paper presented at the Annual Meeting of the Southern Political Science Association, San Antonio, TX.

Mansbridge, Jane. 1999. "Should Blacks Represent Blacks and Women Represent Women? A Contingent Yes." *The Journal of Politics* 61 (3):628–57. doi:10.2307/2647821.

Matos, Yalidy, Stacey Greene, and Kira Sanbonmatsu. 2021. "The Politics of "Women of Color": A Group Identity Worth Investigating." *Politics, Groups, and Identities*:1–22. doi:10.1080/21565503.2021.2008992.

McShane, Julianne. 2021. "For America's 1st Indigenous Transgender Lawmaker, Pride Is `a Statement of Survival'." *NBC Out & Proud*, June 1.

Montoya, Celeste M., Christina Bejarano, Nadia E. Brown, and Sarah Allen Gershon. 2021. "The Intersectional Dynamics of Descriptive Representation." *Politics & Gender*:1–30. doi:10.1017/S1743923X20000744.

Mueller, Tabitha, and Jannelle Carlderon. 2021. "Out of the Shadows: LGBTQ Lawmakers Reflect on past Struggles, Future Goals." *The Nevada Independent*, April 4.

Ogles, Jacob. 2021. "Michele Rayner-Goolsby Aims to Be Florida's 1st Out Person in Congress." *The Advocate*, June 14.

Orey, Byron D'Andra, Wendy Smooth, Kimberly S. Adams, and Kisha Harris-Clark. 2007. "Race and Gender Matter: Refining Models of Legislative Policy Making in State Legislatures." *Journal of Women, Politics & Policy* 28 (3–4):97–119. doi:10.1300/J501v28n03_05.

Osborn, Tracy L. 2012. *How Women Represent Women: Political Parties, Gender and Representation in the State Legislatures*. New York: Oxford University Press.

Palmer, Barbara, and Dennis Simon. 2008. *Breaking the Political Glass Ceiling: Women and Congressional Elections*. 2nd ed. New York: Routledge.

Perry, Ravi K., X. Loudon Manley, and Susan Burgess. 2017. "Case Studies of Black Lesbian and Gay Candidates: Winning Identity Politics in the Obama Era." In *LGBTQ Politics: A Critical Reader*, eds. Marla Brettschneider, Susan Burgess, and Christine Keating. New York: NYU Press, 295–308.

Pettey, Samantha. 2018. "Female Candidate Emergence and Term Limits: A State-Level Analysis." *Political Research Quarterly* 71 (2):318–29. doi:10.1177/1065912917735175.

Phillips, Christian Dyogi. 2021. *Nowhere to Run: Race, Gender, and Immigration in American Elections*. Oxford, UK: Oxford University Press.

Pitkin, Hanna F. 1967. *The Concept of Representation*. Berkeley and Los Angeles, California: University of California Press.

Pyeatt, Nicholas, and Alixandra B. Yanus. 2016. "Shattering the Marble Ceiling: A Research Note on Women-Friendly State Legislative Districts." *Social Science Quarterly* 97 (5):1108–18. doi:10.1111/ssqu.12294.

Pyeatt, Nicholas, and Alixandra B. Yanus. 2017. "Increasing Women's Political Participation: The Role of Women-friendly Districts." *Representation* 53 (3–4):185–99. doi:10.1080/00344893.2018.1438306.

Pyeatt, Nicholas, and Alixandra B. Yanus. 2021. "Gender, Entry, and Victory in State Legislative Primary Elections." *Journal of Women, Politics & Policy* 42 (4):352–68. doi:10.1080/1554477X.2021.1958667.

Reingold, Beth, Kirsten Widner, and Rachel Harmon. 2020. "Legislating at the Intersections: Race, Gender, and Representation." *Political Research Quarterly* 73 (4):819–33. doi:10.1177/1065912919858405.

Sanbonmatsu, Kira. 2015a. "Electing Women of Color: The Role of Campaign Trainings." *Journal of Women, Politics and Policy* 36 (2):137–60. doi:10.1080/1554477X.2015.1019273.

Sanbonmatsu, Kira. 2015b. "Why Not a Woman of Color? The Candidacies of US Women of Color for Statewide Executive Office." *Oxford Handbooks Online*.

Sanbonmatsu, Kira, Susan J. Carroll, and Debbie Walsh. 2009. *Poised to Run: Women's Pathways to the State Legislatures*. Center for American Women and Politics, Eagleton Institute of Politics. Newark: Rutgers University.

Schmitt, Carly, and Hanna K. Brant. 2019. "Gender, Ambition, and Legislative Behavior in the United States House." *Journal of Women, Politics & Policy* 40 (2):286–308. doi:10.1080/1554477X.2019.1570757.

Shah, Paru, Jamil Scott, and Eric Gonzalez Juenke. 2019. "Women of Color Candidates: Examining Emergence and Success in State Legislative Elections." *Politics, Groups, and Identities* 7 (2):429–43. doi:10.1080/21565503.2018.1557057.

Silva, Andrea, and Carrie Skully. 2019. "Always Running: Candidate Emergence among Women of Color over Time." *Political Research Quarterly* 72 (2):342–59. doi:10.1177/1065912918789289.

Smooth, Wendy. 2011. "Standing for Women? Which Women? The Substantive Representation of Women's Interests and the Research Imperative of Intersectionality." *Politics & Gender* 7 (3):436–41. doi:10.1017/S1743923X11000225.

Swift, Clint S., and Kathryn VanderMolen. 2021. "Marginalization and Mobilization: The Roots of Female Legislators' Collaborative Advantage in the States." *State Politics & Policy Quarterly* 21 (4):355–79. doi:10.1017/spq.2020.9.

Thomas, Sue, and Susan Welch. 1991. "The Impact of Gender on Activities and Priorities of State Legislators." *The Western Political Quarterly* 44 (2):445–56. doi:10.1177/106591299104400212.

Uhlaner, Carole Jean, and Becki Scola. 2016. "Collective Representation as a Mobilizer: Race/Ethnicity, Gender, and Their Intersections at the State Level." *State Politics & Policy Quarterly* 16 (2):227–63. doi:10.1177/1532440015603576.

Her Honor: Black Women Judges' Experiences with Disrespect and Recusal Requests in the American Judiciary

Taneisha N. Means

ABSTRACT

Existing scholarship has mainly focused on the experiences of Black women judges as they ascend to the bench and has largely overlooked the experiences of these judges once they reach the court. I address the topic of Black women's experiences in the judiciary by drawing on an original survey with 163 Black women judges and centering their voices, reflections, and perspectives. These women report substantial disrespect by litigants and attorneys and share how they experience questioning about their ability to render fair decisions. These jurists' experiences highlight how many Black women judges deal with disruptive, demeaning, intimidating, and passive-aggressive behavior, dismissive treatment, and insidious nonverbal behavior.

Those gains we have made were never graciously and generously granted. We have had to fight every inch of the way.

Jane Bolin[1]

I have been disrespected by both attorneys and unrepresented litigants too many times to explain.

Anonymous Black woman state court judge[2]

"I believe you have a mindset that may tend, without your being aware of it, to influence your judgment."

Attorney Ephraim London[3]

In 2017, seventeen Black women made history winning judicial seats in Harris County, Texas, under the coordinated electoral campaign "Black Girl Magic Texas."[4] Most of us have seen these women – their iconic picture standing together in a courtroom taken by the Harris County Democratic Party after their historic election was shared widely across popular social media platforms. Judge Tonya Jones, one of the Harris County judges elected, explained these women's victory in the context of the broader Black Girl Magic movement: "The idea of 'Black Girl Magic' in and of itself is just a celebration of the accomplishments of African-American women in various sectors within society, and typically those where we're underrepresented, such as the judiciary here in Harris County."[5] In late February 2022, news sites have published countless articles on Ketanji Brown Jackson, the Black women President Biden nominated to replace Justice Stephen Breyer on the United States Supreme Court. Although Black women state and federal judges have received unprecedented media and scholarly attention in recent years, they are not as well represented as the stories and papers might lead one to believe (Blackburne-Rigsby 2009). In fact, Jackson's confirmation would be a historic moment for the country and SCOTUS as there has never been a Black woman Supreme Court justice.

Black women represent less than 10% of state and federal judges (e.g., George and Yoon 2017; Solberg and Diascro 2018). As of February 2022, there are 45 active Black women federal judges in the United States, comprising about 5% of all sitting Article III judges and 42% of all Black sitting Article

III judges.[6] At the state level, it is unclear exactly how many Black women judges there are because organizations do not track this information regularly and, because judges at the state level lack the lifetime tenure their colleagues in the federal judiciary enjoy, they regularly enter and leave the profession. However, a recent article notes that women of color as a whole make up only about 8% of all state court judges despite representing roughly 20% of the population (George and Yoon 2017). Suffice to say, Black women are underrepresented on the bench irrespective of the level of the court, and their underrepresentation in the judiciary is true even though Black women have been judges in this country since the mid-20th century when the nation's first Black women judges – Jane Bolin, the first state court judge, and Constance Baker Motley, the first Black woman appointed to the federal judiciary, paved the way for later Black women judges (Means 2021).[7]

Black women's underrepresentation amongst judges in the 21st century is puzzling because Black women make up a significant proportion of the United States population and the law school population (Sokoloff 2014).[8] According to a recent report on diversity amongst law school students, "nearly twice as many Black women as Black men study law every year. There were 1,889 Black women in the 2019 incoming class, but only 988 Black men. The same trend has existed in undergraduate higher education for decades."[9] Nonetheless, the judiciary remains an institution where men, especially white men, continue to be overrepresented (Goelzhauser 2019; Means, Eslich, and Prado 2019).

Still, Black women's current representation in the courts is significant compared to their historical representation. But what do we know about these women? Scholars already study what happens during judicial selection for racial and gender minorities (Engstrom 1989; Hurwitz and Lanier 2012), but they generally overlook Black women judges' experiences once they ascend to the bench. Thus, questions that remain unanswered in the existing literature are what are Black women judges' experiences once they make it to the bench? How are they treated in those legal spaces by the individuals they engage with regularly? I tackle this topic by drawing on an original survey with 163 Black women judges and exploring how these jurists report being treated while on the bench by litigants and attorneys.

Studying Black women judges' experiences on the court highlights the challenges these women face in the profession, which may impact judicial diversity because their experiences may influence whether they are able and willing to remain in the profession. This topic is also significant because, generally speaking, we know very little about the experiences of judges, irrespective of race and gender, but especially Black women judges. By focusing on these judges' experiences on the bench, this article contributes to the growing body of research focusing on women of color political elites, especially women of color in the legal profession and judiciary (e.g., Brown 2014; Brown and Lemi 2021; Collins, Dumas, and Moyer 2017; Dawuni 2018; Dowe 2020; Fricke and Onwuachi-Willig 2012). This article also contributes to the substantial body of literature on women judges (e.g., Cook 1984; Johnson et al. 2008; Kenney 2013; Palmer 2001) and Black judges in the United States (e.g., Alozie 1988; Chenault 1981; Cook Jr. 1996; Mitchell 1987; Taslitz 1998; Washington 1971) and those judging outside of the United States (Gomez Mazo 2020; Solanke 2018). In sum, this article is important because it puts us in a better position to understand Black women judges' experiences in the judiciary and helps us to consider at least one factor that may influence why Black women might persist in being underrepresented in the judiciary and how these women can be better supported.

Evaluating Black and women judges

Since the mid-20th century, the American Bar Association's (ABA) Standing Committee on the Federal Judiciary has evaluated federal judicial nominees at some point during those nominees' judicial selection process. The committee maintains that it evaluates nominees to the federal courts based on their professional qualifications and the following categories of criteria: legal ability, integrity/impartiality, communication skills, professionalism/temperament, and administrative capacity. The committee claims that nominees' personal characteristics such as race, gender, ideology, or political affiliation are not taken into account and do not influence the evaluation (ABA 2009), but legal scholars and political scientists find significant evidence to the contrary (Haire 2001; Sen 2014; Smelcer, Steigerwalt, and Vining 2012). For instance, white nominees are more likely than minority nominees to receive higher ratings, and men nominees are more likely than women nominees to receive higher ratings (i.e., qualified and well qualified; Sen 2014). The issue is not quality of the nominees; this finding that men and white judicial nominees fair better before the ABA standing committee stands even when one takes into account important factors such as nominees' educational and professional backgrounds and reversal rates.

Just as the ABA evaluations are meant to help those involved in the federal judicial selection process to appoint quality federal judges, Judicial Performance Evaluations (JPEs), completed chiefly by attorneys, are intended to help voters select quality state judges via publications of their evaluations (ABA 2009). Whether or not the JPEs are used in state judicial selection is a different issue (Gill 2017). Still, unfortunately, just like the bias that has been discovered in ABA ratings, scholars have also noted racial and gender bias in the JPEs. Specifically, racial minority judges and women judges are consistently given evaluation scores that are significantly lower than white and men judges (Gill 2014).

In addition to the evaluations by political elites (i.e., primarily attorneys), recent studies have attempted to understand how the public perceives judges. Fix and Johnson (2017) focused on perceptions of female state court judges, and Means and Unah (2019) and Ono and Zilis (2021) focused on perceptions of judges who are racial minorities. All these scholars find some evidence that gender and racial minorities are perceived more negatively than their counterparts. Their findings are consistent with the work of Harris and Sen (2019) who find that minority judges are perceived as biased and affected by their racial identities in ways that differ from how the public perceives white judges' bias. Combined, this literature on state and federal evaluations, and public perceptions, shows that racial minority judges and women judges are perceived and evaluated more negatively than white and men judges, generally speaking.

Evaluating Black women (judges)

While racial minority judges and women judges are often viewed and evaluated less favorably than their white and men counterparts by attorneys and members of the general United States population (e.g., Fix and Johnson 2017; Gill 2014; Haire 2001; Harris and Sen 2019; Means and Unah 2019; Ono and Zilis 2021; Sen 2014; Smelcer, Steigerwalt, and Vining 2012), we do not yet know how Black women judges are viewed or treated prior to reaching the bench nor once on the bench because scholars have generally not taken an intersectional approach to assess how women of color, especially Black women, are perceived, evaluated, and treated. Theoretical and empirical work in various disciplines highlight how women of color do not behave the same and are likely not perceived the same as men of color and white women (e.g., Alexander-Floyd 2019; Carbado, Crenshaw, and Mays 2013; Cho, Crenshaw, and McCall 2013; Crenshaw 1989, 1991; Hancock 2007; Jordan-Zachery 2007; Livingston, Rosette, and Washington 2012; Simien 2007). This work shows how, because racial and gender categories overlap uniquely for women of color given that they belong to two subordinate groups, they have life experiences that have often been marked by racism and sexism distinctively. The distinctive impact of racism and sexism often leads women of color to be perceived and treated in ways unique or distinctive to them.

While not coined as a concept until the late-20th century by renowned critical race theorist Kimberlé W. Crenshaw (1989), intersectionality as a philosophy and way of thinking about identity, oppression, and privilege has been around for a long time (Hancock 2015). Intersectionality describes women of color as having been disadvantaged based on race and gender and not on a single, categorical axis. Crenshaw (1991, 1467–1468) notes that "the dynamics of racism and sexism intersect in our [i.e., women of color's] lives to create experiences that are sometimes unique to us [i.e., women of color]."

Intersectionality, therefore, also provides space to think about women of color as not being "doubly disadvantaged" but benefitting uniquely from their positionality at the intersection of race and gender (Bowleg 2008; Purdie-Vaughns and Eibach 2008). The theory suggests that their life experiences can be similar to those of Black men (their racial counterparts) and white women (their gender counterparts), but that it is often true that women of color experience discrimination and privilege in ways very distinctive from their racial and gender counterparts. This is the case even of Black women attorneys (Burleigh and Benson Goldberg 1988; Collins, Dumas, and Moyer 2017; Reyes 2020). Given what we know about intersectionality, and the fact that Black women and other women of color are most underrepresented in the judiciary (George and Yoon 2017; Stubbs 2016), scholars must continue to build on the work that has only ever considered how United States judges are viewed and evaluated along one single axis (i.e., race or gender, and not race and gender).

We also cannot assume that, just because we know how Black and women judges are perceived and evaluated by attorneys and the public (i.e., ABA ratings and JPEs), we know something about Black women judges' experiences once on the bench. We have nothing to go by when it comes to considering how Black women judges in the 21st century are treated in their courtrooms because this is a topic understudied amongst academics and judges themselves are not vocal about these topics. I address this topic by intentionally centering Black women judges' reflections on how they are treated on the bench and assessing whether/how they are disrespected and how they perceive their race and gender impact their experiences.

Theorizing Black women judges' experiences on the bench

Like their counterparts, Black women judges spend much of their work time in their courtrooms. This means that the people with whom they are most likely to interact are litigants and attorneys. Therefore, understanding Black women judges' experiences require assessing how they are treated in their courtrooms by these two groups of people. Because existing literature has very little-to-nothing to say about how litigants and attorneys treat judges (Cross 2003), irrespective of race, but especially Black women judges, the theory and expectations for this study are informed by how Black women are generally treated in American society and how Black and women judges have been evaluated by elites and members of the public.

One way to explore Black women judges' experiences is to consider whether/how they are respected or disrespected. Respect is an essential concept in the legal profession. Legal actors, including lawyers and judges, are expected to regard and treat other legal actors with respect and without contempt and rudeness. In their Model Rules of Professional Conduct, the American Bar Association says as much.[10]

> A lawyer's conduct should conform to the requirements of the law, both in professional service to clients and in the lawyer's business and personal affairs. A lawyer should use the law's procedures only for legitimate purposes and not to harass or intimidate others. A lawyer should demonstrate respect for the legal system and for those who serve it, including judges, other lawyers, and public officials. While it is a lawyer's duty, when necessary, to challenge the rectitude of official action, it is also a lawyer's duty to uphold [the] legal process.

Because respect is such a fundamental expectation in the court system, when I considered how to assess Black women judges' experiences on the bench, it was clear that examining whether and how these women feel they are respected/disrespected was important.

According to some judges, disrespect is a growing issue within the courts (Cross 2003) because the courts are spaces where some of the most personal and sensitive matters are being handled (i.e., criminal justice, divorce, and child custody) and attorneys and their clients are motivated to win in the adversarial system. But the respect or disrespect experienced within the courtroom by Black women warrants attention because these are jurists who despite being historically excluded, now hold significant power in the legal system and are racial and gender minorities in a profession and position that is predominantly white and male (Norwood 2020).

How disrespect manifests itself may vary because disrespect is a broad category of verbal and nonverbal behaviors. I conceptualize respect as polite attitudes or behaviors that can be considered or described as deference, admiration, esteem, and regard. Respect also means honoring rules, showing consideration, and treating others courteously. Disrespect is the opposite of respect, and disrespect is not uncommon in the courts. This is not a popular topic in the literature, in fact, there is very little scholarship on disrespect in the courtroom. But one recent autoethnographic article provides some helpful information about disrespect faced by United States judges, at least according to a Colorado county clerk judge.

In his short law review article, Christopher C. Cross (2003) highlights what he has been witnessing and experiencing in the courtroom in terms of disrespect from attorneys and litigants. Cross (2003) writes that there is a "growing number of outward signs of disrespect toward the court by attorneys." But in his opinion, and based on his experience as a white male judge, Cross believes that disrespect in the courts is not often done in writing nor is it verbalized, but instead, is subtle and through body language (Cross 2003).

I expect Black women judges will have experiences with disrespect because it seems that disrespect is not altogether abnormal in the courts, mainly because the stakes are high and courts are stressful environments. Disrespect may not be a daily issue for Black women in the judiciary. Still, they are likely to have had at least some experiences with disrespect like their Black women counterparts who are employed outside of the court (Scarborough 1989). Additionally, I anticipate that, contrary to Cross's suggestion that disrespect is rarely verbal and in written form, Black women will report subtle disrespect and also much more blunt and bold disrespect. They will likely note that attorneys and litigants have been disrespectful toward them by being aggressive with their speech and mannerisms.

This expectation is informed by the fact that Black women judges are relative newcomers to the judicial profession because racism and sexism obstructed significant integration in the judicial system until the mid-20th century, and only after considerable activism during the Black Civil Rights Movement. These newcomers are likely to experience distinctive challenges as judges because racism and sexism continue to impact the profession, especially for Black women. Like other women of color in the judiciary, Black women jurists belong to not one but two marginalized groups by being simultaneously a gender minority *and* racial minority. Therefore, they may find themselves being treated with hostility and aggression that stems from bias against them as women of color and as holding such high positions of power in a largely white profession. Consequently, I anticipate that Black women judges will have subtle experiences with the disrespect that Cross (2003) describes. Still, they will also have experiences that Cross (2003), a white male judge, has not had much experience dealing with because of his racial and gender identities that protect him from racism and sexism. I expect at least some Black women to report being verbally disrespected, because of the perceptions of and experiences of racism and sexism reported by Black women in other contexts (e.g., Collins, Dumas, and Moyer 2017).

Beyond disrespect, Black women judges may also experience their decision-making and ability to be fair questioned by attorneys and litigants. Rendering decisions in court cases is one of the most common and vital responsibilities of judging. Both state and federal judges are expected and mandated to make fair decisions, and they are encouraged to be mindful of (the appearance of) impropriety. Recusal requests are one tool that can help improve the appearance of impropriety because it is a motion filed by attorneys and litigants to have judges disqualified from hearing or rendering decisions in cases when there are serious questions or doubts about judges' ability to be fair and unbiased (Ifill and Segall 2011). Because there is no tracking system for recusal requests, it is unclear how many judges are asked to recuse themselves from the cases they have been assigned to preside over. But it seems that recusals are relatively common in the judiciary.[11]

Some recusal requests are warranted when there truly is a question about whether a judge can render a fair decision. But some requests are frivolous. Take, for example, the excessive recusal requests that ask Black judges to disqualify themselves or be disqualified from rendering decisions in particular cases (Ifill 1997). Ifill (1997) notes that there are times "in which white litigants have sought to disqualify African American judges in cases in which racial discrimination is an issue. The claims of bias asserted by white litigants in these recusal cases have compelled African American judges to question and challenge a racially-constructed definition of 'impartiality'" (Ifill 1997, 114). This does not appear to be a settled issue because even in the 21st century, some Black judges are still being asked to recuse themselves from cases concerning race or involving Black litigants (Means and Unah 2019). Thus, recusals based on prejudice (i.e., a Black judge deciding a case with a racialized context such as a racial discrimination case) are not altogether uncommon nor surprising.

Although they do not necessarily determine and dictate which judge hears their case, because lawyers are authorized to submit recusal requests and can do so without much oversight, the system imbues them with substantial power to have a say in which judges are (not) able to preside over their cases. One danger for Black judges is that recusal requests might be weaponized by biased attorneys who wish to threaten and signal to Black judges that they are perceived as incapable of rendering fair decisions, especially in cases with racialized contexts like racial discrimination cases. While this is impossible to test here, recusal requests, therefore, can at the very least be understood as powerful tools that attorneys can use to challenge the authority and legitimacy of judges to decide the cases they have been randomly assigned to preside over.

In addition to disrespect, I expect that Black women in the judiciary will have had experience being asked to recuse themselves from cases. Recusal requests are meant to address and mitigate the appearance and possibility of impropriety. These requests stem from some perceived conflict of interest that could impact judges' ability to render fair, unbiased decisions for many judges. But, because Black judges are perceived by some Americans to be incapable of rendering fair decisions in cases, especially those involving racial issues (Means and Unah 2019), I anticipate that Black women judges will attribute at least some of their recusal requests to their identities as Black women. In other words, I anticipate that some Black women judges will report their race and gender identities as partly influencing recusal requests they have received.

To summarize the expectations:

H1 – I expect that Black women judges will report having had experience with disrespect, and that that disrespect will be both subtle (i.e., nonverbal behavior) and not subtle (i.e., verbal).

H2 – I expect that Black women judges will have experience being asked to recuse themselves from court cases they have been assigned, and that many of these judges will attribute at least some of their recusal requests to their gender and racial identities.

Data and methodology

I draw on surveys with Black women state court jurists to examine and better understand Black women judges' courtroom experiences with respect/disrespect and recusal requests. With the help of my research team, I invited all Black state court judges (<1,000) in the country to participate in the survey via a letter sent to their courthouses. Our outreach required my research team and I to build a database with judges' contact information that we gathered from court administration websites. Each judge received a packet from the research team that contained a recruitment letter, a sheet with frequently asked questions about the project and principal investigator, and a document with the research team's short biographies. Judges could fill out a paper copy of the survey, but were encouraged to complete the survey online via the survey platform Qualtrics. The surveys were very detailed and comprehensive in nature, asking jurists to share information about their social backgrounds, childhoods, pre-bench careers, and work on the bench.

Because this article is focusing on Black women judges' experiences on the bench, I restrict my analysis to the surveys completed and submitted by Black women judges and I limit my analysis to the questions that focus on these jurists' experiences with respect/disrespect and recusal requests. In the subsequent section, I present the responses of the 163 Black women judges who completed their survey as of July 2021.[12] The following questions were asked of each judge surveyed:

(1) Generally speaking, to what extent do you feel respected by litigants and lawyers in the courtroom? [Response options: Not at all respected, slightly respected, moderately respected, very respected, extremely respected]

(2) If you have experienced any disrespect while on the bench, please briefly describe the experience(s) and generally describe any parties involved.

(3) Have you ever been asked to recuse yourself from a case? [Response options: Yes, no]

(4) If you've ever been asked to recuse yourself from a case, which of the following things, if any, do you feel influenced the request? Check all that apply. (Response options: Your race, your ideology, your gender, your sexual orientation, your religion, your perceived conflict of interest, other)

These questions provide me with an opportunity to analyze and understand Black women judges' experiences with (dis)respect and disqualification requests. Drawing on both open-ended and closed-ended survey questions allows for me to take a mixed method analytical approach to triangulate and understand Black women jurists' experiences in their courtrooms. With the data, I can simultaneously highlight whether there are any trends amongst respondents regarding their experiences with recusal requests and disrespect, and can present the nuances and specifics of some of their experiences as a result of their willingness to provide details about the disrespect they have faced.

Black women judges' experiences with (dis)respect

To assess Black women judges' experiences with respect/disrespect in the courtroom, I asked the Black women judge survey participants: "Generally speaking, to what extent do you feel respected by litigants and lawyers in the courtroom?" The overwhelming majority of respondents (74%) said they were either very or extremely respected by litigants and lawyers in the courtroom, and interestingly, no respondent indicated they were not at all respected. Figure 1 presents all of the responses to this question. Despite many of the judges feeling as though they are respected in their courtrooms, slightly more than half of the Black women judges (55%) reported experiencing disrespect at some point while on the bench. Thus, it would seem that disrespect does happen, but that it is not a frequent experience and is not experienced by every single Black woman judge on the bench. To this point, one judge commented: "I have generally felt respected, but you get the occasional litigant, or defendant who will behave disrespectfully." For some perspective, only 38% of Black men who responded to the survey (n = 109) said they had experienced disrespect.

Disrespect can be manifested in a wide variety of ways. To understand Black women judges' experiences with disrespect, I asked all of the judges surveyed: "If you have experienced any disrespect while on the bench, please briefly describe the experience(s) and any parties involved.)." Eighteen percent of respondents did not provide much in terms of detail, but their responses are still significant. For instance, one judge said, "Too much to explain," suggesting that disrespect is a pervasive issue affecting her as a Black women judge. Another judge stated, "I have been disrespected by both attorneys and unrepresented litigants too many times to explain." Yet another judge said, "can't explain briefly," insinuating that to describe the disrespect she has faced would take significant space and time. Despite not providing much description, these judges highlight the experience of at least some Black women judges – they face some disrespect as judges and that the disrespect comes from various people in the courtroom.

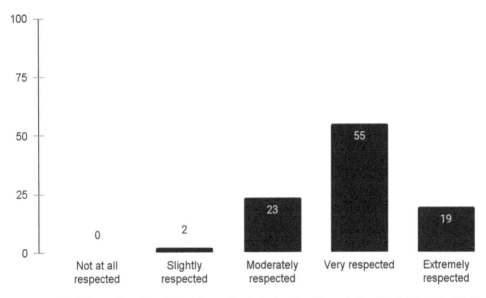

Figure 1. Percent of Black Women State Court Judges' Responding to the Question: "Generally Speaking, to What Extent Do You Feel Respected by Litigants and Lawyers in the Courtroom?."

Most of the judges (82%) who stated that they experienced disrespect provided clear examples to illustrate their point. Analyzing their responses reveals some discernible patterns of disrespect that these judges experience and endure, and shows that many Black women judges have common experiences irrespective of their geographical location, how they reached the bench (i.e., judicial selection method), and the type of court they sit on (i.e., trial court vs. appellate court). Three distinctive patterns are present in the data (see Table 1): First, Black women judges have often been spoken to or treated in aggressive/confrontational, threatening, and inappropriate ways; Second, these judges have had their legitimacy, authority, and competence questioned; Finally, they have not always been referred to or called by their appropriate name or title. Taken together, these Black women judges have experience dealing with disruptive, demeaning, intimidating, and passive-aggressive behavior, dismissive treatment, and non-verbal insidious behavior. I discuss each of these patterns in detail below and, as much as possible, center Black women judges' voices by incorporating examples directly from the surveys.

Table 1. Coding Themes and Examples from the Black Women Judge Participants' Responses.

Code/Short Description	Percent of Participants Who Reported Experience with this Disrespect	Examples
Aggressive/Confrontational, Threatening, and Inappropriate Language and Behavior	52%	• "Lawyers/litigants in custody cases refuse to accept my rulings on separate notices." • "Argument on the court's ruling of objections in the courtroom before a jury." • "Condescending lawyers."
Legitimacy, Authority, and Competence Questioned	61%	• "On occasion an attorney would be disrespectful because he or she did not like a ruling." • "On occasion a white male attorney will attempt to be dismissive toward my experience and opinion." • "Treated as though I'm incompetent."
Not Being Called Their Appropriate Name or Title	19%	• "Some attorneys refuse to address me as 'judge' and insist on 'yes ma'am' or 'no ma'am'." • "I have been called a 'bitch.'" • "Men calling you darling."

Black women judges' experiences with litigants' and attorneys' aggressive/confrontational, threatening, and inappropriate language and behavior

One of the most common experiences amongst the Black women judges in this study is that they have been disrespected by being spoken to and treated in aggressive/confrontational, threatening, and inappropriate ways. More than half (52%) of the judges reported examples that are aggressive, confrontational, threatening, and inappropriate. Nineteen percent of respondents who reported disrespect shared interactions that involved confrontation and aggression. Many of the judges noted that some litigants and lawyers (try to) argue with or out-talk them and "argue with rulings beyond advocacy." For instance, one judge said, "I have had young, white, male attorneys argue with me to the point of near contempt." Some of the judges mentioned attorneys, especially male attorneys, interrupting them and talking over them by speaking too loudly, and shouting or yelling at them. Black women judges also deal with litigants and lawyers talking back to them. Despite the fact that emotions are high in court, these judges experience, and perceive these interactions as disrespectful, and we should understand them as such.

Judges also signaled that sometimes, it is not what litigants and lawyers are saying that is disrespectful, but their tone and behavior can make their remarks inappropriate. Twenty-nine percent of respondents who said they had been disrespected shared incidents involving general inappropriate behavior. For example, judges signaled that being spoken to condescendingly was inappropriate and disrespectful. Numerous judges shared that some attorneys even yell, make faces, and then storm out of the courtroom when they disagree with the court's decision. And another judge said, "I have had attorneys interrupt me while I am giving a ruling." Part of the issue is not just that these attorneys and litigants are behaving this way, but that these judges feel that "those same attorneys don't do that with [their] other colleagues." Thus, this behavior is being experienced as unique to them as Black women judges.

Some of the aggressive behavior that Black women endure is threatening to the judges' safety and careers. Four percent of judges shared that attorneys who are unhappy with the court's decision threaten to appeal while court is still in session. One judge shared her experience of being threatened to render a decision in a specific manner: "One party, in a divorce case, threatened to file a complaint with the Judicial Inquiry Commission, if his case was not decided favorably towards him." Still, another judge reported that rendering decisions that she thought were appropriate led to litigants and attorneys filing complaints against her: "I've also had two grievances – one older white male and one older white female – two different cases, accused me of being racist." Yet another judge said that she once had to get reinforcements to help her deal with a disorderly attorney who was threatening her: "I once had a lawyer whose tone became so aggressive with me that I had to order him to step away from the bench with my bailiffs standing at the ready if necessary." Beyond just threatening court action, one judge said some attorneys even threatened her safety by "directing litigants to come to [her] home to attempt to intimidate [her]."

Ten percent of respondents mentioned that attorneys and litigants had used profanity while in conversation with them. One judge said, "I was recently told by a pro se litigant that I was going to have to give her 'a good mother f . . . .ing reason' for my ruling." Not only was the judge cursed at, but the litigant expected the judge to justify the ruling and, importantly, do so in a way that the litigant approved. Another judge said a litigant told her to "kiss [their] ass," and a third judge said an example of disrespect is a "disgruntled defendant who curses on the way out the door because they don't like your decision." Shockingly, cursing did not just come from litigants, but also attorneys, with one judge saying "[a] lawyer used profanity toward me because he couldn't get his way."

Black women judges' experiences with having their legitimacy, authority, and competence questioned

Every Black woman surveyed for this study reached the bench. Yet, 61% of the judges who said they faced disrespect while on the bench shared that their disrespect involved having their legitimacy, authority, and competence questioned. Some Black women judges report lawyers and litigants questioning their legitimacy as judges. People have condescendingly commented that the Black women judges do not seem old enough to have the position or that their youthfulness makes it difficult for them to understand the way things work in the profession. One judge said she was told, "'You haven't been around long enough to know.'" Another judge said that "during a first appearance calendar, an accused questioned my age based upon my appearance." A third judge said, "Disrespect has been received from older and what they perceive to be more experienced in certain matters."

Beyond experiences with people questioning whether Black women judges can/do belong in the judiciary and are legitimate judicial officers, 51% of Black women judges who said they faced disrespect also mentioned experiencing their authority as a judge being challenged. One Black woman judge reported that when asking questions to witnesses like social workers, her questions will go unanswered or she will have to repeat her question and push for an answer. Another Black woman suggests that some people who come before her despise her in that role and then question her ability to judge by questioning her authority. She has had to learn how to sit in her power and respond to those challenges firmly.

> Older white men simply had no stomach for a Black woman telling them no, which is what a judge does on a daily basis. I decided the only way to deal with it was to run the Court, strictly by the rules. And so we dotted every 'i' and crossed every 't' twice. I refused to rule on objections unless counsel stood to address the Court. I only ruled on legal objections; speaking objections were left hanging until they decided to ask their next questions.

Twelve percent of Black women judge respondents who said they faced disrespect also report having their legal and judicial competence called into question. Despite being knowledgeable about the law and also familiar with the role and responsibilities of judges, these women are still questioned about their competence as legal professionals. One judge said lawyers used "buzz words to question [her] knowledge," and another judge said that "Early in [her] judicial career, an attorney approached the bench with a volume of the rules of procedure to show [her] how to find an applicable rule." A different judge said she has "had a handful of white male attorneys attempt to challenge [her] ... competency in the law. A couple of others come off as if [she does not] know what [she is] doing." Lastly, a judge reported that she has "experienced instances where it seems that the attorney thinks that [she] may not know the law only to discover that they were unfamiliar with the law, but until advised of their mistaken belief, will advocate on this mistaken belief." Other women indicated that these challenges to their authority include not accepting their decisions, interrupting them, facial expressions that show disdain or contempt, and arguing with them even after a ruling.

Black women judges also reported having their authority questioned via litigants and attorneys deciding to lie or disobey them. Most conversations in the courtroom happen under oath, and the expectation is that litigants and lawyers alike are not lying in court to the judge. Additionally, judges expect their orders and rulings to be obeyed and complied with, and to be responded to appropriately when engaged. Numerous respondents shared that they had faced disrespect reported instances in which they were lied to or disobeyed. One judge noted being lied to about an administrative matter: "An attorney who is per diem for many firms and appears before me daily for months lied to me and stated that she represented another attorney who answered the calendar call as pro se; said attorney retracted her statement of representation but only after I had to make a record."

Disobedience and encouraging insubordination happened occasionally, with some judges reporting that they were either disobeyed or were aware that there was an effort to encourage people to defy and disregard them. Judges noted that attorneys have approached the bench, excused witnesses, and even adjourned cases. Attorneys have also told their clients not to appear in court. These are typical actions in a courtroom, and these actions in and of themselves are not problematic. What makes them an issue is that these actions require permission from the judge, and these attorneys are bold and doing what they want to do irrespective of judges' orders and expectations. One judge's comment reflects this dynamic: "A prosecutor excused witnesses, effectively ending court early, without consulting or seeking permission from the court; and when confronted, said, 'what's the big deal?'" By not requesting permission when that is the norm and the rule, attorneys are disobeying these Black women judges and sending a signal to the judges that they believe these Black women's rules (i.e., the court's rules) do not need to be obeyed.

Other examples of disobedience in Black women judges' courtrooms include not following protocols, such as not addressing the judge before speaking and not complying with court rulings. One judge remarked that "Rather than entering notice of appeal, a prosecutor indicated in open court, before a full gallery, that he did not intend to comply with the court's ruling." Another judge reported that "White police officers attempt to disregard evidentiary rulings." Again, these behaviors reveal how litigants and attorneys are being disrespectful to Black women judges by questioning the authority and legitimacy of Black women judges with their actions and rhetoric in the courtroom.

Black women judges' experiences with not being called their appropriate name or title

Judicial officers in the United States typically go by "Judge," "Justice," and "Honorable." It is disrespectful to not refer to judicial officers in their courtroom using one of these titles. Yet, 19% of Black women judge participants report being disrespected by not being referred to by one of their accepted professional titles. In some cases, disrespectful lawyers do not even speak before addressing the judge. But in most cases, Black women judges report the use of derogatory and inappropriate names.

Four judges noted being called (Black) b****es, and two judges reported being called the n-word. Two judges reported not being referred to as a judge when on the bench, with one of the judges saying she was called "Ms." Another judge reported that attorneys and litigant alike called her "honey, sweetie, [and] dear," and one judge said she has been called "darling." One judge said she had been called "a fat Black lady" in writing by a party, and one judge said she had been called "shug," which she suspects is a southern thing. Another judge mentioned being called out of her name but did not share the context nor what she was called. Two judges shared that they were called "ma'am" instead of your honor, and another judge said a litigant called her "girlfriend." Lastly, one judge reported recurring mistaken identity because she had been repeatedly called a different Black woman judge's name: "Unable to differentiate between me and another Black female judge by counsel on numerous occasions." These experiences are consistent with the experiences of other women in the legal profession (Reyes 2020).

In line with my expectations, a significant number of Black women judge respondents report having had experience with disrespect while on the bench. Moreover, as is evident from the data, this disrespect has been both subtle (i.e., nonverbal behavior) like Cross (2003) suggested was prevalent, but it was also not subtle/crude (i.e., verbal). Now, I assess whether the Black women jurists in this study have experience being asked to recuse themselves from court cases and if they perceive their race and gender identities as factors influencing those recusal requests.

"People know that I am very fair": (race) recusal requests and Black women judges' experiences with questions about the fairness of their decision-making

In addition to substantial disrespect, Black women in this study report receiving recusal requests, which inevitably signal that some attorneys question their ability to render fair decisions. To get a sense of how common recusal requests are, I asked each Black woman judge survey participant, "Have you ever been asked to recuse yourself from a case?" Seventy percent of the respondents said they had been asked to recuse themselves from a case. This percentage is not unexpected, given that recusal requests are pretty standard.[13]

Even more important than the number of Black women judges with experience being asked to recuse themselves is whether they believe the recusals are unfounded and the result of bias. To address this topic, survey respondents were also asked to share what they thought influenced the requests they received. Close to half of the respondents (48%) who indicated they had been asked to recuse themselves from a case said "perceived conflict of interest" alone influenced the request(s). This response is expected because a perceived conflict of interest or appearance of impropriety is the primary justification to submit recusal requests. But social identities should not necessarily determine whether a judge should be asked to recuse themselves. Yet, there is a history of race recusal cases and even some contemporary examples (Ifill 1997).

As I expected, some Black women judges believe their social identities played a role in the recusal requests they received. Slightly more than one-fifth of the respondents (23%) who reported experiences with recusal requests said they believed the requests were at least partially influenced by their race. Six percent of respondents said they thought their gender at least partially influenced their requests for recusal. Two judges (i.e., 2%) said they thought their sexual identity influenced their recusal requests, with one judge writing, "motions have been made to recuse me as a judge because I am lesbian." And finally, some Black women (10%) felt their perceived ideology played a role in their disqualification requests.

To some judges, recusal requests are evidence of disrespect, especially if and when they are seen as baseless. One Black woman judge commented that her experience with disrespect was related to disqualification requests she had received. "I have experienced disrespectful posturing by white males in [a] few instances, but those instances were motions for recusals – 3 have been filed by white males and denied." The fact that all three were filed by white males of a Black woman judge is significant and highlights the continued racial dynamics of recusals. Moreover, the fact that all three requests were denied suggests they were frivolous at the outset.

To summarize all of the findings, some Black women judges comment that they have been spoken to or treated in aggressive, confrontational, threatening, and inappropriate ways. They have had their legitimacy, authority, and competence questioned. Additionally, their appropriate name or title has not always been used when speaking or referring to them. Furthermore, Black women judges report having their decision-making and ability to make fair decisions called into question. They understand at least some of the recusal requests they receive to be motivated by their own political and social identities. Thus, at least some Black women jurists are reporting that they experience both disrespect and requests to recuse themselves from cases that are steeped in bias.

Black women judges and white men in the courtroom

Being a judge is hard irrespective of the judges' identities. It can be particularly isolating by the nature of the job and the desire for judges not to appear too political. The Black women judges who participated in my study highlight how many of them face particular challenges. Patterns in the data reveal Black women judges have had challenges with being mistreated and disrupted. Taken together, Black women judges have experience dealing with disruptive, demeaning, intimidating, and passive-aggressive behavior, dismissive treatment, and nonverbal insidious behavior.[14]

Judges interviewed were clear that many of the attorneys and litigants who have been most disrespectful to them are men, especially white men. Thirteen percent of respondents reported that their experiences with disrespect involve male attorneys or litigants generally, and 8% of respondents say their experiences involve white attorneys or litigants. Twelve percent of respondents shared that their incidents of disrespect involved white men specifically. That Black women judges attribute this much of their disrespect and challenges to (white) men attorneys and litigants highlights significant racial and gender dynamics.

One Black woman judge described these dynamics: "I have felt disrespect by older (usually male) attorneys, talking down or challenging my decisions." A second judge said, "I have been challenged daily by male attorneys, primarily white males, although some Black males have challenged my authority also." A third judge said, "I've had a handful of white male attorneys attempt to challenge my authority ... One in particular often attempts to challenge and argue with me."

In addition to the racial and gender dynamics, the fact that so many Black women judges surveyed had these feelings suggests that these issues are not random and are, in fact, pervasive. Black women judges across the country, sitting on different courts and having reached the bench using various selection methods, highlight how Black women judges share some professional experiences. Although there is a lot that they may have in common, unfortunately, amongst those things are the fact that some Black women judges have experience with disrespect and endure challenges to their judging.

To be precise, litigation and attorneys' problematic behaviors and ways do not always go unaddressed by Black women in the judiciary. One judge noted that she has had litigants and attorneys speak out of turn but that when she is "respectful and firm, the situation is quickly handled." Thus, the judge's redirection resolves what she sees as slight disrespect. This particular experience that a judge reported having raises a question about whether Black women are consistently addressing the disrespect they face and whether, over time, they become desensitized to this type of extreme behavior as a way to survive those occasional moments that can be/are demoralizing. This type of desensitivity may be a conscious or unconscious process, but regardless, desensitization can mean that Black women judges will not always explicitly address these situations when they occur as the judge did in this example involving spitting. In fact, one Black woman judge said she sometimes tries to hold off on responding in the moment because she does not want to respond in anger and wants to allow people to be heard. This approach sometimes is at odds with what her staff wishes she would do because the staff members believe the litigants are intentionally being disrespectful.

Conclusion

This article highlighted the experiences and perspectives of a group of legal actors that we rarely hear about – Black women judges. Drawing from an original survey with 163 Black women judges, a significant number of Black women judges in this country, respondents reveal that despite holding powerful positions and high-status jobs, many of these women jurists face challenges while on the bench. I find that Black women judges' experiences involve substantial disrespect from litigants and lawyers, and there is an important racial and gender dynamic to the disrespect aimed at these judges that highlights the continued impact of racism and sexism for Black women in America, including the legal profession. Additionally, I find that these judges contend with outsiders' doubts about their ability to be impartial because they receive requests to recuse themselves from cases, and importantly, these Black women judges attribute these recusals at least partly to their race and gender, highlighting how racism and sexism is manifested in the courtroom for those on the bench. All in all, Black women judges' experiences on the bench highlight that Black women in the judiciary continue to endure opposition, mistreatment, and challenges, and their experiences are influenced by their race and gender identities.

What Black women judges' report experiencing sheds light on how litigants and attorneys treat Black women judges once they reach the bench. How these women are treated helps us better discern how race and gender continue to influence Black women's lives, even as judges. Their treatment can help us better understand what obstacles may stifle the ongoing quest to create more diverse judiciaries and how to counter those issues.

I maintain that judicial diversity is not just about Black women and other minorities reaching the bench but also involves caring for and treating these judges appropriately and respectfully (Kang et al. 2020). So, why should we care about the incidents of disrespect and recusal challenges endured by Black women judges? Work-related challenges and experiences affect Black women's satisfaction with their jobs, mental health, and life chances (Mays, Coleman, and Jackson 1996). The extent to which this is true for Black women judges is unclear. In the future, scholars should determine the specific relationship between Black women judges' experiences, their feelings about the system and their profession, their mental health, and their career goals and aspirations (Jensen and Martinek 2009). Despite being unable to determine precisely what causes or is correlated with Black women judges' satisfaction with being a judge, their mental health, and desire to remain in or exit the judiciary, I maintain that we should still care about Black women judges' experiences with these topics in mind as potential implications of their courtroom experiences that impacts their work.

Black women judges' courtroom experiences may also influence whether these judges are able and willing to stay in their current judicial position. Diversity in the state judiciary is significant because state court judges often have the final say in most cases concerning state laws, and they render decisions in a wide variety of cases that profoundly shape how people live their lives. Moreover, Black women judges' experiences may also affect whether these judges are able and willing to climb the judicial ladder. State appellate jurists and federal judges/justices often come from lower state courts. Suppose Black women are not well-represented at the state court level. In that case, it will be difficult, if not impossible, to diversify at the upper levels of the judiciary. If we can increase the number of lower federal court judges and state court judges, it is more feasible to get Black woman appointed to the federal courts, especially the appellate courts (Dawson 2016). We witnessed this recently when Biden's shortlist for the recent Supreme Court of the United States vacancy was comprised of three Black women, all of whom were either current state or federal court judges.

Finally, Black women judges' experiences could influence whether they maintain their mental health and are satisfied with their judicial career. The implications of employment-related stress and dissatisfaction are significant. For example, the mysterious and tragic death of Judge Sheila Abdus-Salaam was ruled a suicide by the office of New York City's medical examiner (Acosta 2018). Abdus-Salaam was the first Black woman to serve on the New York Court of Appeals, the state's highest court and court of last resort in most cases. When friends and family were questioned about Judge Abdus-Salaam's mental health, they reported that she had been stressed at work.[15]

What needs to happen now? What do we need to do to improve the representation of Black women in the judiciary by way of maintaining diversity (i.e., help Black women remain on the bench)? Based on Black women judges' experiences, I argue that these judges need court administrators to keep workspaces that are not toxic and hostile. This may mean giving Black women additional tools to address the disrespect they experience. Currently, most Black women judges possess the means of declaring misconduct and disrespect as contempt of court. This ensures that Black women judges have a way to punish or at least respond to those who misbehave in the courts. Moreover, those responsible for disrespecting Black women judges should be held accountable by the appropriate legal institutions including bar associations and court administrations.

Beyond creating better work environments, Black women judges need to be supported. They can be financially and electorally supported while pursuing judgeships or trying to retain their judicial positions. They can also be financially supported by being compensated appropriately, especially given what they endure as Black women in the judiciary. Lastly, they can be backed as individual judges with the creation and support for organizations that center them and care for them. For instance, a newly-created organization centers current and prospective Black women judges – the National Society of Black Women Judges (NSBWJ). NSBWJ is similar to the National Association of Women Judges, except that NSBWJ focuses on Black women in the judiciary and maintaining a healthy judicial pipeline for Black women (Rossman 1980).

This is one of the first articles to assess Black women judges' experiences on the bench by assessing how these women are respected/disrespected and have their decision-making challenged. Moving forward, scholars should aim to assess how Black women's experiences compare to those of other judges, especially their racial counterparts (i.e., Black men judges), gender counterparts (i.e., white, Latina, Asian, and Native American women judges), and white men judicial colleagues. Researchers should also determine the relationship between Black women judges' experiences and mental health, perceptions of the courts, and career aspirations (Rothmann and Rossouw 2020).

This article demonstrates that by asking Black women judges directly, we can understand some of what they experience on the bench. This information is significant because this group is under-theorized and studied in the academic literature, but also because of the potential implications and impact of the treatment of Black women judges. That is, this study gives us some factors that may be influencing the persisting underrepresentation of Black women judges and how we can better support these women as prospective judges and actual judges by considering and acknowledging what many of them experience once they reach the bench.

Notes

1. This quote is included in a biography of Jane Bolin, the nation's first Black woman state court judge. The biography is available online: https://herdacity.org/jane-bolin/.
2. This remark is the response by one of the Black women state court judges that I surveyed for my research when I asked her to share whether/how she has ever experienced any disrespect while on the bench.
3. This quote was pulled from the disqualification request submitted by Attorney Ephraim London in the case *Blank v. Sullivan & Cromwell*, a lawsuit that challenged the antidiscrimination principles of Title VII of the Civil Rights Act of 1964. London, the defense attorney, claimed that the judge to hear the case, Constance Baker Motley, the nation's first Black woman federal court judge, should be disqualified because she might be biased as a result of her own race and gender and a likelihood that she had personal experiences dealing with racist and/or sexist employment discrimination that would make it difficult for her to render a fair ruling. In his recusal motion, London implied that "only white men could properly preside in a sex discrimination suit" (Brown-Nagin 2017).
4. https://www.npr.org/2019/01/16/685815783/meet-Black-girl-magic-the-19-african-american-women-elected-as -judges-in-texas.
5. https://www.npr.org/2019/01/16/685815783/meet-Black-girl-magic-the-19-african-american-women-elected-as -judges-in-texas.
6. https://www.fjc.gov/.
7. Jane Bolin became the first Black woman state judge in the United States when Mayor Fiorello H. La Guardia appointed her to the New York City Domestic Relations Court (i.e., Family Court) in 1939. Twenty-seven years later, Constance Baker Motley was appointed to the United States District Court for the Southern District of New York, one of the nation's largest federal trial courts.
8. https://www.usnews.com/education/blogs/law-admissions-lowdown/articles/what-underrepresented-law-school -applicants-should-k.
9. This report is available online: https://www.enjuris.com/students/law-school-race-2019.html.
10. https://www.americanbar.org/groups/professional_responsibility/publications/model_rules_of_professional_ conduct/model_rules_of_professional_conduct_preamble_scope/.
11. https://www.reuters.com/investigates/special-report/usa-judges-misconduct/.
12. This response rate may be shocking to readers who anticipate high response rates (i.e., 30%+), but this is quite typical for a population of elites that, for the most part, choose not to participate directly in political science research. One discernible pattern amongst the judges that responded to the survey is that they are trial court judges, but this is not surprising because Black judges are overrepresented amongst trial court judges and not appellate-level judges. Beyond that pattern, there are no age patterns, and no region patterns in terms of who responded to the survey and the responses to the survey.
13. https://www.law.com/texaslawyer/2020/01/16/judges-dont-like-your-recusal-requests-and-theres-data-to-prove -it/?slreturn=20210603045154; https://iaals.du.edu/sites/default/files/documents/publications/judicial_recusal_ procedures.pdf.
14. Even though they were not writing about judges, Leape et al.'s (2012) categorization of disrespect is a helpful guide that I consulted when analyzing the experiences with disrespect that Black women judges reported in the survey. https://www.ismp.org/resources/disrespectful-behaviors-their-impact-why-they-arise-and-persist-and- how-address-them-part.
15. https://www.cnn.com/2017/07/26/us/abdus-salaam-death-ruled-suicide/index.html.

Disclosure statement

No potential conflict of interest was reported by the author(s).

References

Acosta, Rolando T. 2018. "Sheila Abdus-Salaam: The Value of Contribution." *Columbia Law Review* 118 (1): 1–4.

Alexander-Floyd, Nikol. 2019. "Why Political Scientists Don't Study Black Women, but Historians and Sociologists Do: On Intersectionality and the Remapping of the Study of Black Political Womens." In *Black Women in Politics*, eds. Julia S. Jordan-Zachery and Nikol Alexander-Floyd. Albany: State University of New York Press, 3–17.

Alozie, Nicholas O. 1988. "Black Representation on State Judiciaries." *Social Science Quarterly* 69 (4): 979–86.

Blackburne-Rigsby, Anna. 2009. "Black Women Judges: The Historical Journey of Black Women to the Nation's Highest Courts." *Howard Law Journal* 53 (3): 645–98.

Bowleg, Lisa. 2008. "When Black+ Lesbian+ Woman≠ Black Lesbian Woman: The Methodological Challenges of Qualitative and Quantitative Intersectionality Research." *Sex Roles* 59 (5): 312–25.

Brown, Nadia E. 2014. *Sisters in the Statehouse: Black Women and Legislative Decision Making*. Oxford: Oxford University Press.

Brown-Nagin, Tomiko. 2017. "Identity Matters: The Case of Judge Constance Baker Motley." *Columbia Law Review* 117 (7): 1691–739.

Brown, Nadia E., and Danielle Casarez Lemi. 2021. *Sister Style: The Politics of Appearance for Black Women Political Elites*. Oxford: Oxford University Press.

Burleigh, Nina, and Stephanie Benson Goldberg. 1988. "Black Women Lawyers Coping with Dual Discrimination." *ABA Journal* 74 (6): 64–68.

Carbado, Devon W., Kimberlé Williams Crenshaw, Vickie M. Mays, and Barbara Tomlinson. 2013. "Intersectionality: Mapping the Movements of a Theory." *Du Bois Review: Social Science Research on Race* 10 (2):303–12. doi:10.1017/S1742058X13000349.

Chenault, Renee. 1981. "Pennsylvanians on the Bench: Profiles of Black Judges." *Black Law Journal* 7 (1): 226–42.

Cho, Sumi, Kimberlé Williams Crenshaw, and Leslie McCall. 2013. "Toward a Field of Intersectionality Studies: Theory, Applications, and Praxis." *Signs: Journal of Women in Culture and Society* 38 (4):785–810. doi:10.1086/669608.

Collins, Todd A., Tao L. Dumas, and Laura P. Moyer. 2017. "Intersecting Disadvantages: Race, Gender, and Age Discrimination among Attorneys." *Social Science Quarterly* 98 (5):1642–58. doi:10.1111/ssqu.12376.

Cook, Beverly B. 1984. "Women Judges: A Preface to Their History." *Golden Gate University Law Review* 14 (3): 573–610.

Cook, Julian Abele, Jr. 1996. "Dream Makers: Black Judges on Justice." *Michigan Law Review* 94 (6):1479–94. doi:10.2307/1289957.

Crenshaw, Kimberlé. 1989. "Demarginalizing the Intersection of Race and Sex: A Black Feminist Critique of Antidiscrimination Doctrine, Feminist Theory, and Antiracist Politics." *University of Chicago Legal Forum*: 139–68.

Crenshaw, Kimberlé. 1991. "Race, Gender, and Sexual Harassment." *Southern California Law Review* 65 (3): 1467–76.

Cross, Christopher. 2003. "Disrespect in the Court: A Judge's Perspective." *Denver University Law Review* 80 (4): 765–69.

Dawson, April G. 2016. "Missing in Action: The Absence of Potential African American Female Supreme Court Justice Nominees-Why This Is and What Can Be Done about It." *Howard Law Journal* 60 (1): 177–220.

Dawuni, Josephine. 2018. "African Women Judges on International Courts: Symbolic or Substantive Gains?" *University of Baltimore Law Review* 47 (2): 199–246.

Dowe, Pearl K. Ford. 2020. "Resisting Marginalization: Black Women's Political Ambition and Agency." *PS: Political Science & Politics* 53 (4): 697–702.

Engstrom, Richard L. 1989. "When Blacks Run for Judge: Racial Divisions in the Candidate Preferences of Louisiana Voters." *Judicature* 73 (2): 87–89.

Fix, Michael P., and Gbemende E. Johnson. 2017. "Public Perceptions of Gender Bias in the Decisions of Female State Court Judges." *Vanderbilt Law Review* 70 (6): 1845–86.

Fricke, Amber, and Angela Onwuachi-Willig. 2012. "Do Female Firsts Still Matter: Why They Do for Female Judges of Color." *Michigan State Law Review* 2012 (5): 1529–54.

George, Tracey E., and Albert H. Yoon. 2017. "Measuring Justice in State Courts: The Demographics of the State Judiciary." *Vanderbilt Law Review* 70 (6): 1887–910.

Gill, Rebecca D. 2014. "Implicit Bias in Judicial Performance Evaluations: We Must Do Better than This." *Justice System Journal* 35 (3):301–24. doi:10.1080/0098261X.2013.873290.

Gill, Rebecca D. 2017. "Do Judicial Performance Evaluations Influence Retention Election Results?." In *Judicial Elections in the 21st Century*, eds. Chris W. Bonneau and Melinda Gann Hall. New York, NY: Routledge, pp. 197–214.

Goelzhauser, Greg. 2019. *Intersectional Representation on State Supreme Courts. Forthcoming*. Judicial Politics Reader.

Gomez Mazo, Daniel 2020. "Afro-Descendant Representation On Latin American Courts." *SJD Dissertation*.

Haire, Susan. 2001. "Rating the Ratings of the American Bar Association Standing Committee on Federal Judiciary." *Justice System Journal* 22 (1): 1–17.

Hancock, Ange-Marie. 2007. "When Multiplication Doesn't Equal Quick Addition: Examining Intersectionality as a Research Paradigm." *Perspectives on Politics* 5 (1):63–79. doi:10.1017/S1537592707070065.

Hancock, Ange-Marie. 2015. "Intersectionality's Will toward Social Transformation." *New Political Science* 37 (4):620–27. doi:10.1080/07393148.2015.1089049.

Harris, Allison P., and Maya Sen. 2019. "Bias and Judging." *Annual Review of Political Science* 22 (1):241–59. doi:10.1146/annurev-polisci-051617-090650.

Hurwitz, Mark S, and Drew Noble Lanier. 2012. "Judicial Diversity in Federal Courts: A Historical and Empirical Exploration." *Judicature* 96 (2): 76–84.

Ifill, Sherrilyn A. 1997. "Judging the Judges: Racial Diversity, Impartiality and Representation on State Trial Courts." *Boston College Law Review* 39 (1): 95–150.

Ifill, Sherrilyn A., and Eric J. Segall. 2011. "Judicial Recusal at the Court." *University of Pennsylvania Law Review* 160: 331–48.

Jensen, Jennifer M., and Wendy L. Martinek. 2009. "The Effects of Race and Gender on the Judicial Ambitions of State Trial Court Judges." *Political Research Quarterly* 62 (2):379–92. doi:10.1177/1065912908319574.

Johnson, Susan W., Ronald Stidham, Robert A. Carp, and Kenneth L. Manning. 2008. "The Gender Influence on U.S. District Court Decisions: Updating the Traditional Judge Attribute Model." *Journal of Women, Politics & Policy* 29 (4):497–526. doi:10.1080/15544770802092675.

Jordan-Zachery, Julia S. 2007. "Am I A Black Woman or A Woman Who Is Black? A Few Thoughts on the Meaning of Intersectionality." *Politics & Gender* 3 (2):254–63. doi:10.1017/S1743923X07000074.

Kang, Alice J., Miki Caul Kittilson, Valerie Hoekstra, and Maria C. Escobar-Lemmon. 2020. "Diverse and Inclusive High Courts: A Global and Intersectional Perspective." *Politics, Groups, and Identities* 8 (4):812–21. doi:10.1080/21565503.2020.1782948.

Kenney, Sally J. 2013. "Wise Latinas, Strategic Minnesotans, and the Feminist Standpoint: The Backlash against Women Judges." *Thomas Jefferson Law Review* 36 (1): 43–82.

Leape, Lucian L., Miles F. Shore, Jules L. Dienstag, Robert J. Mayer, Susan Edgman-Levitan, Gregg S. Meyer, and Gerald B. Healy. 2012. "A Culture of Respect, Part 1: The Nature and Causes of Disrespectful Behavior by Physicians." *Academic Medicine* 87 (7):845–52. doi:10.1097/ACM.0b013e318258338d.

Livingston, Robert W, Ashleigh Shelby Rosette, and Ella F Washington. 2012. "Can an Agentic Black Woman Get Ahead? the Impact of Race and Interpersonal Dominance on Perceptions of Female Leaders." *Psychological Science* 23 (4): 354–58.

Mays, Vickie M., Lerita M. Coleman, and James S. Jackson. 1996. "Perceived Race-based Discrimination, Employment Status, and Job Stress in a National Sample of Black Women: Implications for Health Outcomes." *Journal of Occupational Health Psychology* 1 (3):319–29. doi:10.1037/1076-8998.1.3.319.

Means, Taneisha N. 2021. "Why Do so Few Black Women Serve in High-level Federal Posts?" *The Washington Post*, June 24 https://www.washingtonpost.com/politics/2021/06/24/why-do-so-few-Black-women-serve-high-level-federal-posts/

Means, Taneisha N., Andrew Eslich, and Kaitlin Prado. 2019. "Judicial Diversity in the United States Federal Udiciary." In *Research Handbook on Law and Courts*, eds. Susan M. Sterett and Lee D. Walker. Cheltenham, UK: Edward Elgar Publishing, 231–45.

Means, Taneisha N., and Isaac Unah. 2019. "Judging Black Judges in Racialized Conflicts." Unpublished manuscript.

Mitchell, David B. 1987. "A Salute to Black Judges of the Maryland Judiciary." *Law Forum* 18 (3): 26–27.

Norwood, Kimberly Jade. 2020. "Gender Bias as the Norm in the Legal Profession: It's Still a [White] Man's Game." *Washington University Journal of Law & Policy* 62: 25–50.

Ono, Yoshikuni, and Michael A. Zilis. 2021. "Do Americans Perceive Diverse Judges as Inherently Biased?" *Politics, Groups, and Identities*: 1–10.

Palmer, Barbara. 2001. "Women in the American Judiciary: Their Influence and Impact." *Women & Politics* 23 (3):91–101. doi:10.1300/J014v23n03_04.

Reyes, Maritza I. 2020. "Professional Women Subjugated by Name-Calling and Character Attacks." *Journal of Gender Race & Justice* 23 (2):397–450.

Rossman, Lynn C. 1980. "Women Judges Unite: A Report from the Founding Convention of the National Association of Women Judges." *Golden Gate University Law Review* 10 (3): 1237–66.

Rothmann, Sebastiaan, and Elna Rossouw. 2020. "Well-being of Judges: A Review of Quantitative and Qualitative Studies." *S.A. Journal of Industrial Psychology* 46 (1): 1–12.

Scarborough, Cathy. 1989. "Conceptualizing Black Women's Employment Experiences." *The Yale Law Journal* 98 (7):1457–78. doi:10.2307/796750.

Sen, Maya. 2014. "How Judicial Qualification Ratings May Disadvantage Minority and Female Candidates." *Journal of Law and Courts* 2 (1): 33–65.

Simien, Evelyn M. 2007. "Doing Intersectionality Research: From Conceptual Issues to Practical Examples." *Politics & Gender* 3 (2):264–71. doi:10.1017/S1743923X07000086.

Smelcer, Susan Navarro, Amy Steigerwalt, and Richard L Vining Jr. 2012. "Bias and the Bar: Evaluating the ABA Ratings of Federal Judicial Nominees." *Political Research Quarterly* 65 (4): 827–40.

Sokoloff, Natalie J. 2014. *Black Women and White Women in the Professions: Occupational Segregation by Race and Gender, 1960-1980.* New York: Routledge.

Solanke, Iyiola. 2018. "Where are the Black Judges in Europe?" *Connecticut Journal of International Law* 34 (3): 287–316.

Solberg, Rorie Spill, and Jennifer Segal Diascro. 2018. "A Retrospective on Obama's Judges: Diversity, Intersectionality, and Symbolic Representation." *Politics, Groups, and Identities* 8 (3):471–87. doi:10.1080/21565503.2018.1478736.

Stubbs, Jonathan K. 2016. "Demographic History of Federal Judicial Appointments by Sex and Race: 1789-2016, a." *Berkeley La Raza LJ* 26: 92–128.

Taslitz, Andrew E. 1998. "An African-American Sense of Fact: The O.J. Trial and Black Judges on Justice." *Boston University Public Interest Law Journal* 7 (2):219–50.

Valerie, Purdie-Vaughns, and Richard P Eibach. 2008. "Intersectional Invisibility: The Distinctive Advantages and Disadvantages of Multiple Subordinate-Group Identities." *Sex Roles* 59 (5): 377–91.

Washington, Michele. 1971. "Black Judges in White America." *Black Law Journal* 1 (3): 241–46.

The Black Women of the US Congress: Learning from Descriptive Data

Nadia E. Brown, Christopher J. Clark, and Anna Mitchell Mahoney

ABSTRACT

Black women have been historically excluded from Congress and the policy-making power available in the institution. This essay shares details about the 52 Black women who have navigated this raced and gendered institution (Hawkesworth 2003) since 1969. We discuss data on these Black congresswomen, including, but not limited to, their educational attainment, occupations prior to serving in Congress, and ties to Black Greek Letter organizations. We argue that this descriptive data will prompt new questions for legislative scholars and open conversations about disciplinary norms and assumptions which may need revision in light of Congress' increasing diversification.

On January 28, 2022, the *Washington Post* released a database based on archival and census records revealing that 1,767 members of Congress born before 1840 enslaved other human beings. These members represented 37 different states in all regions of the country and were all contributors to the production of Congress' procedures, processes, and policies. Indeed, the average American may know something about these now more than 1,800 Members of Congress who were also enslavers.[1] They have schools, roads, and national monuments named after them. Men such as Thomas Jefferson, Daniel Webster, and Sam Houston are enshrined in American history. Yet, little is known about the descendants of the enslaved, many of whom are now elected members of Congress. With a special focus on Black women, we posit that the wretched history of this institution has contributed to why there have only been two Black women senators. Much of what we know about Congress is based on the legacies that enslavers left for generations of Americans to follow. Yet, we turn this narrative on its head to focus on Black Congresswomen to show how they have found their way to the Capitol despite every effort to keep them out. In this paper, through the use of descriptive data we demonstrate who Black Congresswomen are and their paths to the national legislature.

Much of what we know about the behavior of Members of Congress (MoCs) is based on studies that nearly exclusively focus on White men. Likewise, what scholars have written about Congress as a political institution has centered androcentric understandings of the legislature. Scholars of Gender and Politics as well as Racial and Ethnic Politics – among others – have highlighted how the "universal truths" of the first branch of government have excluded nonwhite male members from upper class backgrounds (Duerst-Lahti 2002; Dittmar et al 2018; Sanbonmatsu 2020). This systematic exclusion should solicit further exploration into how minoritized members interact with, adhere to, or disrupt congressional norms. Acknowledging that identities shape institutions has been well established by gender and race scholars (Casellas 2011; Heideman 2020; Minta 2021; Rosenthal 2002). Too often the story of institutions is told without proper attention to the White male identities of the creators of those institutions. By centering Black women, we learn about the pathways that they take to Congress which helps to broaden the scholarly scope of which members are elected to this body. Doing so requires another set of questions that challenge the core of Congressional studies as well as institutional politics and scholarship on political behavior (Hardy-Fanta, Pinderhughes, and Sierra 2016). Centering the experiences of Black Congresswomen offers an opportunity to explore how pivotal, but often sidelined, lawmakers are elected to Congress.

Data and methods

In this essay, we use descriptive data on Black Congresswomen to explore who these women are and their pathways to the national legislature. Descriptive studies are important when little is systemically known about a topic. These kinds of studies pose questions that center on "who, why, when, and where . . . and so what" (Grimes and Shulz 2002). Our descriptive study seeks to provide an overall picture of Black Congresswomen by describing the situations, political contexts, and socio-political environment in which they were elected and served. To do this, we provide data that identifies variables – or the conditions – that enabled these women to win a seat in Congress. We also highlight individual women to describe the patterns that we uncovered to help make sense of the larger question of how Black women have entered and navigated this racist and sexist institution (Hawkesworth 2003; Jones 2019). Our focus on some individual congresswomen is not to obscure the contributions of some or praise the experiences of others, but rather showcase through example how these women's opportunities, backgrounds, or political achievements are illustrative of larger patterns uncovered in our descriptive analysis. Furthermore, we are not making inferences on the impact that Black Congresswomen have had nor we are attempting to explain or confirm a relationship between independent and dependent variables. Rather, we are describing the conditions in which Black Congresswomen have been elected and served. This descriptive research should enable scholars to refine and clarify the nature of the problem, namely the lack of diversity in Congress. We have organized our findings around classifications, comparisons, and connections between and amongst these Congresswomen.

To collect data on Black Congresswomen, we relied primarily on sources from Congress itself. The "people search" function that is part of the History, Art, and Archives section of the website for the US House of Representatives allowed us to ascertain the total number of Black women who have served in Congress, as well as the number in a given Congress. Moreover, this website pointed us to biographies of Black Congresswomen. These biographies provided information on the partisan identity of each person, their educational attainment, occupation(s) held prior to serving in Congress, Congresses served, chamber represented, the state represented, years served, the lifespan of each member, the committees these individuals served on, as well as whether they chaired committees or subcommittees. These biographies were not always clear about the districts represented, so we relied on Congress.gov for that information.[2] To determine Black Congresswomen's role in the Congressional Black Caucus (CBC) and the Congressional Caucus on Women's Issues (CCWI), we relied on information from the CBC itself as well as the aforementioned History, Art, and Archives website. For information on committees that Senator Harris served on in the 115th and 116th Congresses, we relied on documents provided by the US Government Publishing Office; John Merlino was the author of each document.[3] We also examine whether Black women are members of Black Greek Letter Organizations and relied on several sources when collecting these data including their official biographies, records of the sororities themselves, as well as internet searches.

The early years

Since the 1st Congress convened in 1789, over 11,000 individuals have served in the body. Congress convened for 90 sessions without a single Black woman serving in office. But, in the 91st Congress (1969–71), upon the election of Representative Shirley Chisholm, this trend changed. Representing a district in Brooklyn, Chisholm reached office by besting a Black man, James Farmer in the general election. In her 1970 book, *Unbought and Unbossed*, Chisholm writes, "Farmer's campaign was well oiled; it had money dripping all over it. He toured the district with sound trucks manned by young dudes with Afros, beating tom-toms: the big, black, male image" (Chisholm 1970, 71). Although Farmer appealed to his masculinity throughout the campaign and despite Chisholm becoming severely ill – at one point she was hospitalized and was unable to campaign – she was able to win. Chisholm benefitted from the support of women, who were registered at twice the rate of men in her district, and even more specifically from the backing of women of color. Chisholm spoke Spanish, which also allowed her to appeal to Puerto Rican voters in the district. With these essential sources of support, Chisholm won decisively.

After the passage of the Voting Rights Act, Black Americans were able to vote for and elect descriptive representatives.[4] These lawmakers were elected in areas with sizable Black populations. Indeed, Chisholm was soon joined by three other Black women, who all arrived four years later (the 93rd Congress). Yvonne Braithwaite Burke represented a district in Los Angeles, Barbara Jordan represented a district in Houston, and Cardiss Collins represented a district in Chicago. The fact that each represented districts with large Black populations is consistent with what research has long shown about the jurisdictions that elect Blacks to Congress (Lublin 1997), and it is consistent with what emerging work says about districts that elect women of color (Hardy-Fanta, Pinderhughes, and Marie Sierra 2016).

While Jordan was never appointed to a meaningful leadership role in Congress, she made her mark on the Judiciary committee, providing a compelling statement defending the Constitution as the committee considered articles of impeachment against President Nixon in 1974. Collins, however, served as subcommittee chair on multiple committees (Government Operations and Energy and Commerce). Collins' leadership roles are not surprising since she served over two decades in Congress leveraging institutional norms of seniority. Burke, despite her short tenure on the Hill, was the first female chair of the Congressional Black Caucus and played a pivotal role as chair of the Select Committee on the House Beauty Shop, ensuring the continual operation of the Congressional salon. She was also the first congresswoman to give birth while in office (CSPAN 2015).

Since these four women walked the halls of Congress, 48 additional Black women have served on the Hill as members of Congress. Today, 27 Black women serve in the 117th Congress and none in the Senate. Less than one half of one percent of members of Congress have been Black women (CAWP 2022a; CAWP and Higher Heights 2022). We include nonvoting delegates in the count of Black Congresswomen because of their important representational role they play despite the lack of formal political power these offices hold.

Geography

While Black women have served in regions throughout the country, more have served from more populous states (and thus those with more seats available) and states with larger Black populations (see Table 1). Florida leads all Southern states with five Black women representing the Sunshine State at one point in time, while Georgia has sent four Black women to Congress, followed by three Black women from Texas. North Carolina has sent two Black women to Congress, while Alabama has sent one. More than half of the former Confederate states (6) have failed to send a Black woman to Congress, namely Arkansas, Louisiana, Mississippi, South Carolina, Tennessee, and Virginia. These states that have failed to send a Black woman to Congress are a mixture of Deep Southern and Rim Southern states, suggesting that subregion is not driving the trend. More broadly, although Southern states have a traditionalistic political culture (Elazar 1972), something we might expect would depress the number of Black women sent to Congress (see Hogan 2001), it is clear that Southern states are far from monolithic when it comes to electing Blacks to office, a point echoed in recent work (Bullock et al. 2022).

Name (Lifespan)	Jurisdictions Served (Years Served)	Education (Year)	Occupation(s) and Position(s) Prior to Serving in Congress	Sorority
Chisholm, Shirley (1924–2005)	NY 12 (1969–83)	Brooklyn College, B.A. (1946); Columbia University, M.A. (1952)	nursery school teacher; director of child care center; educational consultant; state legislator	Delta Sigma Theta
Burke, Yvonne Braithwaite (1932-)	CA 28 and 37 (1973–79)	University of California at Los Angeles, B.A. (1953); University of Southern California, J.D. (1956)	lawyer; deputy corporation commissioner; hearing officer; state legislator	Alpha Kappa Alpha
Collins, Cardiss (1931–2013)	IL 7 (1973–97)	Northwestern University, Diploma in Professional Accounting (1967)	secretary; accountant; auditor; committeewoman of a ward	Alpha Kappa Alpha
Jordan, Barbara (1936–96)	TX 18 (1973–79)	Texas State University, B.A. (1956); Boston University, LL.B. (1959)	lawyer, administrative assistant to county judge; state legislator	Delta Sigma Theta
Hall, Katie (1938–2012)	IN 1 (1981–85)	Mississippi Valley State University, B.S. (1960); Indiana University Bloomington, M.S. (1968)	teacher; state legislator	Alpha Kappa Alpha
Clayton, Eva (1934-)	NC 1 (1991–2003)	Johnson C. Smith University, B.S. (1955); North Carolina Central University, M.S. (1962)	director of educational program; assistant secretary; county commissioner	Alpha Kappa Alpha
Collins, Barbara-Rose (1939-)	MI 13 and 15 (1991–97)	Cass Technical High School, Detroit, MI (1957)[a]	school board member; state legislator; city council member	Delta Sigma Theta
Norton, Eleanor Holmes (1937-)	DC At-Large (1991-)	Antioch College, B.A. (1960); Yale University, M.A. (1963); Yale University, LL.B. (1964)	lawyer; law clerk to federal district judge; assistant legal director; adjunct professor; staff of mayor; chair of local commission; chair of federal agency; senior fellow at an institute; professor	
Waters, Maxine (1938-)	CA 29, 35, and 43 (1991-)	California State University, Los Angeles, B.A. (1970)	teacher; volunteer coordinator for federal program; state legislator	
Brown, Corrine (1946-)	FL 3 and 5 (1993–2017)	Florida Agriculture and Mechanical University, B.S. (1969), M.A. (1971); University of Florida, Ed.S. (1974)	faculty member; state legislator	Sigma Gamma Rho
Johnson, Eddie Bernice (1935-)	TX 30 (1993-)	St. Mary's College at the University of Notre Dame, Certificate (1955); Texas Christian University, B.S. (1967); Southern Methodist University, M.P.A. (1976);	chief psychiatric nurse; psychotherapist; state legislator; administrator for federal agency; business owner	Alpha Kappa Alpha
McKinney, Cynthia (1955-)	GA 4 and 11 (1993–2003, 2005–07)	University of Southern California, B.A. (1978); Tufts University Fletcher School of Law and Diplomacy[b]	diplomatic fellow at a university; faculty member; state legislator	
Meek, Carrie (1926-)	FL 17 (1993–2003)	Florida A&M University, B.S. (1946); University of Michigan, M.S. (1948)	educational administrator; educational consultant; board member (2x); chair of local agency; state legislator	Delta Sigma Theta
Moseley Braun, Carol (1947-)	IL (1993–99)	University of Illinois, B.A. (1969); University of Chicago, J.D. (1972)	prosecutor, US Attorney's Office; state legislator; recorder of deeds for county government	Delta Sigma Theta
Jackson Lee, Sheila (1950-)	TX 18 (1995-)	Yale University, B.A. (1972); University of Virginia, J.D. (1975)	lawyer; staff counsel for US House committee; city council member; municipal judge	Alpha Kappa Alpha
Millender-McDonald, Juanita (1938–2007)	CA 37 (1995–2007)	University of the Redlands, B.S. (1981); California State University of Los Angeles, M.A. (1988)	city council member; educator; state legislator	Alpha Kappa Alpha

(Continued)

Table 1. (Continued).

Name (Lifespan)	Jurisdictions Served (Years Served)	Education (Year)	Occupation(s) and Position(s) Prior to Serving in Congress	Sorority
Carson, Julia (1938–2007)	IN 7 and 10 (1997–2007)	Crispus Attacks High School, Indianapolis, IN (1955)[a]	secretary; staff assistant for U.S. Representative; state legislator; center township trustee	Zeta Phi Beta
Christensen, Donna (1945–)	VI At-Large (1997–2015)	St. Mary's College at the University of Notre Dame, B.S. (1966); George Washington University, M.D. (1970)	physician; medical director; territorial assistant for government agency; acting commissioner for government agency; television journalist	
Kilpatrick, Carolyn Cheeks (1945–)	MI 13 and 15 (1997–2011)	Western Michigan University, B.S. (1972); University of Michigan, M.S. (1977)	teacher; state legislator	Delta Sigma Theta
Lee, Barbara (1946–)	CA 9 and 13 (1997–)	Mills College, B.A. (1973); University of California, Berkeley, M.S.W. (1975)	staff of U.S. Representative; state legislator; business owner	
Jones, Stephanie Tubbs (1949–2008)	OH 11 (1999–2008)	Case Western Reserve University, B.A. (1971), J.D. (1974)	municipal court judge; prosecutor for county	Delta Sigma Theta
Watson, Diane (1933–)	CA 32 and 33 (2001–11)	University of California, Los Angeles, B.A. (1956); California State University, Los Angeles, M.S. (1967); Claremont Graduate University, Ph.D. (1987)	psychologist; faculty; health occupation specialist for state agency; school board member; state legislator; U.S. ambassador to the Federated States of Micronesia	Alpha Kappa Alpha
Majette, Denise (1955–)	GA 4 (2003–05)	Yale University, B.A. (1976); Duke University, J.D. (1979)	lawyer; faculty; judge for state court	
Moore, Gwen (1951–)	WI 4 (2005–)	Marquette University, B.A. (1978)	housing officer for state agency; state legislator	
Clarke, Yvette (1964–)	NY 9 and 11 (2007–)	Oberlin College[c]	childcare specialist; staff of state legislator; executive assistant for state agency; youth program director; business development director; city council member	Delta Sigma Theta
Richardson, Laura (1962–)	CA 37 (2007–13)	University of California, Los Angeles, B.A. (1984); University of Southern California, M.B.A. (1996)	businesswoman; teacher; staff of U.S. Representative; city council member; staff of lieutenant governor; state legislator	
Edwards, Donna (1958–)	MD 4 (2008–2017)	Wake Forest University, B.A. (1980); Franklin Pierce Law Center, J.D. (1989)	lawyer; clerk for trial court judge; executive director (3x)	Zeta Phi Beta (honorary)
Fudge, Marcia (1952–)	OH 11 (2008–)	Ohio State University, B.S. (1975); Cleveland State University, J.D. (1983)	lawyer; director of county office/agency (3x); staff of U.S. Representative; mayor	Delta Sigma Theta
Bass, Karen (1953–)	CA 33 and 37 (2011–)	University of Southern California, P.A. (1982); California State University, Dominguez Hills, B.S. (1990); University of Southern California, M.S.W. (2015)	physician's assistant; faculty; state legislator	Delta Sigma Theta
Sewell, Terri (1965–)	AL 7 (2011–)	Princeton University, A.B. (1986); Oxford University, M.A. (1988); Harvard University, J.D. (1992)	lawyer	Alpha Kappa Alpha
Wilson, Frederica (1942–)	FL 17 and 24 (2011–)	Fisk University, B.S. (1963); University of Miami (FL), M.S. (1972)	elementary school principal; school board member; state legislator	Alpha Kappa Alpha
Beatty, Joyce (1950–)	OH 3 (2013–)	Central State University, B.A. (1972); Wright State University, M.S. (1974)	executive director; professor; businesswoman; state legislator; university administrator	Delta Sigma Theta

(Continued)

Table 1. (Continued).

Name (Lifespan)	Jurisdictions Served (Years Served)	Education (Year)	Occupation(s) and Position(s) Prior to Serving in Congress	Sorority
Kelly, Robin (1956-)	IL 2 (2013-)	Bradley University, B.A. (1977), M.A. (1982); Northern Illinois University, Ph.D. (2004)	counselor; community affairs director; state legislator; chief of staff for statewide elected official; chief administrative officer for county government	Sigma Gamma Rho
Adams, Alma (1946-)	NC 12 (2014-)	North Carolina Agricultural and Technical State University, B.S. (1968), M.S. (1972); Ohio State University, Ph.D. (1981)	artist; faculty; school board member; city council member; state legislator	Alpha Kappa Alpha
Lawrence, Brenda (1954-)	MI 14 (2015-)	Central Michigan University, B.A. (2005)	manager for United States Postal Service (USPS); board of education member; city council member; mayor	Delta Sigma Theta
Love, Mia (1975-)	UT 4 (2015–19)	University of Hartford, B.A. (1997)	flight attendant; call center operator; city council member; mayor	
Plaskett, Stacey (1966-)	VI At-Large (2015-)	Georgetown University, B.S.F.S. (1988); American University, J.D. (1994)	Lawyer; professional advocate; staff of U.S. Delegate; assistant district attorney for county; staff of U.S. House committee; staff of U.S. Department of Justice; general counsel for territorial government organization	Delta Sigma Theta
Watson Coleman, Bonnie (1945-)	NJ 12 (2015-)	Thomas Edison State College, B.A. (1985)	state legislator	Alpha Kappa Alpha
Blunt Rochester, Lisa (1962-)	DE At-Large (2017-)	Fairleigh Dickinson University, B.A. (1985); University of Delaware, M.A. (2003)	staff of U.S. Representative; deputy secretary for state agency; secretary of labor for state; personnel director for state agency; chief executive officer; senior fellow at a university	
Demings, Val (1957-)	FL 10 (2017-)	Florida State University, B.S. (1979); Webster University, M.P.A. (1996)	social worker; police officer; police chief	Delta Sigma Theta
Harris, Kamala (1964-)	CA (2017–2021)	Howard University, B.A. (1986); University of California, Hastings College of the Law, J.D. (1989)	deputy district attorney for county; managing attorney; chief of local governmental agency; district attorney for city; state attorney general	Alpha Kappa Alpha
Jones, Brenda (1959-)	MI 13 (2018–2019)	Wayne State University, B.A., graduate certificate[b]	trade union president; city council member	
Hayes, Jahana (1973-)	CT 5 (2019-)	Naugatuck Valley Community College, A.A. (2002); Southern Connecticut State University, B.A. (2005); University of St. Joseph, M.A. (2012)	teacher; public school administrator	
McBath, Lucy (1960-)	GA 6 (2019-)	Virginia State University, B.A. (1982)	flight attendant; professional advocate	Delta Sigma Theta
Omar, Ilhan (1982-)	MN 5 (2019-)	North Dakota State University, B.A., B.S. (2011)	teacher; campaign manager; nonprofit executive; staff for state agency; staff for city council; state legislator	
Pressley, Ayanna (1974-)	MA 7 (2019-)	Francis W. Parker High School, Chicago, IL (1992)[a]	staff of U.S. Representative, staff of U.S. Senator; city council member	

(Continued)

Table 1. (Continued).

Name (Lifespan)	Jurisdictions Served (Years Served)	Education (Year)	Occupation(s) and Position(s) Prior to Serving in Congress	Sorority
Underwood, Lauren (1986-)	IL 14 (2019-)	University of Michigan, B.S.N. (2008); John Hopkins University, M.S.N./M.P.H. (2009)	nurse; professor; senior adviser for a federal agency	Alpha Kappa Alpha
Bush, Cori (1976-)	MO 1 (2021-)	Lutheran School of Nursing, R.N. Diploma (2008)	teacher; nurse; pastor; community organizer	
Strickland, Marilyn (1962-)	WA 10 (2021-)	University of Washington, Seattle, B.A. (1984); Clark Atlanta University, M.B.A. (1992)	marketing executive; staff and member of board of trustees for local library; city council member; mayor	
Williams, Nikema (1978-)	GA 5(2021-)	Talladega College, B.S. (2000)	professional advocate; vice chair, acting chair, and chair of state Democratic Party; state legislator	Alpha Kappa Alpha
Brown, Shontel	OH 11 (2021-)	Cuyahoga Community College, Associate of Science[d]	marketing professional; business owner; city council member; county council member	
Cherfilus-McCormick, Sheila	FL 20 (2022-)	Howard University, B.A. (2001); St. Thomas University School of Law, J.D. (2010)	health care executive	

Notes: These data are accurate as of February 2022. It is common for Black women to be delegates to conventions but these positions were not counted here for the sake of parsimony. The data on sorority membership is for Black Greek organizations only and come from multiple sources.

[a]Indicates that the person enrolled in a college or university but did not finish.

[b]Indicates a lack of clarity about when a degree was completed.

[c]Clarke attended Oberlin College for four years, from 1982 to 1986, but she is not shown to have earned a degree from the institution.

[d]Brown is currently enrolled in four-year degree program and anticipates graduating in 2022.

Sources: Alpha Kappa Alpha Sorority, Inc (2019); Augusta University (2022); Boling (2017); Cassano (2019); Congress.gov (n.d.); Jordan and Hearon (1979); NAACP Connect (2017); Nielsen (2019); North American Interfraternity Conference (n.d.); The Hundred-Seven (n.d.); United States House of Representatives (2019); United States House of Representatives: History, Art, and Archives ("People" n. d.); Zeta Phi Beta Sorority, Inc (2013).

As for states outside of the South, California leads all others, sending a total of eight Black women to Congress, including only the second US Senator (Kamala Harris who is bi-racial, Black and Asian), and has considerably more seats than other states.[5] Illinois elected the nation's first Black woman US Senator (Moseley Braun), and the Land of Lincoln has sent three other Black women to Congress. Michigan, like Illinois, has sent four Black women to Congress. Ohio has sent four Black women to Congress, including Representative Joyce Beatty, the current chair of the CBC. In fact, from 1999 to the present day the Ohio 11th has been represented by a Black woman, albeit three different ones.

Of course, not all Black women have served in US states. The District of Columbia has sent one Black woman to Congress (Eleanor Holmes Norton), and the Virgin Islands has sent two Black women to the storied institution (Donna Christensen and Stacey Plaskett) as delegates.

What research questions emerge from this geographic data? One question is as follows: what is the connection between seat availability and diversity? Turning to the local level, some research suggests more seats on a city council makes each seat less prestigious, which in turns makes it easier for Blacks and women to serve in office (Alozie and Manganaro 1993a, 1993b). On the other hand, Karnig and Welch (1979) show that only Black men benefit from larger council sizes, not Black women. All told, while it appears that more seats benefit Black women, more investigation is needed to disentangle who exactly benefits from the greater availability of seats in a given state delegation. Regional variation of Black residential patterns is also worthy of discussion. In Southern states, Blacks reside in rural and urban areas, but in non-Southern states, Blacks rarely live in rural areas (Grofman and Handley 1989).[6] As a result, an expectation is that Black members of Congress from the South may represent parts of urban areas, but will often represent rural areas, whereas Blacks outside of the South will get often represent urban areas. Although we know that some Black women from these states have represented major cities, such as Yvonne Burke and Cardis Collins, we need to conduct additional research on the type of district Black women have represented in Congress and whether this varies meaningfully across region.

Previous office

Black women running for Congress are strategic in their campaigns, selecting winnable races and acquiring the political experience and resources to win (Gertzog 2002). While a majority of members of the 117th Congress held prior positions in politics or public service, women of color are less likely than their male counterparts to hold local office overall (Hardy-Fanta et al 2016; Congressional; Research Service 2022). However, Black women in Congress are more likely to have served in the state legislature first (Hardy-Fanta et al 2016). Of the 2,300 women serving in state legislatures in April 2022, 367 identify as Black women compared to 1,689 White women (CAWP 2022b).[7] Since nearly 7,400 state legislators serve across the 50 states, this means that Black women were a mere 5% of all state legislators.

While Hardy-Fanta, Pinderhughes, and Sierra (2016) find little evidence of a "career ladder" for officeholders of color, some Black women have served on the local level prior to their Congressional tenure. In fact, 13 of the 52 have served on city councils. In addition, Black women have served as mayors (4) and served local government in some other capacity, such as overseeing administrative agencies (2), consistent with existing research (see Holman 2014). Marilyn Strickland, who was recently elected to represent Washington State, has extensive experience at the local level. She was a member of the board of trustees for a local library, served on the city council, and even served as mayor of Tacoma, Washington, making her the first woman of color mayor of this city.

Furthermore, prior to being elected to Congress, multiple Black women served as staffers for elected officials at the local, state and/or federal level. For example, current US Representative Ayanna Pressley worked as a congressional staffer in both the House and Senate. Laura Richardson worked on the staff of a lieutenant governor, a statewide position, as well as on the staff of a US Representative. Our data reveal that in total 11 of the Black women served as staff to elected officials prior to serving in Congress. Given what we know about the role these actors play in the lawmaking process (Dittmar

2021; Wilson and Carlos 2014), not to mention the real-world experience they earn while engaged in staff work, it is clear that these experiences are important and likely motivate Black women to run for and serve in Congress themselves.

In fact, Julia Carson, who was a district aide for Andy Jacobs, then a US Representative, was encouraged to run for the state legislature by Jacobs. We know that being asked to run for office through a personal relationship is important to the decision to run for candidates of color (Carroll and Sanbonmatsu 2013; Hardy-Fanta 2016). Once Jacobs retired, Carson ran for the seat that became vacant, won the election, and eventually ran for, and won, a seat in Congress. Carson served for a decade before passing away while in office.

If we take seriously the notion that Black women serving as staff is critical for them eventually serving in Congress, and if we assume the pattern observed in Congress is true across offices, then it means that the overrepresentation of white men, or the underrepresentation of Black people in elected office leads to a vicious cycle of suppressing Black faces in government (see also Jones 2022). This lack of diversity is perpetuated because Black members of Congress hire more Black staff than other members, indicating that the dearth of current descriptive representation in Congress yields fewer opportunities for greater representation of Black staffers who might ultimately make their own bids for office (Scott 2018).

Historically Black sororities

Black institutions are key components of Black women's political socialization. These institutions assist in political mobilization, teach democratic norms, and cultivate political activity among its members (Calhoun-Brown 1996). Black Greek Letter Organizations are civil rights organizations that were founded on college campuses between 1906 and 1963. Members in these organizations seek to uplift and transform their communities for the better via civic and social engagement. Many sought to help Blacks attain a higher education. While these organizations mirror White Greek Letter Organizations, they were deeply concerned about Black issues and sought to build supportive communities among like-minded students (Hughey and Parks 2011). All nine BGLOs have produced notable educators, civil rights leaders, musicians, athletes, artists, entrepreneurs, corporate executives and elected officials (Parks 2008).

BGLOs are networks that provide both professional and social support for Black fraternity and sorority members that are fundamental in how Black elites have advanced racial progress (Brown and Lemi 2021). While some traditional civil rights organizations may have closed leadership ranks on Black women, BGLOs remain a place for Black women's political socialization. As Pearl Dowe (2020) notes, membership in BGLOs – Delta Sigma Theta Sorority, Inc. specifically, provides its members with civic skills. These skills are a prerequisite for political participation (Simpson 1998). Dowe (2020) notes that several members of Delta Sigma Theta Sorority, Inc., have sought and gained electoral office because of the skills they gained in the organization as well as support systems or access to networks that were developed through their sorority membership. The emphasis on service may be one explanation for why so many Black women are members of sororities (Brown 2018; Daniels 2021; Dowe 2020).

Several Black women in Congress are members of BGLOs organizations. In fact, our data show 34 Black women have been members of sororities, which is nearly two-thirds of all who have served in Congress (including one honorary member). For example, Representative Joyce Betty, who is a member of Delta Sigma Theta Sorority, Inc., proudly extolled the organizing power of her sorority in helping to confirm Loretta Lynch as President Obama's Attorney General in 2015 over Republican attempts to block the nomination (Brown and Lemi 2021). She credited her fellow sorority sisters in the House such as Marcia Fudge and Yvette Clarke putting pressure on Senate Majority Leader Mitch McConnell to confirm Lynch, who is also a member of Delta Sigma Theta Sorority, Inc. Buoyed by a throng of sorority sisters who used their political power, community organizing skills, affiliational clout, as well as vast social and civic networks, sorority members demonstrated the collective strength of Black women's capacity to influence politics.

Education

Like most members of Congress, Black women are highly educated. As of March 2022, all but four of the Black women who have served in Congress have at least a four-year degree, and even those without such an education attended some college. One trend worth noting is the role of Historically Black Colleges and Universities (HBCUs). Thirteen of the Black women, or one in four, have degrees from HBCUs. The presence of HBCU graduates among Black Congresswomen spans over time, including Barbara Jordan (1973–1979) – who attended Texas Southern University – and Sheila Cherfilus-McCormick (2022-present) – who is a graduate of Howard University.

Similar to BGLOs, HBCUs are Black institutions that help to instill a sense of racial uplift among its students and faculty. HBCUs were established after the Civil War and were a product of Reconstruction era politics. While the vast majority of these universities and colleges are located in the South, there are HBCUs in Pennsylvania, Michigan, and Missouri. These institutions were established to meet the educational needs of newly freed men and women as well as their children. It is important to note that while HBCUs were founded for students of African descent in America, they were never racially exclusive. Moreover, HBCUs sought to advance an abolitionist democracy that would benefit all Americans. Today, these institutions are underfunded but still serve a mighty need. While HBCUs make up only three percent of all US colleges and university, they produce nearly twenty percent of all Black graduates. Graduates, such as the current Vice President of the United States, Kamala Harris, have an eye toward racial justice and expressed commitment to a larger social good. Similar to BGLOs, HBCUs provide Black Congresswomen with a network of alumni who draw on their communal ties to influence politics.

Black women have had educational opportunities outside of HBCUs. Mary Jane Patterson is the first Black woman to receive a B.A. degree in 1862 from Oberlin College.[8] Since then, tomes of Black women have attended schools outside of HBCUs, with the majority of individuals graduating post *Brown* v. *Board of Education* and the advancement of civil rights (Howard-Vital 1989). Some Black women have attended Ivy League institutions. Among Black Congresswomen, Eleanor Holmes Norton, Sheila Jackson Lee, and Denise Majette all attended Yale University, while Terri Sewell attended Princeton University.

Although other Black Congresswomen earned degrees from private universities like Johns Hopkins (Lauren Underwood) and the University of Southern California (Karen Bass, Yvonne Braithwaite Burke, Cynthia McKinney, and Laura Richardson), many others have earned degrees from public universities. Additional research questions may emerge from these patterns including how geography and educational background intersect or how BGLOs membership vs. HBCU attendance shape political development among legislators.

Occupational background

Prior employment before congressional service is important not only because of the skills occupational experience develops in future officeholders but also because of the resources available to candidates' seeking office that are tied to their previous careers (Hardy-Fanta et al 2016). Further, occupations are racialized and gendered with legislators' previous experience influencing their legislative priorities (Barnes, Beall, and Holman 2021). For instance, women's segregation into care industries is correlated with their overrepresentation on social welfare committees as well as agenda priorities for women in legislatures. Thus, we provide descriptive data on the kinds of occupations that Black Congresswomen previously held. This documentation helps to elucidate the career opportunities that may provide a distinct skillset or politically advantageous background for those who hold elected office and the expertise they display while in Congress.

Like most members, Black Congresswomen have worked in the legal field. In total, 13 different Black women worked in the legal field prior to serving in Congress. Nine different women have served as lawyers, four have served as judges, two worked as district attorneys, two worked as prosecutors, and one worked as administrative assistant to a county judge (Barbara Jordan). Some worked in multiple positions within the legal realm. Stacey Plaskett worked as a lawyer and district attorney prior to serving in Congress, while Donna Edwards worked as a lawyer and judge prior to serving in Congress. Stephanie Tubbs Jones worked as a prosecutor and a municipal judge prior to serving in Congress. This representation is not unusual considering the overrepresentation of lawyers in Congress in general and among Black women state legislators (Hardy-Fanta 2016; Robinson 2017).

Black women also have ties to the education field, again a common history among Black women at all levels of politics. In total, 23 Black women, or over 40%, worked in education prior to serving in Congress. Many worked as teachers, such as Katie Hall, teaching K-12 students, while others like Cynthia McKinney worked in university settings. Four Black women worked in education administration, such as Frederica Wilson who was an elementary school principal. Carrie Meek worked for decades as an administrator at a community college in Florida. It is also worth noting multiple Black women (four) have served on school boards, including Barbara Rose Collins, one of the few Black women without a college degree. This previous experience is not surprising given the disproportionate number of women who work as teachers for K-12 schools, but the presence of Black women on faculties at universities is noteworthy given how grossly they are underrepresented (Rucks-Ahidiana 2021) Given that education has been defined as a Black interest (see Clark 2019 for a review), it is not surprising that so many Black women worked in the education field before seeking to influence that policy at the federal level.

Eight Black women worked in health care prior to serving in Congress. Donna Christensen was a medical doctor, Lauren Underwood and Cori Bush worked as nurses, and Eddie Bernice Johnson worked as a psychotherapist and psychiatric nurse, for instance. These previous occupations also have a policy impact with women state legislators with pink-collar backgrounds correlating with larger budgetary outlays for healthcare and social services (Barnes, Beall, and Holman 2021).

Knowing the distinct agenda women in Congress establish (Dittmar et al 2018), documenting the professional experience Black women bring to office is valuable to future studies examining the weight given to Black women's expertise in floor speeches or committee hearings as well as the strategies they employ to achieve their legislative goals.

Leadership of Black women

Positional power in Congress is held by party leadership in posts like majority leader and whip as well as committee chair positions, all of which enable members to wield immense gatekeeping power. The CBC has leveraged their collective power to receive advantageous committee assignments and party leadership positions (Barrett 1975; Holmes 2000). Despite this and Democratic control being associated with higher numbers of women in the top six leadership positions, Black women have held very few formal positions of congressional leadership. Seniority and majority party membership weigh heavily in committee chair selection, and with so few Black women elected, this finding is not surprising. Haynie (2005) show that while Black members of Congress have increased their number of key committee chairmanships and leadership positions over time, no Black women have served in the top five positions (Speaker of the House, Majority/Minority Leader, Majority/Minority Whip, Assistant Speaker, Democratic Caucus Chairman).

Overall, only five Black women have ever chaired committees with Yvonne Burke being the first Black woman to do so (see Table 2). Maxine Waters, Eddie Bernice Johnson, Juanita Millender McDonald, and Stephanie Tubbs Jones are the other four individuals who have chaired congressional committees. Nineteen different Black women have chaired a subcommittee. This difference is not surprising: given the prevalence of subcommittees, Black women have more opportunities to serve in leadership positions.

Table 2. Committee Membership, Committee Leadership, and Identity Caucus Leadership Positions Held by Black Congresswomen.

Name	Jurisdiction(s) (Years Served)	Committees	Committee Leadership Positions Held (Committee)	Caucus (Co-) Chair (Years)
Chisholm, Shirley	NY 12 (1969–83)	Education and Labor; Rules; Veterans' Affairs	–	–
Burke, Yvonne Braithwaite	CA 28 (1973–75) and CA 37 (1975–79)	Appropriations; Interior and Insular Affairs; Public Works; Select Committee on Assassinations; Select Committee on the House Beauty Shop	Chair (Select Committee on the House Beauty Shop)	Chair of Congressional Black Caucus (1976–77)
Collins, Cardiss	IL 7 (1973–97)	Commerce; District of Columbia; Energy and Commerce; Foreign Affairs; Government Operations; Government Reform and Oversight; International Relations; Public Works; Select Committee on Narcotics Abuse and Control; Select Committee on Population	Chair of Commerce, Consumer Protection, and Competitiveness Subcommittee (Energy and Commerce); Chair of Government Activities and Transportation Subcommittee (Government Operations); Chair of Manpower and Housing Subcommittee (Government Operations)	Chair of Congressional Black Caucus (1979–81)
Jordan, Barbara	TX 18 (1973–79)	Government Operations; Judiciary	–	–
Hall, Katie	IN 1 (1981–85)	Post Office and Civil Service; Public Works and Transportation	Chair of Census and Population Subcommittee (Post Office and Civil Service)	–
Clayton, Eva	NC 1 (1991–2003)	Agriculture; Budget; Small Business	–	–
Collins, Barbara-Rose	MI 13 (1991–93) and MI 15 (1993–97)	Government Operations; Government Reform and Oversight; Post Office and Civil Service; Public Works and Transportation; Science, Space, and Technology; Select Committee on Children, Youth, and Families; Transportation and Infrastructure	Chair of Postal Operations and Services Subcommittee (Post Office and Civil Service)	–
Norton, Eleanor Holmes	District of Columbia At-Large (1991-)	District of Columbia; Government Reform; Government Reform and Oversight; Homeland Security; Oversight and Government Reform; Oversight and Reform; Post Office and Civil Service; Public Works and Transportation; Select Committee on Homeland Security; Small Business; Transportation and Infrastructure; Joint Committee on the Organization of Congress	Chair of Judiciary and Education Subcommittee (District of Columbia); Chair of Compensation and Employee Benefits Subcommittee (Post Office and Civil Service); Chair of Economic Development, Public Buildings, and Emergency Management Subcommittee; Chair of Highways and Transit Subcommittee (Transportation and Infrastructure)	Cochair of Congressional Caucus for Women's Issues (1997–99)
Waters, Maxine	CA 29 (1991–93), CA 35 (1993–2013), CA 43 (2013-)	Banking and Financial Services; Banking, Finance, and Urban Affairs; Financial Services; Judiciary; Small Business; Veterans' Affairs	Chair (Financial Services); Chair of Housing and Community Opportunity Subcommittee (Financial Services)	Chair of Congressional Black Caucus (1997–99)
Brown, Corrine	FL 3 (1993–2013) and FL 5 (2013–17)	Government Operations; Public Works and Transportation; Transportation and Infrastructure; Veterans' Affairs	Chair of Railroads, Pipelines, and Hazardous Materials Subcommittee (Transportation and Infrastructure)	–
Johnson, Eddie Bernice	TX 30 (1993-)	Public Works and Transportation; Science; Science and Technology; Science, Space, and Technology; Transportation and Infrastructure	Chair (Science, Space, and Technology); Chair of Water Resources and Environment Subcommittee (Transportation and Infrastructure)	Chair of Congressional Black Caucus (2001–03)
McKinney, Cynthia	GA 11 (1993–97) and GA 4 (1997–2003, 2005–07)	Agriculture; Armed Services; Banking and Financial Services; Budget; Foreign Affairs; International Relations; National Security	–	–
Meek, Carrie	FL 17 (1993–2003)	Appropriations; Budget; Government Reform and Oversight	–	–
Moseley Braun, Carol	IL (1993–99)	Banking, Housing and Urban Affairs; Finance; Judiciary; Small Business	–	–

(Continued)

Table 2. (Continued).

Name	Jurisdiction(s) (Years Served)	Committees	Committee Leadership Positions Held (Committee)	Caucus (Co-) Chair (Years)
Jackson Lee, Sheila	TX 18 (1995-)	Budget; Foreign Affairs; Homeland Security; Judiciary; Science; Select Committee on Homeland Security	Chair of Transportation Security and Infrastructure Protection Subcommittee (Homeland Security)	–
Millender-McDonald, Juanita	CA 37 (1995–2007[a])	House Administration; Small Business; Transportation and Infrastructure; Joint Committee on Printing; Joint Committee on the Library	Chair (House Administration)	Cochair of Congressional Caucus on Women's Issues (2001–03)
Carson, Julia	IN 10 (1997–2003) and IN 7 (2003–07[a])	Banking and Financial Services; Financial Services; Transportation and Infrastructure; Veterans' Affairs	–	–
Christensen, Donna	Virgin Islands At-Large (1997–2015)	Energy and Commerce; Homeland Security; Natural Resources; Resources; Select Committee on Homeland Security; Small Business	Chair of Insular Affairs Subcommittee (Natural Resources)	–
Kilpatrick, Carolyn Cheeks	MI 15 (1997–2003) and MI 13 (2003–11)	Appropriations; Banking and Financial Services; House Oversight; Oversight; Joint Committee on the Library	–	Chair of Congressional Black Caucus (2007–09)
Lee, Barbara	CA 9 (1997–2013) and 13 (2013-)	Appropriations; Banking and Financial Services; Budget; Financial Services; Foreign Affairs; International Relations; Science	–	Chair of Congressional Black Caucus (2009–11)
Jones, Stephanie Tubbs	OH 11 (1999–2008)	Banking and Financial Services; Financial Services; Small Business; Standards of Official Conduct, Ways and Means	Chair (Standards of Official Conduct)	–
Watson, Diane	CA 32 (2001–03) and 33 (2003–11)	Foreign Affairs; Government Reform; International Relations; Oversight and Government Reform	Chair of Government Management, Organization, and Procurement Subcommittee (Oversight and Government Reform)	–
Majette, Denise	GA 4 (2003–05)	Budget; Education and the Workforce; Small Business	–	–
Moore, Gwen	WI 4 (2005-)	Budget; Financial Services; Small Business; Ways and Means	–	Cochair of Congressional Caucus for Women's Issues (2011–13)
Clarke, Yvette	NY 9 (2013-) and NY 11 (2007–13)	Education and Labor; Energy and Commerce; Ethics; Homeland Security; Small Business	Chair of Emerging Threats, Cybersecurity, and Science and Technology Subcommittee (Homeland Security)	–
Richardson, Laura	CA 37 (2007–13)	Homeland Security; Science and Technology; Transportation and Infrastructure	Chair of Emergency Communications, Preparedness, and Response Subcommittee	–
Edwards, Donna	MD 4 (2008–2017)	Ethics; Science and Technology; Science, Space, and Technology; Transportation and Infrastructure	–	Cochair of Congressional Caucus on Women's Issues (2013–15)
Fudge, Marcia	OH 11 (2008-)	Agriculture; Education and Labor; Education and the Workforce; House Administration; Science and Technology; Science, Space, and Technology	Chair of Nutrition, Oversight, and Department Operations Subcommittee (Agriculture); Chair of Elections Subcommittee (House Administration)	Chair of Congressional Black Caucus (2013–15)
Bass, Karen	CA 33 (2011–13) and CA 37 (2013-)	Budget; Foreign Affairs; Judiciary	Chair of Africa, Global Health, Global Human Rights, and International Organizations Subcommittee (Foreign Affairs); Chair of Crime, Terrorism, and Homeland Security Subcommittee (Judiciary)	Chair of Congressional Black Caucus (2019–2021)

(Continued)

WOMEN OF COLOR POLITICAL ELITES IN THE U.S.

Table 2. (Continued).

Name	Jurisdiction(s) (Years Served)	Committees	Committee Leadership Positions Held (Committee)	Caucus (Co-) Chair (Years)
Sewell, Terri	AL 7 (2011-)	Agriculture; Financial Services; Permanent Select Committee on Intelligence; Science, Space, and Technology; Ways and Means	Chair of Defense Intelligence and Warfighter Support Subcommittee (Permanent Select Committee on Intelligence)	–
Wilson, Frederica	FL 17 (2011–13) and FL 24 (2013-)	Education and Labor; Education and the Workforce; Foreign Affairs; Science, Space, and Technology; Transportation and Infrastructure	Chair of Health, Employment, Labor, and Pensions Subcommittee (Education and Labor)	–
Beatty, Joyce	OH 3 (2013-)	Financial Services	Chair of Diversity and Inclusion Subcommittee (Financial Services)	Chair of Congressional Black Caucus (2021-)
Kelly, Robin	IL 2 (2013-)	Energy and Commerce; Foreign Affairs; Oversight and Government Reform; Oversight and Reform; Science, Space, and Technology	–	–
Adams, Alma	NC 12 (2014-)	Agriculture; Education and Labor; Education and the Workforce; Financial Services; Small Business	Chair of the Workforce Protections Subcommittee (Education and Labor)	–
Lawrence, Brenda	MI 14 (2015-)	Appropriations; Oversight and Government Reform; Oversight and Reform; Small Business; Transportation and Infrastructure	–	Cochair of Congressional Caucus for Women's Issues (2019–21)
Love, Mia	UT 4 (2015–19)	Financial Services	–	–
Plaskett, Stacey	Virgin Islands At-Large (2015-)	Agriculture; Oversight and Government Reform; Oversight and Reform; Transportation and Infrastructure	Chair of Biotechnology, Horticulture, and Research Subcommittee (Agriculture)	–
Watson Coleman, Bonnie	NJ 12 (2015-)	Appropriations; Homeland Security; Oversight and Government Reform	–	–
Blunt Rochester, Lisa	DE At-Large (2017-)	Agriculture; Education and the Workforce; Energy and Commerce	–	–
Demings, Val	FL 10 (2017-)	Homeland Security; Judiciary; Oversight and Government Reform; Permanent Select Committee on Intelligence	–	–
Harris, Kamala	CA (2017–2021)	Budget; Environment and Public Works; Homeland Security and Governmental Affairs; Judiciary; Select Committee on Intelligence	–	–
Jones, Brenda	MI 13 (2018–2019 [9])	–[a]	–	–
Hayes, Jahana	CT 5 (2019-)	Agriculture; Education and Labor	–	–
McBath, Lucy	GA 6 (2019-)	Education and Labor; Judiciary	–	–
Omar, Ilhan	MN 5 (2019-)	Budget; Education and Labor; Foreign Affairs	–	–
Pressley, Ayanna	MA 7 (2019-)	Financial Services; Oversight and Reform	–	–
Underwood, Lauren	IL 14 (2019-)	Education and Labor; Homeland Security; Veterans' Affairs	–	–
Bush, Cori	MO 1 (2021-)	Judiciary; Oversight and Reform	–	–
Strickland, Marilyn	WA 10 (2021-)	Armed Services; Transportation and Infrastructure	–	–
Williams, Nikema	GA 5 (2021-)	Financial Services; Transportation and Infrastructure; Select Committee on the Modernization of Congress	–	–

(Continued)

Table 2. (Continued).

Name	Jurisdiction(s) (Years Served)	Committees	Committee Leadership Positions Held (Committee)	Caucus (Co-) Chair (Years)
Brown, Shontel	OH 11 (2021-)	Agriculture; Oversight and Reform	–	–
Cherfilus-McCormick, Sheila	FL 20 (2022-)	Education and Labor; Veterans' Affairs	–	–

Notes: The members listed are those that were in office by January 3, 2021, or the start of the 117th Congress. Some committee names change over time. In an effort to be comprehensive, both older and newer names are listed.
[a]Jones was not assigned to any committees since she served such a short period of time. That said, she is not alone since other women have also served in particular congresses without committee assignments.
Sources: Congress.gov (n.d.; n.d.); Congressional Black Caucus ("About" n.d.); Congressional Black Caucus ("History" n.d.); Merlino (2017, 2018, 2019); United States House of Representatives (2020); United States House of Representatives: History, Art, and Archives ("People" n.d.; "Women" n.d.).

Most of the pioneers who held leadership positions were at the committee and subcommittee level or found alternative paths to leadership among identity caucuses. Nine Black women have served as chair of the CBC. The current chair in the 117th Congress is Joyce Beatty, who was preceded by Karen Bass. Five Black women have served as cochair of the Congressional Caucus for Women's Issues (CCWI). No woman has ever chaired both organizations, suggesting that to climb the leadership ladder of one requires investing in one group more than another. We suspect this is not unique for Black women, as they face the same constraints that other members of Congress do in terms of the time and energy one can devote to a caucus.

Black women's presence in congress

This essay is meant to provide the proverbial bird's eye view of Black women in Congress. Few studies of Congress center these grossly underrepresented actors.[9] Some of this may be due to the dearth of Black women who have ever served in office. Moreover, when Black women serve they are rarely committee chairs and no Black woman has ever served in one of the top leadership positions. Vice President Kamala Harris providing the tiebreaking vote in the 117th Congress is the closest we have come to consistently having a Black woman be THE pivotal actor in the Congress.

In many ways, because Black women have been underrepresented in Congress, their presence is treated as an anomaly. They are more of a source of intrigue than a substantive subject of study. We offer a different take on these actors. We assert that to best understand Congress it is imperative to center Black women. We learn about the way in which identity matters by studying how members function within an institution that wields power and that is trying to come to terms with how to adjust to this increasing diversity. That is, we learn about institutions and identities by studying the two concepts together and how they mutually construct one another. Studies which consider institutions independent of identity fail to provide a complete picture of how institutions function. A study of identity outside of the constraints imposed by an institution only provides a partial picture of the relevance of one's identity and how identity shapes behavior (see also Hancock 2007).

When we center critical aspects of one's identity like race and gender, we learn what is actually true about American politics. We do not paint the picture of American politics that we wish were true, but we study American politics as it is, namely something where race and gender have always mattered for who wields power. In short, when we center Black women, individuals who against the odds made it to one of the most visible and powerful legislative chambers in the world, one that was founded and sustained by slaveholders who would never have imagined a Black woman standing at its dais as Vice President of the United States, we learn about politics as it is.

Black women are trailblazers. They are advocates. They are voices for the marginalized. They are alike in many ways but are not identical. Despite sharing the same race and gender identities, Black women may respond differently to the realities of racism and sexism inherent in political institutions. By centering these 52 Black women (and counting!), we can expand scholarly knowledge about the way Congress works. As Black women increase their congressional representation, it is imperative we better understand the paths they have taken to get there and the history upon which new Black women members stand.

Notes

1. Following the initial release of the data, more enslavers have been identified and added to the database.
2. Due to redistricting, it is very difficult to ascertain the demographic nature of all the districts Black women have represented over the past 50 years, although the role of majority-minority districts has been critical to the election of Black women (Lubin 1997; Hardy-Fanta, Pinderhughes, and Sierra 2016).
3. We ascertained the committees that Sen. Carol Moseley Braun served on through her biography that we accessed by using the aforementioned "people search" function.
4. A descriptive representative shares a characteristic in common with their constituents, commonly included are race and gender as examples of politically salient identities (Dovi 2002).
5. For more on the challenges facing women of color candidates in statewide races, see Sanbonmatsu (2016).
6. We are also aware that a majority of Blacks actually live in suburban areas (Frey 2011), something that further complicates the study of the types of districts represented by Black Congresswomen.
7. https://cawp.rutgers.edu/facts/levels-office/state-legislature/women-state-legislatures-2022.
8. https://www.blackhistory.com/2019/11/mary-jane-patterson-first-black-woman-graduate-college.html.
9. For a comprehensive view of women of color elected at all levels of government, see (Hardy-Fanta, Pinderhughes, and Sierra 2016). Citations for authors' reviews of this invaluable work can be found in the references. For personal interviews with Black women in Congress, see (Dittmar 2018).

Acknowledgments

We would like to thank Kelly Dittmar for helpful feedback on the paper. Kira Goeking provided invaluable research assistance.

Disclosure statement

No potential conflict of interest was reported by the author(s).

References

Alozie, Nicholas O., and Lynne L. Manganaro. 1993a. "Women's Council Representation: Measurement Implications for Public Policy." *Political Research Quarterly* 46 (2):383–98. doi:10.1177/106591299304600210.

Alozie, Nicholas O., and Lynne L. Manganaro. 1993b. "Black and Hispanic Council Representation: Does Council Size Matter?" *Urban Affairs Review* 29 (2):276–98. doi:10.1177/004208169302900205.

Alpha Kappa Alpha Sorority, Inc. 2019. "Pioneering Members." http://akapioneers.aka1908.com/index.php (Accessed February 2022).

Augusta University. 2022. "Delta Sigma Theta Sorority, Inc." https://www.augusta.edu/student-life/greeklife/national panhellenicblackhistorymonth/delta.php (Accessed February 2022).

Barnes, Tiffany D., Victoria Beall, and Mirya R. Holman. 2021. "Pink Collar Representation and Policy Outcomes in U.S. States." *Legislative Studies Quarterly* 46 (1):119–55. doi:10.1111/lsq.12286.

Barnett, Marguerite Ross 1975. "The Congressional Black Caucus." Proceedings of the Academy of Political Science 32 (1): 34–50.

Boling, Louis. 2017. "Sisters in Service: DSTs with Distinguished Civil Service, Leadership Records." *HuffPost*, May 8. https://www.huffpost.com/entry/sisters-in-service-dsts-with-distinguished-civil-service_b_590fe00ae4b056aa2363d69d

Brown, Nadia E. 2018. "Hardy-Fanta, Carol,Pei-te Lien,Dianne Pinderhughes, and Christine Marie Sierra.Contested Transformations: Race,Gender, and Political Leadership in 21st Century America, Cambridge University Press, 512 Pp., \$39.99 (Paperback)." *Journal of Women, Politics, and Policy* 39 (3):399–401. doi:10.1080/1554477X.2018.1477366.

Brown, Nadia E, and Danielle Casarez Lemi. 2021. *Sister Style: The Politics of Appearance for Black Women Political Elites*. New York: Oxford University Press.

Bullock, Charles S., III, Susan A. MacManus, Jeremy D. Mayer, and Mark J. Rozell. 2022. *African American Statewide Candidates in the New South*. New York: Oxford University Press.

Calhoun-Brown, Allison. 1996. "African American Churches and Political Mobilization: The Psychological Impact of Organizational Resources." *The Journal of Politics* 58 (4): 935–53.

Carroll, Susan J., and Kira Sanbonmatsu. 2013. *More Women Can Run: Gender and Pathways to the State Legislatures*. New York: Oxford University Press.

Casellas, Jason P. 2011. *Latino Representation in State Houses and Congress*. New York: Cambridge University Press.

Cassano, Erik. 2019. "County Democratic Party Chair Started Her Path at Tri-C." *Tri-C*, March 15. https://www.tri-c.edu/news-and-events/news/county-democratic-party-chair-started-her-path-at-tri-c.html (Accessed February 2022).

Center for American Women and Politics (CAWP). 2022a. "Women Officeholders by Race and Ethnicity." New Brunswick, NJ: Center for American Women and Politics, Eagleton Institute of Politics, Rutgers University-New Brunswick. https://cawp.rutgers.edu/facts/women-officeholders-race-and-ethnicity (Accessed January 28, 2022).

Center for American Women and Politics (CAWP). 2022b. "Women in State Legislatures 2022." *New Brunswick, NJ: Center for American Women and Politics, Eagleton Institute of Politics, Rutgers University-New Brunswick*. https://cawp.rutgers.edu/facts/levels-office/state-legislature/women-state-legislatures-2022 (Accessed January 31, 2022).

Chisholm, Shirley. 1970. *Unbought and Unbossed*. Boston: Houghton Mifflin.

Clark, Christopher J. 2019. "Contested Transformation: Race, Gender, and Political Leadership in 21st Century America. By Carol Hardy-Fanta, Pei-te Lien, Dianne Pinderhughes, and Christine Marie Sierra. New York: Cambridge University Press, 2016. 512p. 41.99 Paper." *Perspectives on Politics* 17 (3):888–89. doi:10.1017/S1537592719002330.

Congress.gov. n.d.a *Committees of the U.S. Congress*. Accessed January 2021. https://www.congress.gov/committees

Congress.gov. n.d.b *Members*. https://www.congress.gov/search?q={%22source%22:%22members%22} &searchResultViewType=expanded (Accessed February 2021).

Congressional Research Service. 2022. *Membership of the 117th Congress: A Profile*. Washington, DC: CRS. R46705. https://crsreports.congress.gov/product/pdf/R/R46705 (Accessed March 4, 2022).

Congressional Black Caucus. n.d.a *About: About the Chair*. https://cbc.house.gov/about/about-the-chair.htm (Accessed January 2021).

Congressional Black Caucus. n.d.b *History: Past CBC Chairs*. https://cbc.house.gov/history/past-cbc-chairs.htm (Accessed January 2021).

Crayton (2010). Here is the Full Citation: Crayton, *Kareem*. 2010. "Here is the full citation: Crayton." Kareem 19(3): 473–500. https://gould.usc.edu/why/students/orgs/ilj/assets/docs/19-3%20Crayton.pdf

CSPAN. 2015. "Former Rep. Yvonne Brathwaite Burke (D-CA) on Chairing the House Beauty Shop Cmte." https://www.c-span.org/video/?c4559591/rep-yvonne-brathwaite-burke-chairing-house-beauty-shop-cmte (Accessed March 4, 2022).

Daniels, Ashley C.J. 2021. "Unlocking the Power of the Sister (Hood) Vote: Exploring the Opinions and Motivations of NPHC Sorority Black Women Supporting Black Women Candidates." Order No. 28493808. Washington, DC: Howard University.

Dittmar, Kelly. 2021. "Invisible Forces: Gender, Race, and Congressional Staff." *Politics, Groups, and Identities*:1–17. doi:10.1080/21565503.2021.1908370.

Dittmar, Kelly, Kira Sanbonmatsu, and Susan J. Carroll. 2018. *A Seat at the Table: Congresswomen's Perspectives on Why Their Presence Matters*. New York: Oxford University Press.

Dovi, Suzanne. 2002. "Preferable Descriptive Representatives: Or Will Just Any Woman, Black, or Latino Do?" *American Political Science Review* 96 (4):729–43. doi:10.1017/S0003055402000412.

Dowe, Pearl K. Ford. 2020. "Resisting Marginalization: Black Women's Political Ambition and Agency." *PS: Political Science & Politics* 53 (4): 697–702.

Duerst-Lahti, Georgia. 2002. "Knowing Congress as a Gendered Institution: Manliness and the Implications of Women in Congress." In *Women Transforming Congress*, ed. Cindy Simon Rosenthal. Norman: University of Oklahoma Press, 20–49.

Elazar, Daniel J 1972. *American Federalism: A View from the States*. 2nd ed. New York: Crowell.

Frey, William. 2011. "Melting Pot Cities and Suburbs: Racial and Ethnic Change in Metro America in the 2000s." *Brookings Institute*, May 4. https://www.brookings.edu/research/melting-pot-cities-and-suburbs-racial-and-ethnic-change-in-metro-america-in-the-2000s/

Gertzog, Irwin N. 2002. "Women's Changing Pathways to the US House of Representatives: Widows, Elites, and Strategic Politicians." In *Women Transforming Congress*, ed. Cindy Simon Rosenthal. Norman: University of Oklahoma Press, pp. 95–118.

Gregory Parks, ed. 2008. *Black Greek-Letter Organizations in the Twenty-First Century: Our Fight Has Just Begun*. Lexington: University of Kentucky Press.

Grimes, David. A, and F Schulz. Kenneth 2002. "Descriptive Studies: What They Can and Cannot Do." *The Lancet* 359 (9301):145–49. doi:10.1016/S0140-6736(02)07373-7.

Grofman, Bernard, and Lisa Handley. 1989. "Black Representation: Making Sense of Electoral Geography at Different Levels of Government." *Legislative Studies Quarterly* 14 (2):265–79. doi:10.2307/439760.

Hancock, Ange-Marie. 2007. "Intersectionality as a Normative and Empirical Paradigm." *Politics and Gender* 3(2): 248-254.

Hardy-Fanta, Carol, Dianne Pinderhughes, and Christine Marie Sierra. 2016. *Contested Transformation: Race, Gender, and Political Leadership in 21st Century America*. New York: Cambridge University Press.

Hawkesworth, Mary 2003. "Congressional Enactments of Race-Gender: Toward a Theory of Raced-Gendered Institutions." *The American Political Science Review* 97 (4):529–50. doi:10.1017/S0003055403000868.

Haynie, Kerry L. 2005. "African Americans and the New Politics of Inclusion: A Representational Dilemma?" In *Congress Reconsidered*, eds. Lawrence C.Dodd and Bruce Ian Oppenheimer. *8th edition*. Washington, DC: CQ Press, 395–410.

Heideman, Amanda J. 2020. "Race, Place, and Descriptive Representation: What Shapes Trust toward Local Government?" *Journal of Representative Democracy* 56 (2): 195–213.

Higher Heights Leadership Fund and the Center for American Women in Politics. 2021. "By the Numbers: Black Women in the 117th Congress." https://cawp.rutgers.edu/sites/default/files/resources/higher_heights_black_women_in_congress_fact_sheet_12.30.pdf

Hogan, Robert E. 2001. "The Influence of State and District Conditions on the Representation of Women in U.S. State Legislatures." *American Politics Research* 29 (1):4–24. doi:10.1177/1532673X01029001002.

Holman, Mirya R. 2014. *Women in Politics in the American City*. Philadelphia, PA: Temple University Press.

Howard-Vital, Michelle R. 1989. "African-American Women in Higher Education: Struggling to Gain Identity." *Journal of Black Studies* 20 (2):180–91. doi:10.1177/002193478902000205.

The Hundred-Seven. n.d. *HBCU Listing*. http://www.thehundred-seven.org/hbculist.html (Accessed March 2022).

Jones, James R. 2019. "Theorizing a Racialized Congressional Workplace." *Race, Organizations, and the Organizing Process (Research in the Sociology of Organizations)* 60: 171–91.

Jones, James R. 2022. "Racism and Inequality in Congress." *PS: Political Science and Politics* 55 (2): 283–85.

Jordan, Barbara, and Shelby Hearon. 1979. *Barbara Jordan: A Self-Portrait*. Garden City, NY: Doubleday and Company, Inc.

Karnig, Albert K., and Susan Welch. 1979. "Sex and Ethnic Differences in Municipal Representation." *Social Science Quarterly* 60 (3): 465–81.

Lublin, David a. 1997. *The Paradox of Representation: Racial Gerrymandering and Minority Interests in Congress*. Princeton: Princeton University Press.

Matthew W. Hughey and Gregory S. Parks, eds. 2011. *Black Greek-Letter Organizations 2.0: New Directions in the Study of African American Fraternities and Sororities*. Jackson, MS: University Press of Mississippi.

Merlino, John J. 2017. *The Senate of the United States: Committee and Subcommittee Assignments for the One Hundred Fifteenth Congress*. Washington, DC: U.S. Government Publishing Office. https://www.govinfo.gov/content/pkg/GPO-CPUB-115spub4/pdf/GPO-CPUB-115spub4.pdf (Accessed January 2021).

Merlino, John J. 2018. *The Senate of the United States: Committee and Subcommittee Assignments for the One Hundred Fifteenth Congress*. Washington, DC: U.S. Government Publishing Office. https://www.govinfo.gov/content/pkg/GPO-CPUB-115spub10/pdf/GPO-CPUB-115spub10.pdf (Accessed January 2021).

Merlino, John J. 2019. *The Senate of the United States: Committee and Subcommittee Assignments for the One Hundred Sixteenth Congress*. Washington, DC: U.S. Government Publishing Office. https://www.govinfo.gov/content/pkg/GPO-CPUB-116spub2/pdf/GPO-CPUB-116spub2.pdf (Accessed January 2021).

Minta, Michael D. 2021. *No Longer Outsiders: Black and Latino Interest Group Advocacy on Capitol Hill*. Chicago, IL: University of Chicago Press.

NAACP Connect. 2017. *Divine Nine: Sigma Gamma Rho*. http://www.naacpconnect.org/content/post/divine-nine-sigma-gamma-rho

Nielsen, Euell A. 2019. *Carolyn Cheeks Kilpatrick*. https://www.blackpast.org/african-american-history/congresswoman-carolyn-jean-cheeks-kilpatrick-1945/

North American Interfraternity Conference. n.d. *Greek Members of the Congress (117th Congress- updated 01/2021)*. https://nicfraternity.org/ufaqs/greek-members-of-congrestt/# (Accessed January 2022).

Robinson, Nick. 2017. "The Decline of the Lawyer Politician." *Buffalo Law Review* 65 (4): 657–737.

Rosenthal, Cindy Simon, ed. 2002. *Women Transforming Congress*. Vol. 4 Norman:University of Oklahoma Press.

Rucks-Ahidiana, Zawadi "The Systemic Scarcity of Tenured Black Women." Inside Higher Ed, 16 July 2021. https://www.insidehighered.com/advice/2021/07/16/black-women-facemany-obstacles-their-efforts-win-tenure-opinion (accessed July 2021 16).

Sanbonmatsu, Kira. 2016. "Officeholding in the 50 States: The Pathways Women of Color Take to Statewide Elective Executive Office." In *Distinct Identities*, eds. Nadia E. Brown and Sarah Allen Gershon. New York: Routledge, 187–202.

Sanbonmatsu, Kira. 2020. "Women's Underrepresentation in the US Congress." *Daedalus* 149 (1):40–55. doi:10.1162/daed_a_01772.

Scott, Elsie L., Karra W. McCray, Donald Bell, and Spencer Overton. 2018. "Racial Diversity Among Top U.S. House Staff." *Joint Center for Political and Economic Studies*, August 24. https://jointcenter.org/racial-diversity-among-top-house-staff/

Simpson, Andrea Y. 1998. *The Tie That Binds: Identity and Political Attitudes in the Post-Civil Rights Generation*. New York: New York University Press.

United States House of Representatives. 2019. "Congresswoman Stacey E. Plaskett Initiated into Delta Sigma Theta Sorority, Incorporated." Press Release, April 26. https://plaskett.house.gov/news/documentsingle.aspx?DocumentID=3493

United States House of Representatives. 2020. Beatty Elected Congressional Black Caucus Chair." Press Release, December 3. https://beatty.house.gov/media-center/press-releases/beatty-elected-congressional-black-caucus-chair (Accessed January 2021).

United States House of Representatives: History, Art, and Archives. n.d. *People Search*. https://history.house.gov (Accessed February 2022).

United States House of Representatives: History, Art, and Archives. n.d. *Women in Congress: Historical Data*. https://history.house.gov/Exhibitions-and-Publications/WIC/Historical-Data/Representatives–Who-Served-without-Committee-Assignments/ (Accessed January 2021).

United States House of Representatives: History, Art, and Archives. n.d. *Women in Congress: Historical Data*. https://history.house.gov/Exhibitions-and-Publications/WIC/Historical-Data/Women_Caucus/ (Accessed January 2021).

Wilson, Walter Clark, and Roberto Felix Carlos. 2014. "Do Women Representatives Regender Legislative Bureaucracy? Assessing the Effect of Representative Sex on Women's Presence among US Congressional Staff." *The Journal of Legislative Studies* 20 (2):216–35. doi:10.1080/13572334.2013.833392.

Zeta Phi Beta Sorority, Inc. 2013. "Pioneering Lawmaker, Soror Julia Carson to Get Statehouse Bust." December 31. https://zphib1920.org/soror-julia-carson/

Galvanizing Grief: Black Maternal Politics, Respectability, and the Pursuit of Elected Office

Aidan Smith

ABSTRACT

In the aftermath of public outcry of multiple high-profile killings of Black teens at the hands of police or under the auspices of stand-your-ground laws, several bereaved mothers became symbols of resistance to white supremacist policing and surveillance. Known as the "Mothers of the Movement," this paper traces three of these women (Sybrina Fulton, Lucy McBath, and Lezley McSpadden) from the national stage at the Democratic National Convention in 2016 to the transition to candidates themselves. Their engagement in maternal politics is part of a long lineage of Black maternal activists that have sought justice for their fallen children through public advocacy. While McSpadden, Fulton, and McBath all lobby against white supremacist violence, they are most politically successful when they make their case from a rhetoric that affirms a respectability politics that measures the value of Black citizens in their ability to comport themselves within middle-class cultural standards.

"It took my son being shot down to make me stand up. For me who wasn't really paying attention to the things that was going on with this country, it definitely woke me up. It made me pay attention. It made me wanna fight."

Sybrina Fulton, *Rest in Power: The Trayvon Martin Story (2018)*

Introduction

As George Floyd lay dying at the hands of Officer Derek Chauvin, the man summoned his last breath to call for his mother: "Mama, I'm through." This heartbreaking demonstration of desperation resonated with viewers of the nine-minute video of the murder, sparking coverage from media outlets as disparate as *People* magazine and Fox News. Many viewers reacted to that deeply vulnerable and human cry for his mother, as they conveyed a sense of someone worthy of empathy and respect. Understanding the rhetorical power of Floyd's last words, Chauvin's defense team tried to disturb this narrative by claiming he was referring to his girlfriend (D'Abrosca 2021). Speaker of the House Nancy Pelosi reminded Americans of Floyd's last words following Chauvin's conviction noting, "How heartbreaking was that? [To] call out for your mom, 'I can't breathe.'" The speech generated well-deserved criticism for Pelosi's claim that Floyd offered his life as a "sacrifice," but not for her reference to his cry for his mother (Shammas 2021).

Over the past two decades, perhaps no issue has put maternal politics on the national landscape as centrally as efforts to curb gun violence in all its embodiments. Women mobilized around gun reform in 2000, culminating in the Million Mom March that year. Reframing this debate as a child protection issue drew in more participation from women than other efforts around reform (Goss 2003). Today, mothers from across racial and class identities, both those who have lost children and those who have not, unite online and in advocacy groups like Moms Demand Action Against Gun Violence. Yet while these women are united in their efforts to change public policy around guns, another group formed following personal tragedies that rocked the social and political fabric of the United States. Using the same logics as Black maternal activists before them, Black mothers who lost their children, particularly Sybrina Fulton, mother of Trayvon Martin, Lezley McSpadden, mother of Michael Brown, and Lucy McBath, whose son Jordan Davis was killed by a white man who defended his actions under Florida's stand-your-ground laws, reached beyond their public activism to make change in their communities by seeking elected office. In 2019, McSpadden pursued a seat on the Ferguson, Missouri city council, but placed third in the race. Sybrina Fulton ran, unsuccessfully, for Miami- Dade County Commissioner in 2020, and in 2018 and 2020, Lucy McBath ran for and twice won a seat in the House of Representatives, now serving Georgia's 6th congressional district.

This paper locates Fulton, McBath, and McSpadden in a long lineage of Black mothers driven to advocacy following the murder of their children and makes the case that while there is solidarity across racial lines for both Black and white women who advocate against gun violence, Black women are pushing against a set of racial political realities that spurs them to reach for power found in electoral politics. Using theories of Black feminist epistemologies found in Patricia Hill Collins' foundational work, *Black Feminist Thought: Knowledge, Consciousness, and the Politics of Empowerment* (1991), Raisa Williams' work on Black maternal grief (2016), and Judith Butler's work (2003) on what makes for a "grievable life," I center these three bereaved mothers as women struggling to produce and maintain the humanity of their children in a society that always already devalues their lives. Through a discussion of these women's political speech, including their campaign communications, I argue that even though McSpadden, Fulton, and McBath all lobby against white supremacist violence, they are most politically successful when they make their case from a rhetoric that affirms a respectability politics that measures the value of Black citizens in their ability to comport themselves to middle-class cultural standards. McBath and Fulton's status as members of the upper middle-class provides a veil of acceptability among the cultural elite but does little to change the real vulnerability of the less affluent, like McSpadden and other bereaved Black mothers. Though the positions pursued (city council, county commission, House of Representatives) carry different levels of power and status, results of these candidates' elections reveal that those mothers with children that met the demands of white supremacist respectability had more success in their pursuit of political power than their peers. Emotional appeals centered on bereavement are not enough to win, and this paper reflects on factors at work for these mothers turned activists turned candidates, including gendered barriers to office, racial tropes of inferior Black motherhood, and a respectability politics that reinforces colorism and class bias.

Case studies of these three bereaved mothers reveal both their motivation to humanize their children to a nation that has been, at best, indifferent to their lives, and at worst, hostile to their survival. An analysis of their public comments, both before and after they sought office, their campaign communications, and their life writing in the form of autobiography and social media posts, reveals the strategies and tactics they used as they sought justice for their sons as well as a position of power that would allow them to make change for their communities.

The legacy of Black maternal bereavement as a political catalyst

Always already pathologized, Black mothers do not have equal access to claim the vaunted status of mother. Paradoxically, Fulton, McBath, and McSpadden leveraged their identities as mothers in a social context that has historically marginalized Black motherhood and matriarchal leadership. In her 2016 essay, "Toward a Theorization of Black Maternal Grief as Analytic," Rhaisa Kameela Williams argues that this framework "attends to the ways Black women and their relationship with their children are intimately timed to present disempowerment that is reflective of and com-pounded by the afterlives of slavery ... I do not herald Black maternal grief as a celebratory nontraditional mode of resistance. In fact, I contend that it is a tool used by those who are marked as expendable, particularly within a decidedly 'post-racial' nation" (Williams 2016, 29). Black women must navigate around historical, social, and institutional hurdles to access maternal privilege. Historic discourse surrounding Black motherhood has treated it as pathological, from sociologist Franklin Frazier's (1939) study blaming the ills of the Black community on female-headed households and illegitimacy to the 1965 study "The Negro family: The Case for National Action" by then-Assistant Labor secretary Daniel Patrick Moynihan that blamed Black single mothers for poverty and crime. Mass media renderings of the Black crack baby in the 80s and 90s furthered this national narrative (Roberts 1999). More recently, wealthy and powerful Black women have not found themselves exempt from judgment. For instance, Michelle Obama faced criticism from white feminists for calling herself "Mom-In-Chief" during her husband's presidential administration (Cooper 2010).

Sentimentality about Black maternal love flows more freely than the belief that Black women perform this role adequately. Historically, Black women have long been positioned as the strong, overbearing, maternal figure, often at the detriment of their own children. Patricia Hill Collins (1991, 73–74) analyzes the stereotype of the Black "Mammy" figure, simultaneously feminized as a mother but not allowed the cultural power white women could access as a genteel figure of beauty and refinement. She exists to provide labor for a white child, not her own, and her care and concern serves to marginalize her further, a sentimental weakness instead of a signal of strength. Melissa Harris-Perry (2011) describes the triumvirate of stereotypes that frame Black women in America, positioning them as the Jezebel, a wanton sexual actor; the Mammy, as described above, or the Sapphire, an angry harpy that cannot or will not conform to social expectations. These flat stereotypes erase the lived experiences of real people, even when they could be interpreted as positive reflections of behaviors. Williams (2016) speculates that the stereotype of the "strong Black mother" serves to erase the pain suffered by these women and furthers narratives that they are not infused with humanity or capacity for feeling. "Rather, they are defined through continued presence and visibility within their family and throughout their community to enact and model the strength needed by the survivors ... In spite of, or perhaps because of their omnipresence, their interiority remains unseen and unengaged" (Williams 2016, 24). By presenting a public face free of affect, they conform to normative expectations for civil society and the qualities seen as necessary for political leadership.

But how do voters consider these bereaved mothers that seek justice for their dead children from a system that will often not even concede that a crime has been committed? These candidates are angry, but not out of control or unacceptable, almost entirely respectable in their pursuit of justice for their children. They are strategic and rational actors that have martialed their emotions to seek elected office.

Just as all mothers are not given the same merit in the public eye, all children do not carry the same social value. As Judith Butler notes, the consideration of a valuable life is intrinsically entwined with the victim's participation in a particular lifestyle and behavior. "A hierarchy ... could no doubt be enumerated. We have seen it already, in the genre of the obituary, where lives are quickly tidied up and summarized, humanized, usually married or on the way to be, heterosexual, happy, monogamous ... Certain lives will be highly protected, and the abrogation of their claims to sanctity will be sufficient to mobilize the forces of war. Other lives will not find such fast and furious support and will not even qualify as 'grievable'" (Butler 2003, 33). These bereaved Black mothers understood that they needed to make their sons fit within normative expectations of behaviors. These young men were important; their loss is a loss to not only to their families but also to their communities.

Community involvement beyond the nuclear family also demonstrates cultural value. Both Fulton and McBath regularly reference their religious faith as reasons for their pursuit of elected office. In her autobiography, McBath (2018, 25–26) wrote:

> God show me what to do now ... My child was dead. My whole purpose for waking up each morning had been torn away. How would I go on? ... I was too lost in grief and anguish to realize that through Jordan, I was already being guided to a purpose greater than any I could have dreamed for myself. It was a call to action that I would come to understand had been mine all along.

Fulton frequently refers to her son as "Trayvon in heaven," and references her membership in the Missionary Baptist denomination in her campaign material. Religious fervor serves as a common thread that unites these women and others. "A focus on religious experience in the narratives of activist Black women helps to make significant their human conditions – the contexts that produce their co-constitutive expression of religious and racial awakenings as they encounter anti-Black violence" (Booker 2021, 1). The church is central to the Black American experience. At times the institution has either reinforced or challenged the status quo, depending on how members could best benefit from these moves politically (McDaniel 2013). I argue that these bereaved mothers' engagement with religious rhetoric is not only an expression of their personal faith and identity, but an anchor to a conservative institution that furthers their intelligibility to the white public as well as voters.

Patricia Hill Collins' (1991) foundational book, *Black Feminist Thought: Knowledge, Consciousness, and the Politics of Empowermen*t, offers a multifaceted way for scholars to understand the political work of these bereaved mothers. First, she argues that Black women become activists always with a goal of group survival as the key driver. Secondly, Black motherhood has historically been aligned with work, both as domestic workers for white children as well as work done to ensure Black children's survival. Black women's respectability has long determined who may contribute to conversations about race and Black life. Rosa Parks became the icon of the Montgomery Bus Boycott in December 1955 when she refused to give up her seat to a white person. This orchestrated action placed Parks, a married, employed, middle-aged, light-skinned Black woman as the aggrieved party to Jim Crow laws. Yet Claudette Colvin, a 15-year-old girl, had taken the same stance and was arrested in March of that year. Her narrative presented problems to the NAACP and other organizers: she was unwed, pregnant, and did not have what she later called "the right hair and the right look." In a National Public Radio interview in 2009, Colvin reflected on why Parks fit the bill: "Her skin texture was the kind that people associate with the middle-class. She fit that profile" (Adler 2009). Motherhood is always political, and activists and organizations have long understood that the most useful mothers are those that don't transgress social norms. Colvin's teen motherhood, in addition to her appearance that strayed from Eurocentric beauty norms, made her less effective than Parks. Scholarship indicates that Black women candidates and elected officials are judged closely on their appearance (Brown and Lemi 2021), leaving the bereaved mothers-turned-candidates under multiple layers of scrutiny.

Arguably, these women's work has been overshadowed by the #BlackLivesMatter movement, first a hashtag then a grassroots organization that formed after these high-profile deaths at the hands of police. The "Mothers of the Movement" lift the political voice of Black women in tandem with those women of #BlackLivesMatter, a social movement born in the wake of the public visibility of the killings of Martin, Davis, and Brown, in a significantly different way. Allissa V. Richardson (2019) offers a trenchant analysis of the current political moment, noting in her assessment of the BLM move away from respectability politics, "It is also true, however, that the politics of respectability was deeply entrenched in assimilationist thought, which reinforced many of the Black stereotypes it sought to annihilate." As the bereaved mothers speak about and for their dead children, they stand with images of them in graduation gowns and mortarboards, tuxedos, and formal wear, as they did in the *Lemonade* short film (Beyoncé 2016). They are not the "thugs" of hip hop music or conservative political disdain. They are valuable within Butler's framework of a grievable life, respectable members of society that were punished unfairly by racist state structures. And while this is certainly true, what of those who are disrespectable? Who do not have loving parents or prom photos? The profiled maternal activists are operating within a respectability politics framework that does humanize their sons, yet perhaps may reinforce ongoing marginalization of those without the capacity to perform middle-class norms and values.

Black mothers, grief, and American activism

The conversion of mother's love to political work in the wake of Black death is not new. While many Black women were excluded from the concept of republican motherhood as well as the political activism in this era, others also accessed the powers inherent in sentiment about the maternal role and family connections. Scholars have analyzed slave narratives as sites not only of resistance but as pathos appeals to an investment in the inherent value in maternal love and the mother/child relationship. Harriet Jacob's *Incidents in the Life of a Slave Girl* (2015) offered readers a window into the sexual predation Black women suffered, appealing specifically to a female, white middle-class audience, themselves likely mothers (Carby 1987). Literary scholar Stephanie Li argues, "Jacob's reliance upon the trope of motherhood capitalizes on the political import of prevailing beliefs in the sanctity and power of the mother ... For Jacobs, motherhood is not simply a politically astute literary trope and means of describing the abuses of slavery specific to women; it is also a crucial form of female empowerment" (Li 2006, 15).

Following the murder of her 14-year-old son Emmett in 1955, Mamie Till-Mobley insisted on an open-casket funeral for her son that would reveal the brutality done to her child, telling reporters "Let the people see what they did to my boy" (Thornton 2010). *Life Magazine* published photos of the funeral and Mamie in mourning, igniting a national conversation about racialized violence that could no longer be ignored by white America. Till-Mobley detailed in her autobiography her commitment to tell her son's story far and wide throughout the South, leading a speaking tour for the NAACP that resulted in one of its most successful fundraising initiatives (Till-Mobley and Benson 2005). Historian Timothy's (2017, 214) scholarship on the Till trial illuminates the details of the trial and the legacy of the boy's lynching, but eloquently concludes, "American is still killing Emmett Till, and often for the same reasons that drove the violent segregationists of the 1950s and 1960s." Though the murder of Till is well known, today's activists find themselves walking the same reluctant path to political activism. "I never in a million years thought that I would be in the same position," Sybrina Fulton reflected on the work of maternal activists that came before her for a documentary miniseries on her son's case, reflecting in disbelief how she found herself in similar circumstances as Mamie Till (*Rest in Power: The Trayvon Martin Story* 2018).

In 1979, Camille Bell became a national media figure following the murder of her 9-year- old son Yusuf, an early victim in the Atlanta Child Murders that spanned years and took the lives of 29 children. She formed the Committee to Stop Children's Murder, alongside the mothers of other victims. The group was unrelenting in the demand for justice for Black victims from poor communities, insisting the city council and police value the lives of her son and others. Bell, an experienced organizer in the mid-century civil rights movement, did not reserve her anger for white supremacist state apparatus. In a nationally televised interview, she specifically called out Atlanta Mayor Maynard Jackson and other Black elected officials for their lack of concern. "If white people don't care about Black people, that's bad, but if Black people don't care about Black people, that's deplorable" (Gillard 1980). She deployed her pain and anger against anyone who did not act on behalf of the city's most vulnerable.

Motherhood as a political identity

Motherhood has long provided a political pathway for women, operating within a culturally acceptable paradigm for women's involvement beyond the domestic. Transitioning from the "separate spheres" and republican motherhood (Kerber 2000) at the nation's founding to a more public "civic motherhood" during the Progressive era, White women leveraged this identity to become political actors and organizers. As Dolan, Deckman, and Swers (2019, 23) detail in their work on women's political pathways, late nineteenth-century middle-class women engaged in activism ranging from suffrage to temperance to public sanitation, all under the auspices of maternal activism, noting that many "subscribed to a vision of civic motherhood that required women as selfless, moral agents to properly fulfill their roles as mothers and wives."

Motherhood still conveys power, however marginal, that can be used to sway American political thought on issues as crucial to the nation as women's suffrage to those more tangential like drunk driving. These advocates lay claim to a political position based on their status as mothers that is not available to women outside of a traditional reproductive role, and they make the most of this privilege unavailable to those don't participate in child-rearing. Motherhood shapes one's thinking because of the daily care and concern required (Ruddick 1990). Maternal politics reinforces the belief that mothers have a unique position from which to speak about issues that impact not only their children, but all children. An investment in maternal politics is not just the embrace of this role by the mother herself, but also the valuation of this experience by others as something valuable and sacred. Yet all women do not experience the same benefits of this identity. Feminist scholars of motherhood have noted that not all mothers even have equal access to their children. From the lasting legacy of chattel slavery that did not recognize Black women's right to their own offspring, to more contemporary eugenicist policies that surveil disabled mothers to determine fitness (Filax and Taylor 2014), to queer mothers who face legal challenges to parenting as a result of the homophobia, transphobia, and custodial laws that reinforce heteronormative nuclear family dynamics, the cultural capital many white women can access can be hard to come by for others. Recent scholarship demonstrates that being a parent is a gendered political identity that influences how, why, and to what extent women engage with politics (Thomas and Bittner 2017). Kelly Dittmar's (2015) work on the role of gender dynamics in political campaigns sheds light on both the benefits and detriments to an emphasis on a candidate's motherhood. She found that while once a liability, now women candidates "spent more time using their motherhood as a credential for office than assuring voters that it would not be a hindrance to their success" (Dittmar 2015, 119).

For these Black mothers, their motherhood and bereavement are central to their claims on the positions they seek, and often their only past political engagement (Lawson 2018). Yet the contemporary landscape offers a political moment that does not demand previous political experience (see the candidacy and election of Donald Trump). Further, the successful rise of other candidates that embraced a public motherhood across the political spectrum, from Sarah Palin's "hockey mom" to Kristin Gillibrand (Beail and Longworth 2012; Greenlee, Deason, and Langner 2017), provided a tenable pathway. Even Hillary Clinton understood the value of a normative maternal performance, extending her own claims to the valued political role with a cheeky #Grandmothersknowsbest tweet (Rhode and Dejmanee 2016). Embracing the moniker of motherhood as an organizing tool, women in Congress have recently formed a "motherhood caucus," demonstrating recognition of the value of women's organizing across party lines for common cause (Gibson 2019; Mahoney 2018).

Participation in a heteronormative nuclear family carries many political benefits (Greenlee 2014; Smith 2017). Kamala Harris, in her groundbreaking pursuit of the American presidency, made sure to reference her adult stepchildren when given an opportunity, explaining in interviews that her role as stepmother is the most important job she will ever hold. "Of all the titles I've held, my favorite is 'Momala,'" (Williams 2020). A claim to motherhood, no matter how tangential the connection, conveys an essential expertise. While figures like Kamala Harris serve as a victory for descriptive representation, Black women have long been underrepresented in elected positions at all levels and have faced historical exclusion due to their intersecting identities. In 2021, The Center for American Women in Politics reported that that there are more Black women in Congress this session than at any point previously. However, those women found success despite their racial and gender status. Carew (2018) explores how stereotypes of Black women both help and harm these political actors. For Black women pursuing elected office in the wake of the murder of their children or loved ones, these stereotypes can be leveraged strategically to gain traction in the race. As Carew (2018, 109) notes, "Black women seeking office must work hard to present messages that counter any views that are detrimental to their electoral success to overcome stereotypes concerning traits and beliefs. Where they find positive perceptions, they can emphasize these traits to bolster electoral support, and where they find negative perceptions, they can work to demonstrate how those perceptions are not applicable." Culturally, women performing motherhood are rewarded for this normative gender performance requiring perpetual nurture and care, conforming to expectations of gendered behavior. Black women running from a public position of mourning make a claim for positional power that harnesses positive sentiment from voters for occupying the role of caretaker, as well as affirm the stereotype of assertiveness by functioning as vocal advocates for reform.

Smooth's (2005) work on Black women in electoral politics notes that regardless of socioeconomic status, these women are more likely than their male counterparts to be politically active, with their engagement ranging from voting to holding office, as well as club engagement and church attendance. However very little scholarship centers the experience of the Black woman elected official. We have analyses of gendered institutions (Kenney 1996) and of racialized institutions (Jones 2019), but consideration of those who occupy both categories is scant. Mary Hawkesworth's (2003) seminal work on the racing-gender of Congress offers some insight into how these mothers-turned-activists-turned-candidates might experience the halls of power: "The identities of women of color are constituted through an amalgam of practices that construct them as 'other' (to white men, men of color, and white women), challenging their individuality and status as fully human." Yet the category of mother is not "other." It is perhaps one of only a few universal identities that crosses cultural lines.

Seizing the political moment: the "Mothers of the Movement" at the 2016 Democratic National Convention

The nomination of Hillary Clinton to the Democratic ticket offered all mothers an opportunity to see someone like them in a position of power, no matter how far removed they might be from the former first lady, senator, and secretary of state in other aspects of their identity. Clinton leveraged this maternal connection in both 2008 and 2016 and understood its value to soften aspects of her persona often criticized (Smith 2017). But the inclusion of the "Mothers of the Movement" in the nominating convention offered a new avenue for maternal politics, both in terms of who could speak and who was expected to listen. In solidarity with one another Maria Hamilton, Lucy McBath, Gwen Carr, Geneva Reed-Veal, Sybrina Fulton, Annette Nance-Holt, Lezley McSpadden, Wanda Johnson, and Cleopatra Pendleton-Cowley stood on stage together in support of Clinton.

When speaking at the DNC, both McBath and Fulton linked their roles as mothers to an obligation to do the political work to preserve and protect Black lives in the future, not just in pursuit of justice for their fallen sons. Lucy McBath told the audience: "You don't stop being a parent when your child dies. I am still Jordan Davis's mother. His life ended the day he was shot and killed for playing loud music. But my job as his mother didn't." McBath's job was not just to mother Jordan, but it was to mother all Black children that must navigate a cultural landscape that situates them as criminals, predators, or parasites.

Kimberly Killen (2019, 625) offers a nuanced analysis of the language that each woman used as part of their primetime speaking opportunity at the convention, arguing, "Their discourse uses motherhood to challenge institutional practices and statements that position their children as criminals rather than as citizens deserving of justice, restituting blame and fault to a broken system whose promises of equality and justice for all remain unrealized." While this media moment presented a unified wall of bereaved mothers indicting the police state, it happened within a framework that reified Clinton's advocacy as a mother herself. McBath proclaimed, "Hillary Clinton isn't afraid to say Black Lives Matter. She isn't afraid to sit at a table with grieving mothers and bear the full force of our anguish. She doesn't build walls around her heart." Fulton, gesturing toward bipartisanship perhaps, remarked, "This isn't about being politically correct. It's about saving our children ... Hillary is the one mother who can ensure our movement will succeed." It wasn't just that these women's maternal identity was important, it was the appeal to the would-be mother/president that was important. The "Mothers of the Movement" continued to campaign for Clinton well beyond the convention, attending over 20 campaign stops. They were in New York City on election night, poised to celebrate Hillary Clinton's expected victory.

Clinton's loss changed the trajectory of progressive politics in the United States, mobilizing activists to navigate a landscape that was now openly hostile. An assessment of the campaigns and races of Davis, McBath, and McSpadden demonstrates the ways in which maternal politics are an ongoing part of conversations surrounding race and police brutality, the political utility of respectability politics, and the ways that each woman sought a seat at the table to make change in her own community. Though no conclusions can be drawn between cause and effect, I argue that the outcomes of the bereaved mothers' elections align with the adjudication of their children's killers. Davis's killer was convicted, his mother was elected. Martin and Brown's murders walked free; their mothers were not elected. The victim found most innocent, most worthy of justice, perhaps not coincidentally came from the most affluent and light-skinned family. While Martin's and Brown's deaths contributed to the activation of a social movement that has arguably made lasting political change, the state has not recognized that a crime was committed in either case.

A snapshot of the dead: Jordan Davis, Trayvon Martin, and Michael Brown

Jordan Davis, Trayvon Martin, and Michael Brown each occupied their own community differently, carrying with them the burdens of stereotypes about young Black men (Ellis 2014). Law enforcement and the media scrutinized their attire and behavior at the time of their deaths for an assessment of whether they deserved to die. Recently suspended from his high school for marijuana possession, 17-year-old Martin's hooded sweatshirt served as a marker of his criminality, while Davis' loud music signaled his participation in a thug culture that did not defer to white notions of appropriate behavior. Brown's alleged theft of a package of cigarillos from a convenience store sentenced him to death at the hands of a police officer. The killer of each of these young men received a different punishment: Davis' murderer was tried twice, once resulting in a hung jury, with conviction of second-degree murder on the second attempt; Martin's killer, neighborhood watch captain George Zimmerman, was acquitted of all charges under Florida's stand-your-ground laws, and Brown's shooter, a Ferguson, Missouri police officer, was never charged.

The following is an analysis of how each mother defined herself and her political activism in the context of her child's death.

US Representative Lucy McBath

A *Rolling Stone* magazine article describing the Davis shooting opened with a vignette of the teenager at the mall that establishes the victim as just another kid, not a criminal, not a thug:

> The boys did their best impression of premium shoppers, four well-raised black teens from middle-class homes trying hard to stand out by blending in. They talked to – but whiffed with – a few of the upscale "honeys," browsed the stores for high-priced sneakers that they mostly owned already (Tevin bought a new pair every payday; Jordan, who'd just landed his first after-school job, was breaking his father's wallet with his shoe game) and began to make their way toward the exits. (Solotaroff 2013)

This narrative establishes Davis's grievable life in all its required details: middle-class, straight, employed, and an avid participant in consumerist culture. What made these teens "well-raised" made their lives meaningful and valuable. The same assessment was not extended to other Black teens, or their parents, in the wake of their killings. Davis's death was extrajudicial; therefore, a condemnation of his killer does not necessarily require an indictment of police brutality or the surveillance state. Lucy McBath's search for justice and dignity for her son attacked white supremacy but was not an inherent condemnation of government authorities. McBath stated in an interview for a documentary film about her son's case, "If we don't get a guilty verdict, then as a minority it's like another slap in the face.

Constantly telling a race of people that they don't matter" (*3 1/2Minutes, 10 Bullets* 2015). Her son's murderer was ultimately convicted. In 2014, Michael Dunn was given the maximum possible sentence plus 90 years for killing Davis and for the three attempted murders of the other teens in the car.

McBath's campaign announcement press release in 2018 identified her as Jordan Davis' mother in its first 20 words and anchored her desire to serve in Congress to her anti-gun activism: "Her decision to run was influenced in part by the recent events in Parkland and the polarized debate among leaders in Washington and the Administration that followed. 'We need common sense solutions – not heated political rhetoric – to help solve gun violence prevention. I offer my voice in this debate for the safety of my neighbors in Georgia and across the country'" (Friends Of Lucy Mcbath 2018). McBath does not ground her desire for political power in a desire to upend white supremacy, or even change the stand-your-ground law that was evoked to excuse the murder of her son. She presents herself as a relative centrist seeking to defuse a volatile situation, mobilized to seek office after the mass shooting at a predominately white high school in Florida. The press release also references her professional background as a flight attendant for thirty years for Delta Airlines, a career entrenched in the performance of feminine beauty, middle-class manners, and service work. She also calls out her church and sorority membership, nods to her community engagement in culturally valued institutions to further burnish her campaign persona. McBath demonstrates Pierre Bourdieu's (1986) concept of cultural capital in her campaign communications, a framework that privileges symbols, ideas, tastes, and preferences that can be strategically used as resources in social action. McBath's "habitus" as an affluent, professional member of the Atlanta community elevates her claims to office over her fellow "Mothers of the Movement" as well as her electoral opponents. In 2018, McBath narrowly defeated Republican opponent Karen Handel by 3,264 votes, 50.5% to 49.5%. In 2020, McBath defeated Handel again, this time with a wider margin of victory, earning 54.6% of the vote.

Sybrina Fulton

"At first, I didn't want to be the voice for Trayvon after he died but I decided I have no choice. Now, I'm called to act, and called to serve. It became clear to me there's an opportunity to turn our family's tragedy into something positive for many other families," she told viewers in her video campaign announcement, posted on her social media accounts (Fulton 2019). She went on to mention her work with other bereaved mothers, as well as the need for affordable housing, the cost of living, and the amorphous "quality of life for everyday people." Each of these issues is solidly gendered within a domestic framework that aligns with Fulton's core maternal identity. Importantly, she notes that she felt obliged to run. "Until recently, I didn't see myself as someone who would run. But if not me, then who? If not now, then when?" (Simon 2019).

Trayvon Martin's killer George Zimmerman, though not officially a tool of the state, served as neighborhood watch captain appointed by a homeowner's association to privilege the protection of property over civil rights. The police department in Sanford, Florida did not initially charge Zimmerman with a crime, opening a national debate on stand-your-ground laws and the ongoing criminalization of Black youth. Six weeks after the shooting, Zimmerman was finally charged. Debate over the incident ranged from established pundits like Fox News' Sean Hannity to random internet commentors, speculating whether Martin "deserved it" (Capeheart 2012). A jury acquitted Zimmerman in July 2013. Unlike McBath, no court found her son's killer responsible for the crime, and Trayvon's worthiness of life remains publicly debated.

Fulton's campaign, significantly, was not anchored in a platform focused on police reform or racism. Her candidacy was not focused on this movement, and instead centered, as most local elections do, on housing, economic issues, and transportation. At one point, she even was in opposition to some of her supporters who called for a defunding of the police department (Smiley and Robertson 2020). She lost her race to Oliver Gilbert, a Black former mayor of Miami Gardens, by just 331 votes, a razor-thin loss for a metropolitan area with a population of 2.7 million. Her near-success affirms electability is anchored in mainstream political concerns, not a revolution intent on upending the status quo. Fulton has hinted that she plans to run again, undaunted by her narrow loss: "Well, a lot of people have been saying: 'You have to do this again because it was too close.' I can't tell you right now, honestly. That is something I'm exploring, but I definitely will do my research and take a look at it to see if there's another seat I want to run for in the near future" (Rose 2021).

Lezley McSpadden

In 2016, Lezley McSpadden stood on the stage at the DNC among the other women who had lost their children but she did not speak. The mother of Michael Brown, whose killing in 2014 by police in Ferguson, Missouri contributed to the BLM movement, specifically anchored her political ambition in racial justice. When asked why she sought to hold public office, she responded, "If a mother had to watch her son lay on the street for four hours, and watch our community be completely disrespected by the people we elected, what would you do? You would stand up and you would fight, too" (Martinez 2018). Officer Darren Wilson shot Michael Brown from his police cruiser once, and then again seven times as the teen ran for his life. Wilson allegedly believed that Brown was a suspect in a strong-arm robbery of a convenience store. Brown's body lay in the street for over four hours, signifying its lack of value to the victim's family and his community. Much like the Trayvon Martin case, public debate on the killing centered on whether Brown deserved what he got. Media did not focus on his consumer habits. Instead, his height and weight (6 feet, 4 inches tall, 292 pounds) and his alleged strong-arm robbery of a convenience store dominated the narrative. Protests erupted after no charges were brought, and McSpadden could be seen on national television crying in agony over the lack of accountability in her son's death.

Like Fulton, McSpadden cites her son's murder as the moment of her political awakening. She explicitly called out the incumbent elected for their inaction and disrespect to her child, where McBath and Fulton did not. Fulton ran for office in Miami-Dade county, over 200 miles from where her child died, while McBath sought and gained office in the federal government. McSpadden targeted the local government she found responsible for her anguish. "I wanted to go back and do something right in a place that did something so very wrong to my son, and I think that's what my son would want as well," McSpadden said in an interview with the Associated Press (2019). McSpadden had not lived in the community until a year before the election and moved to Ferguson specifically to seek a seat on the council. In her campaign, she articulated a clear platform of police reform: "I think they should work much harder to prove that they are there to protect and serve, because no one believed that in August 2014 and people are still skeptical" (Associated Press 2019).

McSpadden was unsuccessful in her attempt, finishing with only 20% of the vote in a three-way race, but reflected later on the challenges, both personal and political, of her run. "Campaigning was scary. I had to knock on all those doors. I had to listen to people saying they weren't going to vote for me. But it was important to me to go back for those who absolutely did support me, supported me when I couldn't even support myself" (Secret 2020). She links her political work directly back to the community that found value in her son's life and in her pursuit for justice. Her remarks align with Collins' (1991) and Williams' (2016) reflections on the strong Black mother, whose efforts are not only for her family but her community at large, whose emotional needs are omnipresent but often go untended.

While all seven of the "Mothers of the Movement" that took the stage with Hillary Clinton in 2016 had a moment of hypervisibility that would serve as a launchpad for a national campaign, Dowe's (2020) work on Black women's political ambition helps contextualize the profiled bereaved mother's political engagement: "Structural factors undoubtedly affect and determine which political offices women seek. However, what more crucially determines Black women's decision to seek office and specifically higher office is which venue is most likely to provide the greatest impact for their communities." Though Dowe's work focuses on young Black women's political ambition, I would argue that her findings could also be applied here. For Lezley McSpadden, a woman robbed of her son by a local police force that would not prosecute an unlawful shooting, she sought a position of power on the city council that oversaw this organization. Sybrina Fulton, while she had a national platform and persona, sought a seat in the county government where she had served for thirty years as an administrative staffer. McBath, the most economically privileged of those profiled here, set her sights on a legislative position that would allow her to address national gun reform policy and the stand-your-ground laws that were used in the defense of her son's murder.

Bereaved Black mothers in comparison to bereaved white mothers as candidates

Though both white and Black women leverage the value of their culturally rewarded identity as mothers in a nation that values heteronormativity and feminine domesticity, white and Black women have very different experiences and responses. Certainly, white women who lost children and loved ones to gun violence have sought elected office in the United States. Representative Carolyn McCarthy ran for office in the wake of the murder of her husband and the shooting of her son in 1993's Long Island Railroad Massacre that left six dead and 19 wounded. The shooter, Colin Ferguson, was a Black man that targeted commuter train riders as he declared a hatred of whites and white supremacy. McCarthy spent 18 years in office as the "gun lady," often asking her colleagues in Congress to "send me home" by voting for gun control measures. McCarthy's tenure in office saw the deadliest mass shootings in the nation up to that point, from 1999's Columbine Massacre to the Sandy Hook shooting in Newtown, Connecticut in 2012. During her time in office, she was never able to bring about significant gun control legislation that would reduce mass shootings.

Following her electoral victory, a *New York Times* article described her as a reluctant warrior: "She was the Long Island Everywoman, forced into the limelight by a flash of violence, who reluctantly capitalized on her own celebrity to take on-and defeat-one of the most daunting political machines in the nation ... In her loss, Mrs. McCarthy found a mission. She became an anti-gun activist whose simple questions tested the complications surrounding the issue. Why do ordinary citizens need assault weapons? Why are guns so easy to obtain? She was earnest rather than slick, and her message carried resonance" (Barry 1996). McCarthy's efforts to make policy change fit neatly into gendered expectations for women's political success: earnest, not ambitious.

Unlike McBath and Fulton, McCarthy's defense of gun control politics as a result of her bereavement went unquestioned. She did not have to advocate for her husband's innocence or the merits of his life, or to demonstrate the lifelong disability that impacted her son. A middle-aged, straight white man with a wife and children, his life stood in stark contrast to that of young Black men killed due to state or vigilante violence. In fact, *The Washington Post* identified the incident succinctly: "The media could condense the nightmare to a single line: A Black man walked through the LIRR train calmly firing a 9 mm Ruger semiautomatic handgun, killing six riders and wounding 19 in a three-minute racist massacre" (Jones 1996). Though the shootings were not identical to those that left Brown, Davis, and Martin dead, there was no equivocation about the racial implications of the crime. This benefit extended to McCarthy did not equally land on Fulton, McBath, or McSpadden.

All mothers are not part of the movement: Samaria Rice

Fulton, McBath, McSpadden have shown political ambition where others have not, and their pathways are not available to all those who find themselves in this tragic sorority of bereaved mothers. Bereaved Black mothers with public profiles are not a monolith, with some notably disdaining the work of the "Mothers of the Movement" and those who would seek to capitalize on their notoriety. Tamir Rice was a 12-year old boy killed by a police officer in Cleveland, Ohio in 2014. The child only had a toy gun, yet no charges were filed against the shooter. His mother, Samaria Rice, struggling with grief and anger like so many others, understood that she did not fit the requirements of respectability politics that would grant her the cultural capital of the others to speak for her son's life. She was a woman that had been in and out of foster care as a child and was frequently incarcerated as an adult. At the time of the shooting, she was on public assistance and had just gotten her children out of foster care themselves. In the media maelstrom following the death of her son, she felt overwhelmed by the publicity. "A lot of us parents don't know what to say or how we should be acting," she said in May 2021. "There is a certain way you have to go in front of the media to let them know that you want justice for your baby" (Perry 2021). She was angered at the use of her son's image for political purposes and resistant to his story being subsumed in a national narrative. Her pain was hers, not to be shared with the nation.

Rice's rejection of the "strong Black mother as candidate" role serves as a reminder that not everyone seeks engagement in political discourse and even fewer seek a seat in government. Further, it could be argued that Rice's resistance to political involvement is a rational choice, particularly for a low-income single mother with other young children. The risks of political participation are real, even for those with the greatest resources. Discriminatory harassment, from online bullying to death threats to oneself and one's family, particularly targeted at women of color, are valid reasons to avoid engagement. A recent study found that during their campaigns, women faced death threats, threats of sexual assault, stalking, vandalism of their homes and cars, home and car break-ins, and sexual harassment, both online and through other means (Laramie 2020). Beyond the political landscape, researchers have found that women of color receive more negative communications via social media than their white or male counterparts, and that those communications are specifically racist and sexist in nature, deploying slurs and stereotypes anchored in xenophobia and misogyny (Francisco and Felmlee 2022).

Conclusion

How does McBath, the only candidate that won her race, legislate and lead? Much like Carolyn McCarthy did years earlier, she reminds voters that her son's murder is the center of her political worldview. In April 2021, she tweeted an announcement about President Joe Biden's executive actions around gun reform legislation, including increased regulation of homemade firearms and closing loopholes on background checks: "To my Jordan: This day. At the White House. In the Rose Garden. The President announced actions that will help keep families safe. Actions that will protect children across America. Children like you. My dear Jordan, this day is your day" (McBath 2021). McBath included an image of her son as a very young child. Interestingly, this legislation is not specifically child-focused. It's not about school shootings, gun locks, or any of a variety of policies that would necessarily impact youth. McBath's infantilization of her son functions not only to reinforce her identity as a maternal figure, but also rhetorically furthers him as an innocent to be protected.

Biological mothers are not the only ones deploying a campaign of maternalist politics to seek office. In 2020, Princess Blanding, the sister of Marcus-David Peters, a high school teacher who was fatally shot by police in May 2018 during a mental health crisis, launched a third-party bid for governor of Virginia, citing the death of her brother as the catalyst for her campaign. Running as part of the newly launched Liberation Party, the video announcing her candidacy is filled with images of children at play or in the arms of their mothers (Blanding 2020). Blanding, an out queer woman, told voters in the voice-over that her administration would prioritize clean energy, comprehensive health care for all, gender inclusivity, Black Lives Matter, safe schools and "fixing our broken criminal injustice system." She condemned political moments that she posited are just public relations moves, calling out then-Governor Ralph Northam at the signing of a bill in honor of her brother Marcus, telling the gathering of Democrats: "Please take a moment to pat yourselves on the back for doing exactly what this racist corrupt (and broken) system expected you to do." It is not enough to make speeches and posture toward incremental change; Blanding demanded accountability from both enemies and allies.

Her quest for justice for her dead brother functioned within what Patricia Hill Collins might call the framework of the "othermother," a tradition of women-centered kinship networks in Black communities that serve as a defense against the diminution of family networks that dates back to slavery, "that children are 'private property' and can be disposed of as such" (Collins 1991, 122). Black children belong to more than just their nuclear family. "By seeing the larger community as responsible for child-rearing, African Americans challenge prevailing property relations. It is in this sense that traditional bloodmother/othermother relationships in women-centered networks are 'revolutionary'" (Collins 1991, 123). Blanding's activism against police brutality and her entrance into electoral politics on behalf of her brother as a long-shot third-party candidate aligns with the other bereaved mothers seeking justice, solidly part of Collins' othermother revolution. Her efforts at electoral victory, as expected, were unsuccessful. Blanding garnered only 0.07% of the vote in the general election, losing to Republican Glenn Youngkin.

Despite greater attention, there looks to be no shortage of grieving mothers impacted by racialized gun violence. In 2021, names like Ma'Khia Bryant and Andrew Brown Jr. joined the list of Black Americans shot and killed by police. Paula Bryant, Ma'Khia's mother, immediately addressed the media, telling reporters that her daughter was a loving honor roll student. She spoke at a rally in Columbus, Ohio in the aftermath of the shooting, reminding the audience not only of her daughter's academic accomplishments, but of her feminine, nurturing disposition: "She had a beautiful smile, was loving and had a beautiful personality. She was a protector and had a motherly spirit about her" (Ward 2021). The life lost was one that conformed to gendered expectations as well as middle-class standards of productivity and performance. Much as Jordan Davis was everything a young man should be, so too was Ma'Khia Bryant everything a young woman should be. Paula Bryant had to humanize her daughter to a world that would dismiss her death as justified, normal, and unremarkable.

While the lost lives of Black men and boys killed at the hands of state actors has dominated the national media narrative, Paula Bryant's voice joins that of other mothers of Black girls and women killed through similar means. Ma'Khia Bryant joins Sandra Bland, Tanisha Anderson, Rekia Boyd, among so many unknown others, on a list of Black women largely forgotten as part of the national discourse around police brutality. In 2014, the African American Policy Forum began the #SayHerName movement in an effort to retrieve the stories of these women. As happens so often, Black women's lives must be actively centered to avoid erasure in dominant activist narratives.

George Floyd's killer has now been found guilty and was sentenced to over two decades in prison for second degree homicide. Even though justice has been arguably served in this case, true reform on police brutality and white supremacist policing tactics remains elusive. In the summer of 2020, street protests broke out around the country. Today, many of those streets are quiet, though they still bear the marks of a society forced to reckon with the marginalization of many of its citizens. Street art remains that honors both the life and death of George Floyd, at the site of the murder in Minneapolis and beyond. In Portland, Oregon, one mural stands out as symbol of maternal politics at work. The words appear amidst an array of colorful flowers, capitalized block letters that evoke a call to action: "ALL MOTHERS WERE SUMMONED WHEN HE CALLED OUT TO HIS MAMA" (Ruvalcaba 2020). Though George Floyd's mother passed away before her son, other mothers stand in her place, advocating for his life as well as for Black life everywhere. Whether these activists reach their goals of elected office or continue their work in other spheres, they and others have answered the call.

Disclosure statement

No potential conflict of interest was reported by the author(s).

References

3 ½ Minutes, 10 Bullets. 2015. Documentary Film Directed by Mark Silver HBO Films.

Adler, Margot 2009. "Before Rosa Parks, There Was Claudette Colvin." *National Public Radio*, March 15. https://www.npr.org/2009/03/15/101719889/before-rosa-parks-there-was-claudette-colvin

Associated Press. 2019. "Michael Brown's Mother Is Running for Ferguson City Council." April 2. https://www.usatoday.com/story/news/nation/2019/04/02/nstagr-brown-mother-mom-ferguson-city-council-lesley-mcspadden/3340996002/ (Accessed May 29, 2021).

Barry, Dan. 1996. "L.I. Widow's Story: Next Stop, Washington." *The New York Times*, November 7. https://www.nytimes.com/1996/11/07/us/li-widow-s-story-next-stop-nstagram.html (Accessed July 2, 2021).

Beail, Linda, and Rhonda Kinney Longworth. 2012. *Framing Sarah Palin: Pit Bulls, Puritans, and Politics*. New York: Routledge.

Beyoncé. 2016. *Lemonade*. New York: Parkwood Entertainment.

Blanding, Princess. 2020. Campaign Announcement Video. https://video.wixstatic.com/video/0fddde_8e138c675d15414198643e40948f5aa5/1080p/mp4/file.mp4 (Accessed July 2, 2021).

Booker, Vaughn A. 2021. "'Mothers of the Movement': Evangelicalism and Religious Experience in Black Women's Activism." *Religions* 12 (2):141. doi:10.3390/rel12020141.

Bourdieu, Pierre. 1986. "The Forms of Capital." In *Handbook of Theory and Research for the Sociology of Education*, ed. J. Richardson. New York: Greenwood, 241–58.

Brown, Nadia E., and Danielle Casarez Lemi. 2021. *Sister Style: The Politics of Appearance for Black Women Political Elites*. New York: Oxford University Press.

Butler, Judith. 2003. *Precarious Life: The Powers of Mourning and Violence*. London, New York: Verso.

Capeheart, Jonathan. 2012. "A Response to 'Martin Got What He Deserved.'" *The Washington Post*, July 23. https://www.washingtonpost.com/blogs/post-partisan/post/a-response-to-martin-got-what-he-deserved/2012/07/23/gJQA8WIF5W_blog.html (Accessed May 21, 2021).

Carby, Hazel V. 1987. *Reconstructing Womanhood: The Emergence of the Afro-American Woman Novelist*. New York: Oxford University Press.

Carew, Jessica D. Johnson. 2018. "Mothers of the Movement." In *Women of the 2016 Election: Voices, Views, and Values*, ed. Jennifer Schenk Sacco. Lanham, MD: Rowman & Littlefield, 139–56.

Collins, Patricia Hill. 1991. *Black Feminist Thought: Knowledge, Consciousness, and the Politics of Empowerment*. New York: Routledge.

Cooper, Brittney. 2010. "A'n't I a Lady?: Race Women, Michelle Obama, and the ever-expanding Democratic Imagination." *Melus* 35 (4):39–57. doi:10.1093/melus/35.4.39.

D'Abrosca, Peter. 2021. "Chauvin Attorney Destroys Narrative that Floyd Called for Mother before His Death, Media Ignores." *The Minnesota Sun*, April 2. https://theminnesotasun.com/2021/04/02/chauvin-attorney-destroys-narrative-that-floyd-called-for-mother-before-his-death-media-ignores/ (Accessed July 2, 2021).

Dittmar, Kelly. 2015. *Navigating Gendered Terrain: Stereotypes and Strategy in Political Campaigns*. Philadelphia, PA: Temple University Press.

Dolan, Julie, Melissa M. Deckman, and Michele L. Swers. 2019. *Women and Politics: Paths to Power and Political Influence*. Lanham, MD: Rowman & Littlefield.

Dowe, Pearl K. Ford. 2020. "Resisting Marginalization: Black Women's Political Ambition and Agency." *PS: Political Science & Politics* 53 (4): 697–702.

Ellis, Antonio L. 2014. "What Suspicious Looks Like." In *(Re)Teaching Trayvon*, eds. Venus E. Evans-Winters and Magaela C. Bethune. Rotterdam: SensePublishers, 43–54.

Friends Of Lucy Mcbath. 2018. "LucyforCongress.com." Campaign Announcement Press Release. https://lucyforcongress.com/about/ (Accessed June 30, 2021).

Filax, Gloria, and Dena Taylor. 2014. "Disabled Mothers." In *Mothers, Mothering and Motherhood across Cultural Differences: A Reader*, ed. Andrea O'Reilly143–60. Ontario, Canada: Demeter Press.

Francisco, Sara C., and Diane H. Felmlee. 2022. "What Did You Call Me? An Analysis of Online Harassment Towards Black and Latinx Women." *Race and Social Problems* 14 (1):1–13. doi:10.1007/s12552-021-09330-7.

Frazier, E. Franklin. 1939. *The Negro Family in the United States*. Chicago: The University of Chicago Press.

Fulton, Sybrina, and Tracy Martin. 2018. *Rest in Power: The Enduring Life of Trayvon Martin*. New York: Random House.

Fulton, Sybrina. "Sybrina Fulton 2020 Campaign Announcement." *Instagram video*, 2019 May, 20. https://www.instagram.com/p/Bxr1Oe2FtmQ/ (Accessed July 2, 2021).

Gibson, Caitlin. 2019. "A Record Number of Congresswomen are Mothers. Here's A Glimpse inside Their first-ever Caucus." *The Washington Post*, April 16. https://www.washingtonpost.com/lifestyle/on-parenting/a-record-number-of-congresswomen-are-mothers-heres-a-glimpse-inside-their-first-ever-caucus/2019/04/16/b563b964-5c77-11e9-842d-7d3ed7eb3957_story.html (Accessed July 2, 2021).

Gillard, Deric. 1980. "Black Leaders Lashed for 'Lack of Interest' in Missing, Slain Youths." *Atlanta Daily World*, August 14.

Goss, Kristin A. 2003. "Rethinking the Political Participation Paradigm." *Women & Politics* 25 (4):83–118. doi:10.1300/J014v25n04_04.

Greenlee, Jill. 2014. *The Political Consequences of Motherhood*. Ann Arbor: University of Michigan Press.

Greenlee, Jill, Grace Deason, and Carrie Langner. 2017. "The Impact of Motherhood and Maternal Messages on Political Candidacies." In *The Political Psychology of Women in US Politics*, eds. Angela L. Bos and Monica C. Schneider. New York: Routledge, 133–48.

Harris-Perry, Melissa V. 2011. *Sister Citizen: Shame, Stereotypes, and Black Women in America*. New Haven, CT: Yale University Press.

Hawkesworth, Mary. 2003. "Congressional Enactments of race-gender: Toward a Theory of Raced- Gendered Institutions." *The American Political Science Review* 97 (4):529–50. doi:10.1017/S0003055403000868.

Jacobs, Harriet a, and R J. Ellis. 2015. *Incidents in the Life of a Slave Girl*. Oxford: Oxford University Press.

Jones, Tamara. 1996. "A Candidate's Uneasy Station in Life." *The Washington Post*, August 27. https://www.washingtonpost.com/archive/lifestyle/1996/08/27/a-candidates-uneasy-station-in-life/2083fd4d-87b4-4653-8f1d-bd6ccb690f24/ (Accessed July 2, 2021).

Jones, James R. 2019. "Theorizing a Racialized Congressional Workplace." In *Race, Organizations, and the Organizing Process*, ed. Melissa E. Wooten. Bingley, UK: Emerald Publishing Limited, 171–92.

Kenney, Sally J. 1996. "New Research on Gendered Political Institutions." *Political Research Quarterly* 49 (2):445–66. doi:10.1177/106591299604900211.

Kerber, Linda K. 2000. *Women of the Republic: Intellect and Ideology in Revolutionary America*. Chapel Hill: University of North Carolina Press.

Killen, Kimberly. 2019. "'Can You Hear Me Now?' Race, Motherhood, and the Politics of Being Heard." *Politics & Gender* 15 (4):623–44. doi:10.1017/S1743923X18000697.

Laramie, Olivia. 2020. "The Impact of Discriminatory Harassment on Gender Representation in Elected Office in the United States." *RAIS Journal for Social Sciences* 4 (1): 20–31.

Lawson, Erica S. 2018. "Bereaved Black Mothers and Maternal Activism in the Racial State." *Feminist Studies* 44 (3): 713–35.

Li, Stephanie. 2006. "Motherhood as Resistance in Harriet Jacobs's Incidents in the Life of a Slave Girl." *Legacy* 23 (1):14–29. doi:10.1353/leg.2006.0009.

Mahoney, Anna Mitchell. 2018. *Women Take Their Place in State Legislatures: The Creation of Women's Caucuses*. Philadelphia, PA: Temple University Press.

Martinez, Gina. 2018. "Michael Brown's Mother Announces Run For Ferguson City Council, Four Years After Son's Death." *Time Magazine*, April 11. https://time.com/5364781/michael-brown-mother-ferguson-city-council/ (Accessed June 30, 2021).

McBath, Lucy. 2018. *Standing Our Ground: The Triumph of Faith over Gun Violence: A Mother's Story*. New York: Simon and Schuster.

McBath, Lucy. 2021. "@RepLucyMcBath." *Twitter Post*: To My Jordan. April 8, 2018. https://twitter.com/replucymcbath/status/1380233193576599554 (Accessed June 30, 2021).

McDaniel, Eric. 2013. "The Black Church and Defining the Political." *Politics, Groups, and Identities* 1 (1):93–97. doi:10.1080/21565503.2013.760311.

Moynihan, Daniel Patrick. 1965. *The Negro Family: The Case for National Action*. Washington, DC: US Government Printing Office.

Perry, Imani. 2021. "Stop Hustling Black Death: Samaria Rice Is the Mother of Tamir, Not a 'Mother of the Movement.'" *The Cut*, May 24. https://www.thecut.com/article/samaria-rice-profile.html (Accessed June 2, 2021).

Rest in Power: The Trayvon Martin Story. 2018. Miniseries. Directed by Jenner Furst New York:Cinemart Productions

Rhode, Flemming Schneider, and Tisha Dejmanee. 2016. "Effeminate Speech on New Media: @hillaryclinton's Public Intimacy through Relational Labor." *International Journal of Communication* 10 (2016): 486–507.

Richardson, Allissa V. 2019. "Dismantling Respectability: The Rise of New Womanist Communication Models in the Era of Black Lives Matter." *Journal of Communication* 69 (2):193–213. doi:10.1093/joc/jqz005.

Roberts, Dorothy E. 1999. *Killing the Black Body: Race, Reproduction, and the Meaning of Liberty*. New York: Vintage.

Rose, Steve. 2021. "'It Is so Much Bigger than Trayvon': How Bereaved Mother Sybrina Fulton Fought Back." *The Guardian*, February 11. https://www.theguardian.com/us-news/2021/feb/11/it-is-so-much-bigger-than-trayvon-how-bereaved-mother-sybrina-fulton-fought-back (Accessed May 27, 2021).

Ruddick, Sara. 1990. *Maternal Thinking: Toward a Politics of Peace*. New York: Ballantine.

Ruvalcaba, Xochitl 2020. "All Mothers Were Summoned When He Called Out To His MAMA." *Urban Art Mapping Research Project*, August 2. https://georgefloydstreetart.omeka.net/items/show/1390 (Accessed July 2, 2021).

Secret, Mosi. 2020. "Lezley McSpadden Is Still Fighting Six Years Ago, Her Son Michael Brown Was Killed in Ferguson. The Officer Has Faced No Charges." *New York Magazine*, July 31. https://nymag.com/intelligencer/2020/07/lezley-mcspadden-is-still-fighting.html

Shammas, Brittany. 2021. "Pelosi Faces Backlash after Thanking George Floyd for 'Sacrificing Your Life for Justice.'" *The Washington Post*, April 21. https://www.washingtonpost.com/politics/2021/04/21/nancy-pelosi-george-floyd/

Simon, Darran. 2019. "Sybrina Fulton, Trayvon Martin's Mother, Is Running for Political Office." *CNN*, May 20. https://www.cnn.com/2019/05/19/us/sybrina-fulton-trayvon-martin-political-office-run/index.html (Accessed July 2, 2021).

Smiley, David, and Linda Robertson. 2020. "After Tragedy and amid Protests, Sybrina Fulton Seeks Her Own Political Path in Miami." *Miami Herald*, July 7. https://www.miamiherald.com/news/politics-government/article243545997.html (Accessed May 27, 2021).

Smith, Aidan. 2017. *Gender, Heteronormativity, and the American Presidency*. New York: Routledge.

Smooth, Wendy. 2005. "African American Women and Electoral Politics." In *Gender and Elections: Shaping the Future of American Politics*, eds. Susan J. Carroll and Richard L. Fox. Cambridge: Cambridge University Press, 117–42.

Solotaroff, Paul. 2013. "A Most American Way to Die." *Rolling Stone*, April 25. https://www.rollingstone.com/feature/trayvon-martin-stand-your-ground-florida-jordan-davis-93561/

Thomas, Melanee Lynn, and Amanda Bittner. 2017. *Mothers and Others: The Role of Parenthood in Politics*. Vancouver: UBC Press.

Thornton, Brian. 2010. "The Murder of Emmett Till: Myth, Memory, and National Magazine Response." *Journalism History* 36 (2):96–104. doi:10.1080/00947679.2010.12062820.

Till-Mobley, Mamie, and Christopher Benson. 2005. *Death of Innocence: The Story of the Hate Crime that Changed America*. New York: One World/Ballantine.

Tyson, Timothy B. 2017. *The Blood of Emmett Till*. New York: Simon & Schuster.

Ward, Allison. 2021. "Mother of Ma'Khia Bryant Speaks at Saturday Rally." *The Columbus Dispatch*, May 1. https://www.dispatch.com/story/news/local/2021/05/01/mother-makhia-bryant-speaks-saturday-rally/4906701001/

Williams, Rhaisa Kameela. 2016. "Toward a Theorization of Black Maternal Grief as Analytic." *Transforming Anthropology* 24 (1):17–30. doi:10.1111/traa.12057.

Williams, Lilee. 2020. "VP Candidate Kamala Harris' Favorite Title Is 'Momala.'" *Moms*, August 13. https://www.moms.com/vp-candidate-kamala-harris-favorite-title-is-momala/ (Accessed July 2, 2021).

"Better Too Much Than Not Enough": The Nomination of Women of Color to the Federal Bench

Laura Moyer, Allison P. Harris, and Rorie Spill Solberg

ABSTRACT

It is well established that the federal judiciary has been an overwhelmingly White and male institution since its creation and continues to be so today. Even as presidents of both parties have looked to diversify their judicial nominees, this has tended to result in the appointment of White women and men of color rather than women of color. Using data on the confirmed federal district and circuit court judges from presidents Clinton through Trump, we assess how the backgrounds of women of color nominated to the federal judiciary compare with those of other appointees. The results indicate that, compared to White male judges, women of color judges accrue more types of professional experience before their appointments, are more likely to have had prior experience as a judge, and are generally nominated earlier in their careers.

It is well established that the federal judiciary has been and continues to be an overwhelmingly White and male institution (Diascro and Solberg 2018; Millhiser 2019). Even as presidents of both parties have looked to diversify their judicial nominees, they have tended to conceptualize diversification along a single dimension (i.e., gender or race) masking the intersection of the two. Past research on judicial appointment patterns has found that, when looking beyond White male nominees, presidents have tended to prioritize the nomination of White women and men of color over that of women of color (Haire and Moyer 2015; Jeknic, Solberg, and Waltenburg 2021).

In this essay, we leverage an original dataset of judicial appointees to both the US District Courts and US Courts of Appeals to explore how the backgrounds of women of color appointed to the federal judiciary compare with those of other appointees, across four presidents, Clinton through Trump. Our aim is not to determine why some types of nominees are confirmed while others are not.[1] Rather, we argue that even though notions of ideal judging are conflated with the experiences of White men (Kirkpatrick 2020; Sen 2014), for other demographic groups, the White male baseline is a mere minimum. As we note below, our data show that the White male norm consists of only two types of experience: clerkship and private practice. As such, we expect that presidents utilize a strategy of selecting women of color who have longer resumes and who have "proved themselves" with prior judicial and/or other experiences beyond the White male baseline. Our findings reveal that, compared to White male judges, women of color judges accrue more types of professional experience before their appointments, are more likely to have had prior experience as a judge, and are generally nominated earlier in their careers.

Assessing "qualifications" against a white male norm

Obtaining a seat on the federal bench is the apex of a judicial career, and the patterns found in terms of selection and confirmation mirror those found in management and human resources research, generally speaking. Scholars from these fields have found that nonwhite applicants fare worse than their White counterparts when applying for jobs and that gender can moderate the relationship between candidates' perceived "riskiness" and their qualifications (Bendick et al. 1991; Triana et al. 2021; van Esch et al. 2018). A recent meta-analysis spanning two decades of field experiments on hiring and racial discrimination showed that Black and Latinx applicants receive fewer callbacks for employment than White applicants (Quillian et al. 2017). Similarly, women of color who aspire to become federal judges may be perceived as "risky" appointees and may be less likely to be appointed than comparably situated men.

For example, one important metric used in the federal judicial selection process is the rating system administered by the American Bar Association. Since Eisenhower, presidents have generally sent the ABA Standing Committee on the Federal Judiciary names of judicial nominees prior to formal nomination.[2] The Committee screens potential nominees and, based on the evaluation, nominees are then ranked as either well qualified, qualified, or not qualified.

However, the ABA ratings have been shown to be biased in ways that may systematically disadvantage nonwhite women nominees. For example, Sen (2014) found that, even after accounting for education, experience, and partisanship, district court nominees who were nonwhite or women were systematically rated lower, which reduced their likelihood of confirmation. This is consistent with earlier studies of federal appellate nominees that found evidence of gender and racial bias in ABA ratings (Haire 2001). Nominees assigned lower ratings tend to have a more difficult time with Senate confirmation, though the ratings are not correlated with judicial performance (Sen 2014).[3]

Unlike other hiring settings, presidents are not constrained by any official requirements regarding background or professional experience when making selections for federal judgeships,[4] though there are norms that have developed over time.[5] Because not all areas of the legal profession have been equally welcoming to women or to people of color, selecting nominees based on the types of career paths common among White men can be exclusionary in practice (Martin 2004). For instance, overt discrimination in private practice settings in the 1960s and 70s meant that these prestigious, well-paying jobs were largely reserved for White men. As a result, public sector jobs were often a better option for newly minted lawyers who did not identify as White men (Haire and Moyer 2015). Today, partner positions at private law firms are overwhelmingly White and male, as are general counsel positions at Fortune 500 companies (National Association of Women Lawyers 2020; Nelson et al. 2019).[6]

Existing research suggests that presidents may hold women of color to a different standard when it comes to professional experience. Moyer (2021) concludes that "prior judicial experience has been something like an unofficial requirement for women of color" on the federal appeals courts, consistent with the conclusions of other work (Haire and Moyer 2015; Martin 2004). Such an unstated requirement would be normatively problematic given the composition of both state and federal courts; notably, women of color are the most underrepresented race-gender group in state courts, relative to their share of the population, while White men are the most overrepresented group (Adelstein and Bannon 2021; George and Yoon 2017). Beyond prior judicial experience, prosecutorial experience was also more common for women of color than any other race-gender group appointed to circuit court positions by Clinton, Bush, or Obama (Moyer 2021). Taken together, this literature suggests that presidents may seek out nonwhite women with a greater breadth of professional experience than other groups. Such experience could serve as a counterweight to the perception of risk associated with selecting women of color. Therefore, we expect presidents to select women of color who have longer resumes and who have previously served as a judge.

H_1: *Nonwhite women judges will have a greater number of professional experiences than their White male colleagues.*

H₂: *Nonwhite women judges will be more likely to have judicial experience than White men.*

At the same time that nonwhite women may be perceived as less qualified, and therefore may feel pressure to bolster their resumes, they can also be fast-tracked to federal judgeships as presidents seek to diversify the bench. A common practice in the private sector, fast-tracking refers to a process whereby organizations identify and advance candidates in an accelerated manner through a series of developmental opportunities to achieve higher level positions. Fast-tracking can help companies achieve diversity goals for representation in management and other leadership positions. However, there are pitfalls to a speedy pipeline. Perceptions of the likelihood of derailment may be a self-fulfilling prophecy for underrepresented groups (Bono et al. 2017; Braddy et al. 2020). Women and people of color may be perceived as risky investments precisely because they are fast-track candidates.

While delving into the intricacies of derailment is beyond the scope of this study, similar concerns apply to the judicial context. The legal profession's "leaky pipeline" (National Association of Women Lawyers 2020) means that the pool of potential women of color candidates for a federal judgeship is small relative to that of White men, which creates incentives for presidents to identify potential nominees with fewer years of experience. The literature suggests that, to climb the judicial ladder, women of color may forgo depth of experience in favor of breadth, which may create other disadvantages for these individuals (Gulati 2013). In other words, women of color not only must have more types of experience before nomination to the federal bench, they must do so more rapidly than their counterparts. This gives an attorney or judge less time to make their mark and build a reputation that can smooth controversial confirmations.[7]

H₃: *Nonwhite women judges will have practiced law for less time at than White men before nomination.*

So, what does it take for presidents to view a woman of color as sufficiently qualified to become a life-tenured federal judge? Below, we describe our dataset and our expectations.

Data and variables

To investigate the experiential background of federal judges, we draw on data from the Federal Judicial Center (FJC) from the Clinton through Trump presidencies, a period of time in which women of color made relatively big gains compared to previous administrations. While only 15 women of color were confirmed during the Carter, Reagan, and first Bush administrations, the period of Clinton through Trump includes 97 women of color confirmed to the federal bench.[8]

The FJC database includes a short biography of each confirmed judge that includes their previous work history, educational background, nomination information, and self-reported demographic identifiers. From this short vita, we coded their education and work experience into a series of variables, described in Table 1. Next, we used the professional experience variables to create an additive index, which reflects how long or short an individual's resume was upon nomination. The index simply marks whether the judge had each type of experience or not. Though the index does not capture the amount of time spent in each professional setting or if they served in this capacity in several venues (e.g., served as a state trial judge and then an appellate judge), it does allow us to measure the number of different types of experiences accumulated after law school (e.g., clerkship, private practice, and judgeship).[9] To account for career length prior to nomination, we calculated the number of years from law school graduation (JD) to the year first nominated to the federal bench. The professional experience index ranges from a minimum of 1 to a maximum of 7 and has a mean of 2.7 types of experience. The career length variable has a mean of 24 years with a minimum of eight and a maximum of 45.

Table 1. Variables.

Variable name	Description
Gender-race	Categorical variable that indicates whether judge was a White man, White woman, Nonwhite man, or Nonwhite woman.
Law school quality	1 = Top 20 law school; 2 = State flagship; 3 = Lower tier law school (categories are mutually exclusive)
ABA rating	1 = Not Qualified; 2 = Qualified; 3 = Well Qualified
Career length	Number of years from JD to first successful nomination year
Private practice	Worked in a private law firm (0,1)
Clerk experience	Experience as a law clerk at any level (0,1)
US Attorney	Service as either a US Attorney or an Assistant US Attorney (0,1)
State prosecutor	Experience as a state or local prosecutor (0,1)
State court	Experience as a state court judge (includes municipal judges) (0,1)
Non-Article III judge	Experience as a federal magistrate or bankruptcy judge (0,1)
Elevate	Elevated from district court to circuit court seat (0,1)
Professional experience index	Additive index of the following variables: • Private practice • State prosecutor • US Attorney • Non-Article III judge • State court judge • Public defender • Corporate counsel • Law clerk • Academic • Nonprofit • Solicitor General • Elevate
Court level	Nominated to district court seat or circuit court seat
Democrat	Nominated by a Democratic president (1) or a Republican president (0)

Note: Demographic and background attributes drawn from the Federal Judicial Center (2021).

Defining the white male norm for federal judges

Because of the overall composition of the federal judiciary, we argue that the baseline against which women of color have been and continue to be compared is the professional experience of White men.[10] On the professional index scale, White men average 2.6 types of experience and typically practice law about 25 years before they are (successfully) nominated.

Among the different types of professional experiences, one is ubiquitous for White men: private practice. While White men generally need more than private practice on their resume to become federal judges, there is no other type of experience that is more common among or dominated by this group. When comparing across groups, 93% of White men had worked in private practice, compared to 79% for nonwhite women, 87% for White women, and 85% for nonwhite men. The difference between White men and nonwhite women is statistically significant.[11]

The literature suggests that clerkships should also be especially common among White men. However, in our data, this appears to be a weaker norm than that of private practice experience. Forty-seven percent of White men had clerkship experience, lagging slightly behind White women (53%). Among the appellate judges in our data, the rates of clerkship experience for White men and White women are virtually identical (about 66%).[12] Beyond private practice and clerkships, no other type of professional experience – including judgeships or prosecutorial experience – were especially common among White men. In sum, a typical White male federal judge has worked in private practice, served as a clerk, and worked about a two-and-a-half decades before nomination.

How do nonwhite women stack up against these norms over time? Figure 1 shows that while the percentage of White men with private practice experience has not varied much across appointment cohort, the share of nonwhite women with this type of experience increased with the Obama cohort and remained relatively high during the Trump years. The

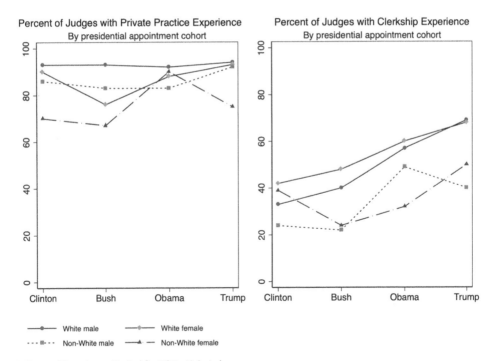

Figure 1. Types of Experiences Typical for White Male Judges.

share of White men who served as clerks increased steadily over that period, while Clinton and Trump both appear to have sought out more nonwhite women with clerking experience than Bush or Obama. If presidents rely on a White male norm of experience for judicial nominees, private practice and, to a lesser extent, clerkship experience may be increasingly expected of women of color.

Women of color and longer resumes

Hypothesis 1 predicts that nonwhite women selected as federal judges will have more types of experience on their resumes than similarly situated White male judges. Compared to other groups, a larger share of White men (15%) have only one type of professional experience before becoming a federal judge, a rate more three times higher than that of nonwhite women (see the Supporting Information). On the other end of the scale, a higher percentage of nonwhite women (9.7%) have five or more types of experiences, compared to White men (4%). While most judges fall somewhere in the middle of the professional experience index, this does suggest that nonwhite women are overrepresented among those with longer resumes.

Next, we graphed the mean index value for race-gender groups over time, so that differences across presidential appointment cohorts could be observed (see Figure 2). For White men, there is a small, steady increase in the mean levels of professional experience over time, regardless of appointing president. Looking at nonwhite women, Clinton appointees tended to have more types of professional experience than was typical under either Bush or Obama, but the trend reverts to higher levels during the Trump years. There is a similar dip in experience for White women, but for nonwhite men, there is little variation in the average level of professional experience.

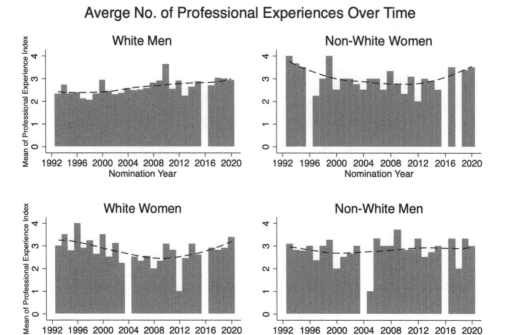

Figure 2. Variation in Professional Experience by Group.

To supplement these descriptive analyses, we constructed an ordered logit model of professional experience.[13] Because there are relatively few observations at the upper end of the professional experience index, we collapsed all observations where there are more than 5 types of experience into a single category, making this a five-category variable. To facilitate comparisons between women of color and other groups, we set nonwhite women as the excluded, reference category for the gender-race variables. Lastly, we include controls for ABA rating, law school quality, party of nominating president, career length, and level of court (district or appellate).[14]

The results shown in Figure 3 offer strong support for our hypothesis that women of color judges will have longer resumes than White men. The coefficient for White men is negative and significant ($p < .001$), indicating that this group has fewer professional experiences than women of color. Interestingly, there are no statistically significant differences in experience between nonwhite women and other comparator groups.[15]

Judicial experience as prerequisite

Next, to test Hypothesis 2, we model the likelihood that nonwhite women will have prior judicial experience before being confirmed to the federal bench, again excluding those judges who were elevated and using the same battery of controls. In Figure 4 (left panel), the results indicate strong support for our hypothesis. White men are significantly less likely to have previous judicial experience than nonwhite women.[16] Comparing the predicted probabilities (Figure 4, right panel) shows the stark differences here. For a Democratic district court appointee who is rated well-qualified by the ABA, graduated from a top law school, and has the average career length, the probability of prior judicial service is 0.61 for a nonwhite woman. The probability drops to a staggering 0.31 for a White man. The same results also hold when we limit the analysis to those with state court experience.

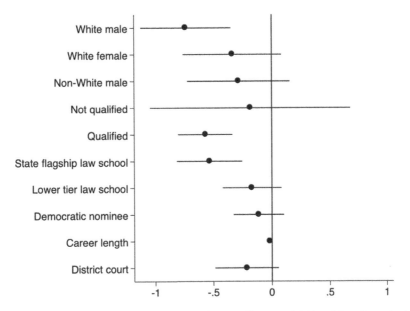

Figure 3. Ordered Logit of Professional Experience. N = 1172. Plot shows coefficients and 95% confidence intervals. Nonwhite female is the excluded reference category for Gender-Race. Well Qualified is the excluded category for ABA rating, and Top 20 law school is the excluded category for Law School Quality. See Supporting Information for full results.

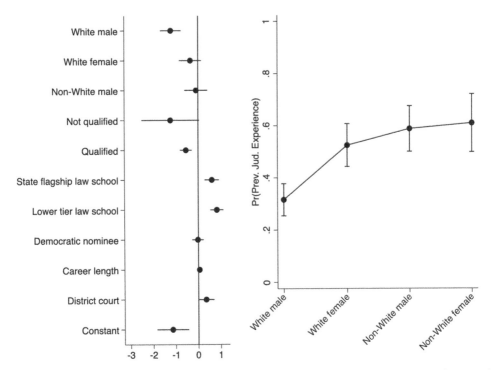

Figure 4. Logit of Prior Judicial Experience and Predicted Probabilities. N = 1172. Left-side plot shows coefficients and 95% confidence intervals. Nonwhite female is the excluded reference category for Gender-Race. Well Qualified is the excluded category for ABA rating, and Top 20 law school is the excluded category for Law School Quality. See Supporting Information for full results. Right-side plot shows predicted probabilities of previous judicial experience generated from the logit model.

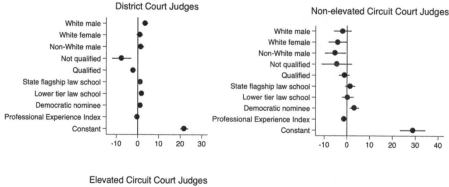
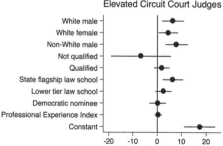

Figure 5. OLS Regression of Career Length before Nomination. Plot shows coefficients and 95% confidence intervals. N = 1001 for district court judges model ($R^2 = 0.1063$). N = 171 for non-elevated circuit court judges model ($R^2 = 0.1508$). N = 63 for elevated circuit court judge model ($R^2 = 0.294$). Nonwhite female is the excluded reference category for Gender-Race. Well Qualified is the excluded category for ABA rating, and Top 20 law school is the excluded category for Law School Quality. See Supporting Information for full results.

The fast track

Lastly, Hypothesis 3 anticipates that nonwhite women will be on a "fast track" to joining the federal bench.[17] Here, we estimate separate OLS models of career length for district court judges, circuit court judges who were not elevated from district court, and elevated circuit court judges. In this model, we add the professional experience index to the set of control variables.

Beginning with the district court model, White men have 3.5 more years in the profession than nonwhite women, consistent with our expectations (See Figure 5). While the differences between nonwhite women and the other groups are not significant, we do see that judges nominated by Democratic presidents had about a year more of experience than those nominated by Republican presidents. Among the circuit court judges who were elevated from district court (N = 63), women of color appear to be on a fast track compared to members of other gender-race groups. Nonwhite men wait almost eight years longer to be elevated, while White men wait a little more than six years longer before they are elevated to an appeals court position. With respect to circuit court appointees who were not elevated to their positions, there is no significant difference in career length between White men and nonwhite women. However, nonwhite men appear to be fast tracked relative to nonwhite women, spending five fewer years practicing law than nonwhite women before they are nominated to a federal appeals court.

In a final comparison, we examined appellate judges who were elevated from the district courts versus those whose first Article III appointment was to the US Courts of Appeals. For most demographics, those who were elevated had similar years of experience prior to elevation, but the difference for nonwhite women is dramatic. For example, White women averaged a little over 23 years in their career before initial appointment and about a year more if they were elevated to the appellate bench. In contrast, nonwhite women worked almost six years *less* if they were elevated, revealing a distinct fast track when compared to their counterparts.

Conclusions

Being selected to serve as a federal judge is a prestigious accomplishment, particularly as presidents increasingly view these appointments as policy statements and as Senate obstruction and delay has increased (Steigerwalt 2010; Slotnick, Schiavoni, and Goldman 2017; but see Dancey, Nelson, and Ringsmuth 2020). This study identifies several ways in which nonwhite women judges' careers differ systematically from those of White men, the overrepresented demographic group in the federal judiciary. Do these differences represent opportunities or obstacles? The answer is complicated.

We found that women of color are, on average, appointed earlier in their careers than White men, but they also have accumulated a more diversified set of professional experiences. On its face, this seems to be an impressive feat, though these differences do vary somewhat by president. Overall, we found that women of color are nominated to district court positions and elevated to circuit court seats earlier in their careers than White men. We speculate that this "fast track" is due to the scarcity of nonwhite women in the legal profession, but we encourage more work to examine how this trend intersects with party priorities in nominations. To wit, nonwhite women who are nominated by Republican presidents to a circuit court seat (without first serving as district court judge) have about four more years of experience under their belts than their White male peers, which may say something about the pool of conservative, nonwhite women. It is also possible that these patterns may be related to the size of the courts. Larger courts tend to diversify more quickly compared to smaller courts (Haire and Moyer 2015), so future work could take a court-by-court approach to unpack these patterns further.

On average, women of color bring more types of professional experiences to the federal bench than any of the other gender-race groups we have considered.[18] However, the differences here also vary by party. Under Republican presidents, nonwhite appointees have more types of experience than White appointees, regardless of gender; both nonwhite men and women average more than three types of professional experiences, while White men and women average 2.6 and 2.7 types, respectively. On the Democratic side, White men have fewer different types of professional experiences (2.48) than other gender-race groups, who each average about 2.9 on the index. To view how the distribution of professional experience has shifted under different presidents, Figure 6 shows histograms of the professional experience index across presidential appointment cohort. Of course, it is important to emphasize that these comparisons are based upon only two Democratic and two Republican presidents and may differ with the inclusion of, say, Biden's appointees.

The history of exclusion from and, later, barriers to entering the legal profession are responsible for the continued underrepresentation of those who do not identify as White men among lawyers and judges. The sources of this underrepresentation have limited the career choices available to women of color. And it may also be driving their quicker path to the federal bench. However, this fast track could create concerns about the depth of appointees' experience, leading to more scrutiny in the Senate confirmation process, lower ABA ratings, or both. Though this study has focused on successful nominations, future research might consider the impact of these differences in career length on the confirmation process.

The combination of the "fast track" and an expectation for a longer resume also suggests that nonwhite women must fit in more types of experience into a shorter period of time than White men before nomination. While future research should unpack this finding more fully (and consider the amount of time in each type of job setting), it may impact the lifetime earnings of women of color. Generally, private practice is the most lucrative of legal professions, and we find that this experience is consistently the norm for White male appointees. In contrast, there appears to be an unofficial norm of prior judicial experience for nonwhite women federal judges, which means that nonwhite women have to step away from more lucrative practice areas to run for more poorly compensated state or local judicial seats before being viewed as viable candidates for federal judgeships. It is also possible that the differences in private practice experience reflect persistent problems with climate that drive women of color out of large firms (Peery, Brown, and Letts 2020) and into other types of work settings.

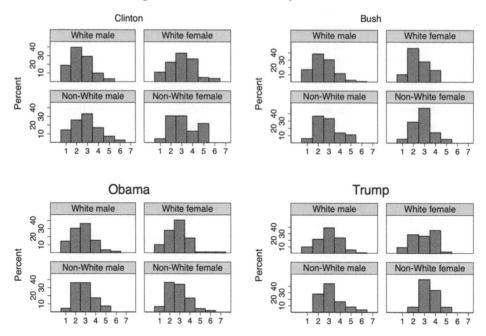

Figure 6. Trends in Professional Experience by Presidential Appointment Cohort. The full 7-category professional experience index, rather than the collapsed 5-category version used in the ordered logit model, is shown.

Although nonwhite women have clearly made inroads at all levels of the legal profession, we find that the pathways for becoming Article III judges differ from those of their White counterparts, particularly White men. To be clear, because our data include only confirmed judges, we are unable to disentangle whether these observed differences are attributable to presidents' decisions to select nominees with particular professional and educational backgrounds, to individual choices in career paths, or to a combination of both. Earlier studies noted that, due to overt discrimination, women and nonwhite lawyers took a different pathway to become judges, often denoted as "nontraditional" careers. As these barriers are reduced or fall, it is clear that new, unstated expectations have been established. This study takes a first step at unmasking these previously unrecognized barriers to women of color as they navigate the current pathways of success.

Notes

1. We only include Article III judgeships from US district courts and the US Courts of Appeals, including the Federal Circuit. While the Federal Circuit has a narrower jurisdiction than the other 13 circuit courts, its judges, like all Article III judges, require presidential nomination and Senate confirmation, and provide for life tenure as well as salary security.
2. Presidents George W. Bush and Trump each involved the ABA only after formal nomination. Although not included in our data, Biden is following this pattern.
3. Dancey, Nelson, and Ringsmuth (2020) find that nominees rated lower face more questions related to their qualifications and are more likely to be considered controversial.
4. Considerations related to selecting lower federal court nominees include the preferences of home state senators (Slotnick, Schiavoni, and Goldman 2017; Steigerwalt 2010), symbolic representation (Diascro and Solberg 2018), ideological or policy goals (Goldman 1997), and even partisan advantages related to diversity (Asmussen 2011).
5. For example, all federal judges confirmed during our time period graduated from an accredited law school, and the vast majority worked in private practice.

6. The same pattern repeats for clerkships. White men held the majority of federal clerkships (53% in 2016), and gains by women were largely limited to White women, with women of color holding less than 10% of federal clerkships (NALP 2017).
7. For these reasons, we do not characterize the fast-tracking phenomenon as an advantage but rather as a mixed bag for nonwhite women, as it may create other difficulties with a smooth confirmation process and reduce their lifetime earnings. With respect to the causal mechanism, the structure of our data do not allow us to assess whether the differences in career paths or career length are attributable to individual choice, systematic bias, or the intersection of the two.
8. While President Carter is often lauded for diversifying the federal bench (Martin 2004), this was mostly in appointing White women and nonwhite men (Haire and Moyer 2015). His two Republican successors, Reagan and G.H.W. Bush largely reverted to the previous norm of appointing white men (Goldman 1997). Thus, our time period spans almost 30 years but only includes four presidents, two from each party. Space limitations prevent a deeper dive into individual presidential cohorts. For more about presidential appointment trends on individual presidencies, see e.g., Slotnick, Schiavoni, and Goldman (2017) and Jeknic, Solberg, and Waltenburg (2021).
9. For clerkships or previous judicial experience, we count all types of experiences, and each type of experience is only counted once. For example, a judge who served as a clerk to a state trial judge and a judge who served as a clerk to a Supreme Court justice are both coded as having a clerkship. Similarly, a judge who served as a local judge and a judge that served as a federal magistrate are both coded as having previous judicial experience. Finally, a judge that held several clerkships only receives one point for clerking. We make no distinctions based on the prestige of the clerkship or judicial position or the length or scope of experience.
10. Fifty-four percent of the federal judges nominated from Clinton through Trump were White men.
11. Using a two-sample test of proportions to assess statistical significance, the difference between White men and White women or nonwhite men is also significant. However, the differences between White women, nonwhite men, and nonwhite women are not.
12. However, White men are the race-gender group most likely to have served in the most prestigious clerkships: those at the Supreme Court.
13. We limit our analysis to district and circuit judges who have not been elevated. Full model results appear in the Supporting Information.
14. For the ABA rating, we follow the Federal Judicial Center coding scheme, which only reports the majority rating (i.e., no split ratings are included).
15. Rotating the excluded reference category (not shown) reveals that White women and nonwhite men also are significantly more likely to have higher levels of professional experience than White men.
16. Nonwhite women are also significantly more likely to have state court and US attorney experience than White men (see the Supporting Information for alternative specifications).
17. To be clear, we are not measuring the time from a president's nomination to confirmation, but rather the number of years from completing the JD until the individual is nominated successfully to the federal bench.
18. On the professional experience index, the mean number of experience types for all White men is 2.58, 2.84 for all White women, 2.91 for all nonwhite men, and 2.98 for all nonwhite women. Figures comparing professional experience by party are shown in the Supporting Information.

Disclosure statement

No potential conflict of interest was reported by the author(s).

References

Adelstein, Janna, and Alicia Bannon. 2021. "State Supreme Court Diversity—April 2021 Update." Brennan Center for Justice. April 20. https://www.brennancenter.org/our-work/research-reports/state-supreme-court-diversity-april-2021-update.

Asmussen, Nicole. 2011. "Female and Minority Judicial Nominees: President's Delight and Senators' Dismay?" *Legislative Studies Quarterly* 36 (4):591–619. doi:10.1111/j.1939-9162.2011.00028.x.

Bendick, Marc, Jr, Charles W. Jackson, Victor A. Reinoso, and Laura E. Hodges. 1991. "Discrimination against Latino Job Applicants: A Controlled Experiment." *Human Resource Management* 30 (4):469–84. doi:10.1002/hrm.3930300404.

Bono, Joyce E., Phillip W. Braddy, Yihao Liu, Elisabeth K. Gilbert, John W. Fleenor, Louis N. Quast, and Bruce A. Center. 2017. "Dropped on the Way to the Top: Gender and Managerial Derailment." *Personnel Psychology* 70 (4):729–68. doi:10.1111/peps.12184.

Braddy, Phillip W., Rachel E. Sturm, Leanne Atwater, Scott N. Taylor, and Rob Austin McKee. 2020. "Gender Bias Still Plagues the Workplace: Looking at Derailment Risk and Performance with Self–other Ratings." *Group & Organization Management* 45 (3):315–50. doi:10.1177/1059601119867780.

Dancey, Logan, Kjersten R. Nelson, and Eve M. Ringsmuth. 2020. *It's Not Personal: Politics and Policy in Lower Court Confirmation Hearings.* Ann Arbor: University of Michigan Press.

Diascro, Jennifer, and Rorie Spill Solberg. 2018. "A Retrospective on Obama's Judges: Diversity, Intersectionality and Symbolic Representation." *Politics, Groups, and Identities* 8 (3): 471–87.

George, Tracey E., and Albert H. Yoon. 2017. "Measuring Justice in State Courts: The Demographics of the State Judiciary." *Vanderbilt Law Review* 70: 1887–910.

Goldman, Sheldon. 1997. *Picking Federal Judges: Lower Court Selection from Roosevelt through Reagan.* New Haven, CT: Yale University Press.

Gulati, Daniel. 2013. "Stop Fast Tracking Your Career." *Harvard Business Review*, March 14. https://hbr.org/2013/03/stop-fast-tracking-your-career.

Haire, Susan Brodie. 2001. "Rating the Ratings of the American Bar Association Standing Committee on Federal Judiciary." *Justice System Journal* 22 (1): 1–17.

Haire, Susan B., and Laura P. Moyer. 2015. *Diversity Matters: Judicial Policy Making in the U.S. Courts of Appeals.* Charlottesville: University of Virginia Press.

Jeknic, Petar, Rorie Spill Solberg, and Eric N. Waltenburg. 2021. *Open Judicial Politics Reader.* 2nd ed. https://open.oregonstate.education/open-judicial-politics/.

Kirkpatrick, Jennet. 2020. "Fairness Has a Face: Neutrality and Descriptive Representation on Courts." *Politics, Groups, and Identities* 8 (4):803–11. doi:10.1080/21565503.2020.1782951.

Martin, Elaine. 2004. "Gender and Presidential Judicial Selection." *Women & Politics* 26 (4):109–29. doi:10.1300/J014v26n03_05.

Millhiser, Ian. 2019. "The Absurd Whiteness of America's Court System, in 2 Charts." *Vox*, October 3. https://www.vox.com/policy-and-politics/2019/10/3/20893643/whiteness-federal-judiciary-diversity-obama-trump.

Moyer, Laura 2021. "Assessing President Obama's Appointment of Women to the Federal Appellate Courts." *British Journal of American Legal Studies* 10 (3):433–55. doi: 10.2478/bjals-2021-0008. Special issue: United States Committee on the Judiciary: Oversight, Scrutiny, and Process

National Association of Women Lawyers. 2020. "2020 Survey Report on the Promotion and Retention of Women in Law Firms." https://www.nawl.org/p/cm/ld/fid=2019.

Nelson, Robert L., Ioana Sendroiu, Ronit Dinovitzer, and Meghan Dawe. 2019. "Perceiving Discrimination: Race, Gender, and Sexual Orientation in the Legal Workplace." *Law & Social Inquiry* 44 (4):1051–82. doi:10.1017/lsi.2019.4.

Peery, Destiny, Paulette Brown, and Eileen Letts. 2020. "Left Out and Left Behind: The Hurdles and Hassles of Achieving Long-Term Legal Careers for Women of Color." American Bar Association. https://www.americanbar.org/products/inv/book/401210758/.

Quillian, Lincoln, Devah Pager, Ole Hexel, and Arnfinn H. Midtbøen. 2017. "Meta-analysis of Field Experiments Shows No Change in Racial Discrimination in Hiring over Time." *Proceedings of the National Academy of Sciences* 114 (41):10870–75. doi:10.1073/pnas.1706255114.

Sen, Maya. 2014. "How Judicial Qualification Ratings May Disadvantage Minority and Female Candidates." *Journal of Law and Courts* 2 (1):33–65. doi:10.1086/674579.

Slotnick, Elliot, Sara Schiavoni, and Sheldon Goldman. 2017. "Obama's Judicial Legacy: The Final Chapter." *Journal of Law and Courts* 5 (2):363–422. doi:10.1086/693347.

Steigerwalt, Amy. 2010. *Battle over the Bench: Senators, Interest Groups, and Lower Court Confirmations.* Charlottesville: University of Virginia Press.

Triana, María del Carmen, Pamela Gu, Olga Chapa, Orlando Richard, and Adrienne Colella. 2021. "Sixty Years of Discrimination and Diversity Research in Human Resource Management: A Review with Suggestions for Future Research Directions." *Human Resource Management* 60 (1): 145–204.

van Esch, Chantal, Margaret M. Hopkins, Deborah A. O'Neil, and Diana Bilimoria. 2018. "How Perceived Riskiness Influences the Selection of Women and Men as Senior Leaders." *Human Resource Management* 57 (4):915–30. doi:10.1002/hrm.21902.

Black and Desi: Indian American Perceptions of Kamala Harris

Danielle Casarez Lemi, Maneesh Arora, and Sara Sadhwani

ABSTRACT
How do voters evaluate descriptive representatives who vary in prototypicality? Specifically, how do Indian American voters evaluate Black women candidates who are also Indian American, or Indian American women candidates who are also Black? Using the case of Kamala Harris, we present findings from an original survey experiment of over 1,000 Indian Americans collected just prior to the 2020 election. We examine the power of shared identity cues for Indian American voters, who represent a growing political bloc of Asian American voters. We find that relative to being framed as Indian alone, Indian American respondents are less likely to support the Biden-Harris ticket when Harris is framed as Black and Indian American. This is true for Indian Americans who believe that Indian Americans have something in common. This study extends our knowledge of Black women in politics, Indian American politics, Asian American politics, and voter evaluations of mixed-race descriptive representatives.

Introduction

Kamala Harris is the first Black woman to serve as Vice President. As she took the stage of the Democratic National Convention in 2020 to accept her party's nomination, she spoke about her ethnoracial backgrounds fully. She told of her experience as a Black woman in America, and as the daughter of immigrants from Jamaica and India. She described her mother's immigrant journey from the southern state of Tamil Nadu, India to California. Like President Obama more than a decade ago, Vice President Harris's mixed-race heritage challenges our notions of ethnoracial identity and leaves open questions about the functionality and practicality of ethnoracial identity in a multiracial democracy, especially with respect to descriptive representation (Mansbridge 1999).

In the aggregate, a majority of Indian Americans – much like African Americans – identify as Democrats and the two racialized communities share a number of ideological perspectives (Arora, Sadhwani, and Shah 2021). Yet, the two communities diverge in important experiential, socioeconomic, and attitudinal ways. As an immigrant community in the US, Indian Americans are largely viewed as a monolith and often compiled together with other east and southeast Asians in the broad ethnoracial categorization of "Asian American." But India is a nation of more than one billion people, distinguishable by region, language, caste, and creed. They bring with them to the US their own belief systems and stereotypes that evolve through the integration and adaptation phases of the immigrant experience as second and third generations of Indian Americans are born and develop. To date, we know little about how Indian Americans evaluate candidates or politicians on any dimensions of race, gender, caste, or creed. Important variations within the community, however, could shape Indian Americans' political attitudes toward Harris, such as divides between North and South Indians, a culturally ingrained sense of colorism (Mishra 2015), and deeply rooted views of traditional gender roles (Chakravarti 1993).

A growing literature on Black women politicians finds that Black women elites contend with colorism, with lighter-skinned Black women being more prevalent in the candidate pool than darker-skinned Black women, and expectations that they style their hair in certain ways, such as being advised to straighten their hair (Brown and Lemi 2021). Kamala Harris is lighter-skinned with straightened hair. Indeed, Barack Obama famously called Kamala Harris "the best-looking Attorney General" (Lemi and Brown 2020). Harris's features, along with the fact that Harris is also Indian American, might lead some Indian American constituents to vary in classifying Harris as a Black politician (see Monk 2022). Conversely, because Harris is also Black, some Indian American constituents might vary in the extent to which they consider Harris Indian American. Some Indian American constituents might evaluate Harris as a politician differently depending on how her group membership is presented. We should not assume that all Indian Americans would embrace Kamala Harris simply because she has an Indian mother.

The election of Harris prompts us to ask: how do voters evaluate descriptive representatives who vary in prototypicality?[1] More specifically, how do Indian American voters evaluate Kamala Harris – a Black woman candidate who is also Indian American? This paper examines the nuances of Indian American evaluations of descriptive representatives through the assessments that Indian Americans have of Kamala Harris. We explore these questions in a survey experiment on Indian Americans conducted before the 2020 Presidential Election. Drawing on social identity theory of leadership (Hogg, van Knippenberg, and Rast 2012), we argue that Indian Americans' assessments of Harris will vary based on the framing of her ethnoracial identity. We provide a test of new work from Lemi (2021), who argues that when a candidate is classified with multiple ethnoracial categories, they are less likely to collect immediate support from members of their own groups because such classification raises the salience that the candidate may not conform to ideas of group prototypicality, or the confines of group membership. Using original survey data of over 1,000 Indian Americans, we find that relative to being framed as Indian alone, Indian American respondents are less likely to support the Biden-Harris ticket when Harris is framed as Black and Indian American. We find this to be true among respondents who believe Indian Americans have common political, cultural, and economic interests. This article charts new territory by examining the complexities of Indian American identity and descriptive representation.

Descriptive representation, mixed candidates, and Asian American Political behavior

As a descriptive representative of multiple ethnoracial groups, Kamala Harris may claim shared group membership with Black Americans, Jamaican Americans, Indian Americans, and Asian Americans. Whether constituents treat mixed politicians as an insider or an outsider, however, remains an open question. Several survey experiments in the political science literature provide insights into how voters evaluate mixed candidates. First, voter evaluations of mixed candidates may depend on how the candidate self-identifies ethnoracially. Masuoka (2015) found that predominantly white participants assessed a mixed Black and white candidate's issue competencies differently depending on how the candidate self-identified, but Leslie et al. (2022) suggest that non-mixed voters' actual vote choice may not hinge on claimed identity. Second, different ethnoracial groups respond differently to mixed candidates. One study featuring former Congressmember Charles Rangel, who is Black and Latinx, found that relative to no information about Rangel's background, Black respondents generally evaluated Rangel favorably whether he was framed as Black or Latinx (Adida, Davenport, and McClendon 2016). By contrast, Adida, Davenport, and McClendon (2016) found that Latinx respondents did not evaluate Rangel differently when information about his heritage was cued. They suggest that these differences might be due to differences in perceptions of group commonality with each other (Adida, Davenport, and McClendon 2016, 831).

Importantly, receptions of mixed candidates depend on their specific ethnoracial combinations, not just their mixed status. Scholars like Hernández (2018), writing about the experiences of mixed persons, find that people do not necessarily discriminate against mixed people on the basis of their mixed identity, but rather based on their specific background, often when someone is Black. This applies to politicians as well. In a conjoint experiment, Lemi (2021) found that Black, white, Hispanic, and Asian American voters reacted differently to mixed candidates depending on candidates' ethnoracial combinations and positioning in the American ethnoracial hierarchy (Masuoka and Junn 2013), but generally not favoring mixed candidates relative to their non-mixed counterparts. This pattern extended to Black Californians' evaluations of Kamala Harris in the 2016 California US Senate election. Regarding Black and Asian candidates like Kamala Harris, Lemi (2021) found that relative to Asian candidates, Black and Asian candidates tended to be disadvantaged among Asian Americans. When it comes to women voters only, overall, Lemi (2020) found that women tended to prefer non-mixed women candidates relative to mixed women candidates.

More recently, Greene, Matos, and Sanbonmatsu (2022) tested whether framing Kamala Harris as a "woman of color," "Black woman," or "South Asian woman" had any effect on Black, Latina, and white women's favorability ratings of Harris. They did not find strong evidence that varying Harris's ethnoracial-gender identities altered Harris's favorability ratings. Importantly, they noted that their results may have been time-dependent, as Harris's heritage was well-known by the time they fielded their study (Greene, Matos, and Sanbonmatsu 2022, 33).

In terms of Asian American preferences for descriptive representatives, recent research finds that Indian Americans have a strong desire for descriptive representation. In an analysis of voter turnout from California State Assembly elections, Sadhwani (2020) found that overall, Asian Americans are more likely to turn out to vote when an Asian American candidate is on the ballot depending on the proportion of Asian Americans residing within a jurisdiction. This was true despite being a community of many different national origin groups. When disaggregated by national origin, however, Indian Americans especially stood out: Their mobilization rate for an Indian American candidate exceeded any other Asian American community, regardless of district demographics. Moreover, in the absence of another Asian American candidate, Asian American voters tend to prefer Asian American candidates (Sadhwani 2021). There is wide heterogeneity among Asian Americans (Lien et al. 2021), and it is possible that Indian Americans are likely to respond favorably to any cue that communicates that a candidate is Indian. Still, we know little about how Asian Americans, and much less about how Indian Americans, evaluate mixed candidates who hold membership to multiple ethnoracial groups.

An important moderating variable that conditions how ethnoracial groups evaluate descriptive representatives is linked fate, or the belief that one's individual outcomes are tied to the broader group (Dawson 1994; Tate 1994; Gay et al. 2016). Linked fate is a measure of group consciousness (McClain et al. 2009). Research by Bejarano et al. (2020) demonstrates variation in how the relevance of linked fate to candidate evaluation differs by ethnoracial-gender combinations. In their analysis of the 2016 Collaborative Multiracial Post-Election Survey, they found that overall, the presence of linked fate with one's own group and with other minority groups was associated with inferences about a Black or Latinx candidate's ability to represent a voter's interests. Considering Latinos/Latinas and Black men and Black women separately also suggested that linked fate with other groups and with one's own group did not consistently condition candidate evaluations. There is less research on how linked fate differs for gender groups among Asian Americans, though research suggests that Asian Americans who report a sense of linked fate are more likely to support Asian American candidates than those who do not (Schildkraut 2012). In terms of evaluating an Asian American candidate who is also Black, Nicholson, Carter, and Restar's (2020) research indicates that linked fate precedes expressing political commonality with Black people, implying that a sense of group consciousness may precede favorable evaluations of a Black and Asian candidate.

Given the breadth of this research, we anticipate that Kamala Harris's ethnoracial membership to both Black Americans and Indian Americans will shape constituents' evaluations of her as a descriptive representative. For Indian Americans in particular, we argue that we must examine those components of Harris's identity that might cue common stereotypes or prejudices within the community. For example, within India, important regional divisions exist between North and South Indians that could influence Indian American's assessments of Harris, who is South Indian. In addition, given the long tradition of colorism within the Indian culture, an important aim of this project is to examine the extent to which Harris's identity as Black might lead to variations in support among Indian Americans.

Theory, research design, & hypotheses

We apply the theoretical framework developed by Lemi (2021) to test how voters evaluate a mixed descriptive representative in a survey experiment on Indian Americans and their evaluations of Kamala Harris. Lemi (2021) draws on a social identity theory framework to argue that when a candidate is classified with multiple ethnoracial categories, they are less likely to collect immediate support from members of their own groups because such classification raises the salience that the candidate may not conform to ideas of group prototypicality, or what it means to be a member of an ethnoracial group (see Hogg, van Knippenberg, and Rast 2012). Although voters may not react much to explicit information about a mixed candidate's claimed identity (Leslie et al. 2022), the mere classification with multiple categories may raise the question about a candidate's group attachments. Mixed classification sends the signal that there may be social distance via ethnoracial differences between the candidate and the group (see Harris 2020), and perhaps political differences. Harris's mixed ancestry conditions how she experiences her ethnoracial identity as a Black woman and an Indian American woman (see Monk 2022). To test the theory, we provide cues to survey respondents about Harris's identity as being either Black and Indian American (mixed), or non-mixed conditions of Black, Indian American, or Tamil. We hypothesize that:

H1: Relative to a non-mixed condition, classifying Harris with multiple ethnoracial categories will have a negative effect on respondents' reported likelihood of voting for the Biden-Harris ticket.

In the non-mixed conditions, we include Harris's South Indian Tamil group membership to assess the extent to which Indian Americans' support might vary based on North-South distinctions. North Indians have been considered descendants of Indo-Aryans who use Sanskrit-based languages, while South Indians are identified as Dravidians using Tamil-based languages (Deshpande and Hook 1979). North Indian climate is known for growing wheat, the primary ingredient for breads such as chapati, roti, and naan, making north-Indians known as "wheat eaters," whereas South Indians are typically referred to as "rice eaters" for the rice-based dietary staples such as idli and dosa (Sarkar et al. 2015).[2] While these distinctions in cuisine may seem small, they play a distinctive role in identifying in-groups and out-groups among Indians and could carry over to the immigrant experience in the United States (Sen 2004). The North-South divide is distinguishable in ethnic histories, languages, foods, religious or cultural celebrations, and therefore included within this study.

Additionally, we include a non-mixed condition that identifies Harris as "Black" to test the impact of Harris's identity as a Black woman on Indian Americans. Recent work from Jayawardene (2016), argues that racialized hierarchies that are prevalent in western societies that have led to conclusions that Blackness, or the qualities of Black people, are somehow inferior, also exist in South Asian societies given the enduring nature of colonial rule. Jayawardene argues that modern Indian society should be analyzed through the lens of what she calls *racialized casteism*, which reveals the ingrained relationship between race, caste, and colorism in modern Indian society. We recognize that there are significant differences in political behavior by ethnic identity among Black Americans, given Harris's heritage as a Jamaican American. For example, while West Indians report similar levels of linked fate as African Americans, West Indians might be less likely to vote or campaign for a party than African Americans (Watts Smith 2014, 142, 167). People may also "elevate" Jamaican immigrants compared to US-born Black Americans (Greer 2013, Chapter 1, 105). Mixed Jamaican Americans might also have more salient ethnic identities as Jamaican than racial identities as Black (Waring and Purkayastha 2017). However, we use the term "Black" within our research design given the prevalence of colorism in South Asian culture. Colorism is particularly relevant for Indians' evaluations of political candidates, as lighter-skinned politicians may have a general advantage in India (Ahuja, Ostermann, and Mehta 2016).

In addition, Harris has referred to herself as "the first black woman from [California]" to serve in the US Senate in her memoir (Harris 2019, 3, 12), and makes only one reference to Jamaica as her father's birthplace in the main text of her memoir. Cueing a Black identity thus reflects how Harris has talked about herself and one of the identities that she has chosen to make salient to the public as part of telling her story. Moreover, cueing Black as opposed to also cueing variations such as "Jamaican American" or "Black immigrant" allowed the sample size to remain large enough to test results across four conditions.

Finally, a third non-mixed cue of "Indian American" is used in the survey experiment, which is the common pan-ethnic term used to identify either immigrants to the United States from India, or those individuals whose heritage comes from India. The term suggests a commonality between individuals who have a shared experience of having a common heritage within the US. As discussed above, however, Indian Americans are diverse on a range of dimensions including language, religion, caste, and socioeconomic status in the United States. To further assess the strength of the Indian American identity we asked a series of questions about the extent to which respondents see commonalities among Indian Americans.

Lemi (2021) also explores whether individuals with stronger group identities are more or less likely to support a mixed candidate. On one hand, those with stronger group identities may be more likely to enforce ideas of group prototypicality on a mixed candidate and withhold their support. On the other hand, those with stronger group identities may embrace mixed candidates because they share group membership. Previous work has shown that Asian Americans do not necessarily have a cohesive pan-ethnic identity (e.g., Wong et al. 2011). Although most studies that measure the politicization of one's ethnoracial identity use linked fate, some research suggests the measure is inappropriate for non-Black Americans and that other measures, such as questions that gauge a belief that one's ethnoracial group has something in common, may be more appropriate (Sanchez and Vargas 2016). Using this logic, we test our second hypothesis:

H2: Strong perceptions of Indian American group commonality will condition respondents' support for Kamala Harris.

Data and methods

We used the firm Lucid to collect an online sample of 1,003 Indian Americans living in the United States. About 59% of respondents were born overseas, mostly in India. Respondents or their families hail from 25 of India's 28 states and the Delhi region. The survey was conducted October 13–30, 2020, just before the 2020 presidential election. The sample was Census-matched for age, gender, education level, political party and geographic region. We did not construct the sample for representativeness of religion, but the sample includes Hindus, Muslims, Christians, and respondents of other religious backgrounds.

We included an experiment in which respondents were randomly assigned to different frames of Kamala Harris's ethnorace. Respondents were told that Kamala Harris had recently been chosen as Joe Biden's vice-presidential nominee for the 2020 election. We then described Harris as: Black, Indian American, Tamil, or Black and Indian American. Respondents were then asked, *"Does Harris being on the ticket make you more or less likely to vote for Joe Biden for President?"* Response options were: More likely (1); Less likely (0); or Neither more nor less likely (0.5). We also asked respondents a series of demographic questions, questions that gauged their political identity and political behavior. We use this question to examine our first hypothesis by comparing the results based upon the four cues given for Harris's identity.

Table 1. Summary Statistics of Sample.

	Our sample	Indian American Attitudes Survey 2020
Age	35	35
Bachelor's	76%	79%
Women	56%	45%
Hindu	57%	54%
First generation	59%	62%
Democrat	53%	56%
Republican	19%	15%
Independent/other party	27%	22%

Table 2. Descriptive Statistics of Key Variables.

	Mean	Min.	Max.
Support for Biden/Harris ticket	0.67	0	1
Common cultural interests	0.69	0	1
Common economic interests	0.69	0	1
Common political interests	0.63	0	1
Commonality index	0.67	0	1
Racial resentment	0.42	0	1

Our second hypothesis required assessing the strength of group identity as Indian Americans. To do so, respondents were asked a three-part question about whether they believe Indian Americans have common political, economic, and cultural interests. Respondents were asked, *"Do you believe that Indian Americans have common ... [Political interests/Economic interests/ Cultural interests]?"* A five-point response scale was used, which included the following options: Definitely yes; Probably yes; Might or might not; Probably not; Definitely not. We use each measure separately, and we also pooled the three questions together to form a commonality index.

Finally, building on Jayawardene (2016), Hernández (2018), and Lemi (2021), we included in the survey a two question "racial resentment" scale, to capture a measure of anti-Blackness. Racial resentment is an index variable that combines two questions using a five point agree-to-disagree scale.[3] Responses to these questions that indicate negative assessments of African Americans were coded as having high levels of racial resentment. The combined scale ranges from 0 (low levels of racial resentment) to 1 (high levels of racial resentment).

Table 1 reports the summary statistics of the sample. The median age of this sample is about 35 years, most participants have Bachelor's degrees, and a majority are first-generation Americans and identify as Democrats. The demographic characteristics of our sample compare favorably to the 2020 Indian American Attitudes Survey (IAAS), a nationally representative sample of 1,200 Indian Americans collected through the firm, YouGov (Badrinathan et al. 2021). The only major discrepancy between the samples is that 56% of the respondents in our sample are women while 45% of the IAAS sample is women. Across all other characteristics, the samples are relatively similar.

Results

How do Indian American voters evaluate Kamala Harris – a Black woman candidate who is also Indian American? Table 2 summarizes participants' general support for the Biden-Harris ticket, their perceptions of commonality, and their responses to the racial resentment items. Overall, participants expressed higher levels of support for Biden-Harris, higher levels of group commonality, and lower levels of racial resentment.

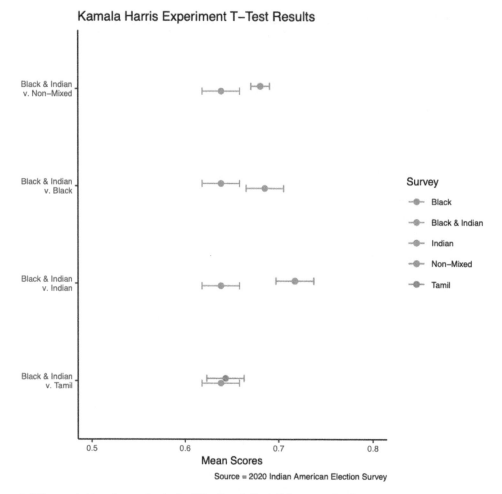

Figure 1. Differences in Mean Support for the Joe Biden/Kamala Harris Ticket across Conditions.

Testing hypothesis 1

To further evaluate Indian American's assessment of Kamala Harris, we examine the mean support for the Biden/Harris ticket across the different identity conditions. Figure 1 displays the mean likelihood of voting for Joe Biden and Kamala Harris when Harris is described as Black and Indian American compared to the other identity frames. We use "non-mixed" to refer to pooled conditions of Black, Indian American, and Tamil. Table A1 in the Appendix reports the full results of Figure 1.

Overall, we find tacit support for H1. The mean likelihood of voting for the ticket is lower when Harris is described as Black and Indian American compared to mean support for the ticket pooled across the three other treatment groups. Participants were less supportive of the ticket by about 4.4 percentage points (p = 0.095). When we disaggregate the non-mixed conditions, we find that support for the ticket is lower when Harris is described as Black and Indian American relative to when Harris is described as Indian alone. Relative to being framed as Indian alone, respondents were about 7.9 percentage points less likely to support the Biden-Harris ticket (p = 0.015), supporting H1. There are no statistically significant differences between framing Harris as Black and Indian American and Black alone or Tamil alone. These findings suggest that for Indian American respondents, these frames carry some weight and that seeing Harris framed as Indian American is particularly mobilizing. Given this finding, we might further anticipate that seeing Indian Americans as having a lot in common may be influential in assessments of Harris and the Biden/Harris ticket.

Testing hypothesis 2

In Tables 3–5, we compare mean support for the Biden and Harris ticket when Harris is described as Black and Indian American compared to mean support for the ticket within the other treatment groups among respondents who said Indian Americans "Definitely" or "Probably" have common political, economic, or cultural interests. We find some support for H2, specifically when we compare framing Harris as Black and Indian American to pooled non-mixed conditions and to framing as Indian alone.

In Table 3, generally, among Indian American respondents who believe Indian Americans have something in common, participants are less likely to support the Biden-Harris ticket when Harris is presented as Black and Indian American, relative to being presented as Black alone, Indian American alone, or Tamil alone. In particular, those who believe Indian Americans have common cultural interests were about 5.8 percentage points less likely to support Biden-Harris ($p = 0.071$) and those who believe Indian Americans have common economic interests are about 6.5 percentage points less likely to support Biden-Harris ($p = 0.063$) when Harris is presented as Black and Indian American.

Table 3. Commonality Measures Black & Indian V. Non-Mixed.

Commonality Measures Black & Indian v. Non-Mixed				
Scenario	Black & Indian	Non-Mixed	Difference	p-value
Commonality index	0.654	0.703	**−0.050**	**0.112**
Common political interests	0.663	0.702	**−0.039**	**0.301**
Common cultural interests	0.660	0.719	**−0.058**	**0.071**
Common economic interests	0.641	0.702	**−0.065**	**0.063**

Note: *$p < 0.05$, **$p < 0.01$, ***$p < 0.001$

Table 4. Commonality Measures Black & Indian V. Black.

Commonality Measures Black & Indian v. Black				
Scenario	Black & Indian	Black	Difference	p-value
Commonality index	0.654	0.706	**−0.053**	**0.182**
Common political interests	0.663	0.722	**−0.059**	**0.205**
Common cultural interests	0.660	0.701	**−0.048**	**0.231**
Common economic interests	0.641	0.700	**−0.059**	**0.161**

Note: *$p < 0.05$, **$p < 0.01$, ***$p < 0.001$

Table 5. Commonality Measures Black & Indian V. Indian.

Commonality Measures Black & Indian v. Indian				
Scenario	Black & Indian	Indian	Difference	p-value
Commonality index	0.654	0.747	**−0.093***	**0.016**
Common political interests	0.663	0.739	**−0.076**	**0.098**
Common cultural interests	0.660	0.776	**−0.115****	**0.004**
Common economic interests	0.641	0.747	**−0.106****	**0.007**

Note: *$p < 0.05$, **$p < 0.01$, ***$p < 0.001$

In Table 4, we test how those who perceive group commonality evaluate Biden-Harris when Harris is framed as Black. Table 4 shows that while participants were generally less likely to support the ticket when Harris was framed as Black and Indian American, the differences do not reach statistical significance.

Table 5 shows consistency with H2. Indian Americans who report any group commonality are less likely to support the Biden-Harris ticket when Harris is framed as Black and Indian American compared to when she is framed as Indian American alone. Those with any commonality are about 9.3 percentage points less likely to support Biden-Harris ($p = 0.016$). Those who perceive political commonality are about 7.6 percentage points less likely to support Biden-Harris ($p = 0.098$). The difference jumps to over 10 percentage points among those who perceive common cultural interests (-0.115, $p = 0.004$) and those who perceive common economic interests (-0.106, $p = 0.007$). In Table A2 in the Appendix, we do not find statistically significant differences by lower or higher levels of racial resentment.

Discussion

There are a few explanations for the results we found in this study. One question regards the null effects of framing Harris as Black and Indian American relative to framing Harris as Tamil alone. These findings suggest that Indian Americans were not motivated by North-South divisions or internal divisions more generally in their assessment of Biden-Harris. While such divisions may hold significant weight culturally, they did not manifest into variations in political attitudes. Instead, this null effect suggests that Indian American identity is consolidated on a political dimension among generations of Indians in the United States.

Two other notable findings are the null effect of classifying Harris as Black and Indian American relative to Black alone and the statistically significant effect of classifying Harris as Black and Indian American relative to Indian American alone. Perhaps the public is generally aware that Harris self-identifies as a Black woman, and therefore classifying Harris as Black and Indian American has no effect. After all, Harris was already prominent on the national stage as a US Senator and having run for the presidency in the primary. In addition, to the extent that colorism might be at play or some level of anti-Blackness that was not revealed in the racial resentment questions, both of these categories identify Harris as Black, and therefore might be tapping the same kinds of assessments from Indian Americans. In other words, any time a candidate is identified as Black – either as Black alone or as Black and something else – could impact an Indian American's assessment of the candidate.

When Harris is classified as Indian American alone, Indian American constituents, especially those who hold a feeling of in-group commonality, may evaluate Harris more favorably because the classification may signal Harris's conscious self-identification with Indian Americans. Taken together, these findings show that treating "Asian Americans" as a monolith is inappropriate for understanding how different Asian American ethnic groups evaluate different Asian American candidates.

In terms of evaluations of Black women candidates, these findings suggest that assignment to an additional non-Black ethnoracial "outgroup," like Indian American, in addition to Black, may not cause non-Black constituents to react differently. Determining whether this finding is unique to Harris or generalizable to Black women candidates is somewhat of a challenge with Harris because she was nationally known by 2020 and generally understood as a Black politician. Cueing her as Black and Indian versus Black by 2020 may have been unlikely to move voter evaluations (also see Greene 2022). This experiment did not manipulate features used for ethnoracial classification (e.g., Brown and Lemi 2021; Monk 2022; Sims, Pirtle, and Johnson-Arnold 2020), and future research should explore whether ethnoracial classification interacts with a candidate's appearance to produce distinct evaluations.

These findings also raise questions about the malleability of ethnoracial classification for mixed Black women. Previous research suggests that women may have more fluid ethnoracial identification than men (Davenport 2016), and that Black men may generally be perceived as Black alone (Penner and Saperstein 2013; Sims and Joseph-Salisbury 2019). Harris's biography in particular indicates a strong Black identity – she holds membership to a Black Greek letter organization (Brown and Lemi 2021, Chapter 5), she graduated from a historically Black university, and her mother raised her within a Black community in Berkeley/Oakland, California (Harris 2019). This research raises the question of whether, in an arena with so few Black women, mixed Black women *politicians* experience ethnoracial fluidity.

Regarding voter evaluations of mixed candidates generally, these findings provide additional evidence that mixed candidates appeal to different ethnoracial groups depending on the candidate's specific ethnoracial backgrounds (Lemi 2021). The historical one-drop rule for Black Americans offers context for interpreting how non-Black constituents evaluate mixed Black candidates like Kamala Harris (see Daniel 2001; Davis 1991). In the case of Kamala Harris, Indian Americans were more responsive to framing Harris as Indian alone than Black and Indian American. Whether we would see the same patterns for Indian Americans evaluating a mixed Indian and white candidate, mixed Indian and Latinx candidate, or Indian American and another Asian American ethnicity, for example, remains an open question. Overall, these findings demonstrate that descriptive representatives who hold multiple ethnoracial group memberships may experience different reactions, on the basis of their classification, from their ethnoracial constituents.

Conclusion

While Indian Americans make up less than 2% of the US population overall, they are concentrated in traditional immigrant-receiving states like California, New York, and New Jersey, as well as politically important battleground states like Georgia, Pennsylvania, Texas, and Virginia. They have the highest median average income of any ethnoracial group in America,[4] including whites, and are becoming important and strategic political donors (Shah 2020). The election of Kamala Harris was largely viewed in the popular press as a win for the Indian American community, with some calling the election an "early Diwali gift."[5]

This study breaks new ground to examine the relationship between the Indian American community and our nation's first Indian American – and Black American – vice president. What we find is that while framing Kamala Harris as either Black or Black and Indian matters little to Indian American respondents, among those who see their community as sharing in cultural and economic common traits, cuing Kamala Harris as Indian American drives support for a Biden-Harris ticket. This suggests that Indian Americans hold a desire for descriptive representation and to see "one of their own" reaching the highest levels of political power in the United States.

Furthermore, the study identifies the importance of Indian Americans as seeing common political interests. While Indian Americans are often considered a homogenous group in the United States – one of many national origins that make up the pan-ethnic Asian American identity – they in fact are a pan-ethnic group themselves, complete with internal divisions, variations in immigration and socioeconomic status, and with important linguistic, cultural, regional, caste, and religious differences that must be reconciled through the immigrant experience. They carry their own set of prejudices, stereotypes, and notions of in-group and out-group identity. These findings suggest that if the media focuses on a mixed Black and Indian American candidate's mixed heritage, that Indian Americans may not respond as favorably as they would if the candidate's Indian American heritage was highlighted alone. While the commonality measure used here is distinct from traditional measures of linked fate typically used in studies of African American political behavior, we find it to be an important predictor of political attitudes.

The 2020 US Census found that the rate of people identifying with multiple ethnoracial categories has grown in the last decade, yet much of the conceptualization and theorizing of ethnoracial politics in the US is based on strict ethnoracial categorization. As these categories evolve, so must our understanding of the ethnoracial landscape of America. The presence of Kamala Harris and her identity as a Black and Indian American woman in the office of Vice President represents a time period

Notes

1. For a more comprehensive discussion of the role of "typicality" in the study of ethnoracial inequality, see Monk (2022).
2. See also Sanghvi, Vir. "Rude Food: Our Rich Rice Legacy." The Hindustan Times. June 15, 2013. Available: https://www.hindustantimes.com/brunch/rude-food-our-rich-rice-legacy/story-m2v0Xw3TSdpHEccKyv7JNN.html.
3. The two questions are: "It's really a matter of some people not trying hard enough. If African Americans would only try harder they could be just as well off as Asians," and "Generations of slavery and discrimination have created conditions that make it difficult for African Americans to work their way out of the lower class." Scholars have used several different questions to measure racial resentment or other forms of symbolic racism including the two and four battery racial resentment scale, Henry and Sears' Symbolic Racism 2000 Scale, and the color-blind racial attitudes scale. While there is debate over the use of these two questions or a four-question battery, or even developing a set of new measures, the use of these two questions is consistent with the racial resentment scale used in the Congressional Election Survey (CCES) as well as recent work from Garcia and Stout (2020); Nteta and Tarsi (2016); and Citrin, Levy, and Wong (2017). Both questions are also included in the Symbolic Racism 2000 Scale.
4. "Indians in U.S. Wealthier with average household earning of 123,700: Report." https://www.businessstandard.com/article/international/indians-in-us-wealthier-with-average-household-earning-of-123-700-report-121082501016_1.html.
5. "Celebrating Diwali, some see Kamala Harris' rise reflected in stories of good over evil." Los Angeles Times. November 14, 2020. Available: https://www.latimes.com/politics/story/2020-11-14/california-hindusdiwali-festival-kamala-harris-biden.

Disclosure statement

No potential conflict of interest was reported by the author(s).

References

Adida, Claire L., Lauren D. Davenport, and Gwyneth McClendon. 2016. "Candidate Cueing across Minorities: A Survey Experiment in the United States." *Public Opinion Quarterly* 80 (4):815–36. doi:10.1093/poq/nfw029.

Ahuja, Amit, Susan L. Ostermann, and Aashish Mehta. 2016. "Is Only Fair Lovely in Indian Politics? Consequences of Skin Color in a Survey Experiment in Delhi." *Journal of Race, Ethnicity, and Politics* 1 (2):227–52. doi:10.1017/rep.2016.6.

Arora, Maneesh, Sara Sadhwani, and Sono Shah. 2021. "Unpacking Identity: Opportunities and Constraints for cross-racial Collaboration." *RSF: The Russell Sage Foundation Journal of the Social Sciences*. https://www.rsfjournal.org/content/rsfjss/7/2/93.full.pdf

Badrinathan, Sumitra, Devesh Kapur, Jonathan Kay, and Milan Vaishnav. 2021. "Social Realities of Indian Americans: Results from the 2020 Indian American Attitudes Survey." *Carnegie Endowment for International Peace*. https://carnegieendowment.org/files/Vaishnav_etal_IAASpt3_Final.pdf

Bejarano, Christina, Nadia E. Brown, Sarah Allen Gershon, and Celeste Montoya. 2020. "Shared Identities: Intersectionality, Linked Fate, and Perceptions of Political Candidates." *Political Research Quarterly* 74 (4):970–85. doi:10.1177/1065912920951640.

Brown, Nadia E., and Danielle Casarez Lemi. 2021. *Sister Style: The Politics of Appearance for Black Women Political Elites*. New York: Oxford University Press.

Chakravarti, Uma. 1993. "Conceptualising Brahmanical Patriarchy in Early India: Gender, Caste, Class, and State." *Economic and Political Weekly* 28 (14): 579–85.

Citrin, Jack, Morris Levy, and Cara J. Wong. 2017. "Politics and the English Language in California: Bilingual Education at the Polls." *California Journal of Politics and Policy* 9 (2): 2. doi:10.5070/P2cjpp9234853.

Daniel, G. Reginald. 2001. *More than Black? Multiracial Identity and the New Racial Order*. Philadelphia, PA: Temple University Press.

Davenport, Lauren D. 2016. "The Role of Gender, Class, and Religion in Biracial Americans' Racial Labeling Decisions." *American Sociological Review* 81 (1):57–84. doi:10.1177/0003122415623286.

Davis, F. James. 1991. *Who Is Black? One Nation's Definition*. University Park, PA: Penn State University Press.

Dawson, Michael C. 1994. *Behind the Mule: Race and Class in African-American Politics*. Princeton, NJ: Princeton University Press.

Madhav M. Deshpande and Peter Edwin Hook, eds. 1979. *Aryan and Non-Aryan in India*. Ann Arbor: University of Michigan.

Garcia, Jennifer R., and Christopher T. Stout. 2020. "Responding to Racial Resentment: How Racial Resentment Influences Legislative Behavior." *Political Research Quarterly* 73 (4):805–18. doi:10.1177/1065912919857826.

Gay, Claudine, Jennifer Hochschild, and Ariel White. 2016. "Americans' Belief in Linked Fate: Does the Measure Capture the Concept?." *Journal of Race, Ethnicity, and Politics* 1 (1):117–44. doi:10.1017/rep.2015.3.

Greene, Stacey, Yalidy Matos, and Kira Sanbonmatsu. 2022. "Women Voters and the Utility of Campaigning as 'Women of Color.'" *Journal of Women, Politics & Policy* 43 (1):25–41. doi:10.1080/1554477X.2022.2007467.

Greene, Stacey, Yalidy Matos, and Kira Sanbonmatsu. 2022. "Women Voters and the Utility of Campaigning as "Women of Color." *Journal of Women, Politics & Policy* 43 (1): 25–41. doi:10.1080/1554477X.2022.2007467.

Greer, Christina M. 2013. *Black Ethnics: Race, Immigration, and the Pursuit of the American Dream*. New York: Oxford University Press.

Harris, Kamala. 2019. The Truths We Hold: An American Journey. New York: Penguin Press. Google Book.

Harris, Adam S. 2020. "At the Borders of Identity: Identity Construction and Racial Bloc Voting." *Journal of Race, Ethnicity, and Politics* 5 (2):326–55. doi:10.1017/rep.2019.35.

Hernández, Katerí Tanya. 2018. *Multiracials and Civil Rights: Mixed-Race Stories of Discrimination*. New York: NYU Press.

Hogg, Michael A., Daan van Knippenberg, and David E. Rast III. 2012. "The Social Identity Theory of Leadership: Theoretical Origins, Research Findings, and Conceptual Development." *European Review of Social Psychology* 23 (1):258–304. doi:10.1080/10463283.2012.741134.

Jayawardene, Sureshi. 2016. "Racialized Casteism: Exposing the Relationship between Race, Caste, and Colorism through the Experiences of African People in India and Sri Lanka." *Journal of African American Studies* 20 (3–4):323–45. doi:10.1007/s12111-016-9333-5.

Lemi, Danielle Casarez. 2020. "Voting for multi-racial Women." In *Politicking while Female: The Political Life of Women*, ed. Nichole M. Bauer. Baton Rouge: Louisiana State University Press, 55–70.

Lemi, Danielle Casarez. 2021. "Do Voters Prefer Just Any Descriptive Representative? the Case of Multiracial Candidates." *Perspectives on Politics* 19 (4):1061–81. doi:10.1017/S1537592720001280.

Lemi, Danielle Casarez, and Nadia E. Brown. 2020. "The Political Implications of Colorism are Gendered." *PS, Political Science & Politics* 53 (4): 669–73.

Leslie, Gregory John, Natalie Masuoka, Sarah E. Gaither, Jessica D. Remedios, and A. Chyei Vinluan. 2022. "Voter Evaluations of Biracial-Identified Political Candidates." *Social Sciences* 11 (4):171–202. doi:10.3390/socsci11040171.

Lien, Pei-te, Loan Le, Okiyoshi Takeda, Sara Sadhwani, and Andrew L. Aoki. 2021. "Are Asian Americans a Meaningful Political Community?" *PS, Political Science & Politics* 54 (2): 232–34.

Mansbridge, Jane. 1999. "Should Blacks Represent Blacks and Women Represent Women? A Contingent 'Yes.'" *Journal of Politics* 61 (3):628–57. doi:10.2307/2647821.

Masuoka, Natalie. 2015. "Racial Identification in a Post Obama Era: Multiracialism, Identity Choice, and Candidate Evaluation." In *American Identity in the Age of Obama*, eds. Amilcar Antonio Barreto and Richard L. O'Bryant. New York, NY: Routledge, 42–69.

Masuoka, Natalie, and Jane Junn. 2013. *The Politics of Belonging: Race, Public Opinion, and Immigration*. Chicago, IL: University of Chicago Press.

McClain, Paula D., Jessica D., Johnson Carew, Eugene Walton, and S Watts. Candis 2009. "Group Membership, Group Identity, and Group Consciousness: Measures of Racial Identity in American Politics?." *Annual Review of Political Science* 12:471–85. doi:10.1146/annurev.polisci.10.072805.102452.

Mishra, Neha. 2015. "India and Colorism: The Finer Nuances." 14 *Wash. U. Global. Stud. Law Rev.* 725–50.

Monk, Ellis P., Jr. 2022. "Inequality without Groups: Contemporary Theories of Categories, Intersectional Typicality, and the Disaggregation of Difference." *Sociological Theory* 40 (1):3–27. doi:10.1177/07352751221076863.

Nicholson, Harvey L., Jr., J. Scott Carter, and Arjee Restar. 2020. "Strength in Numbers: Perceptions of Political Commonality with African Americans among Asians and Asian Americans in the United States." *Sociology of Race and Ethnicity* 6 (1):107–22. doi:10.1177/2332649218785648.

Nteta, Tatishe M., and Melinda R. Tarsi. 2016. "Self-selection versus Socialization Revisited: Military Service, Racial Resentment, and Generational Membership." *Armed Forces and Society* 42 (2):362–85. doi:10.1177/0095327X15580115.

Penner, Andrew M., and Aliya Saperstein. 2013. "Engendering Racial Perceptions: An Intersectional Analysis of How Social Status Shapes Race." *Gender & Society* 27 (3):319–44. doi:10.1177/0891243213480262.

Sadhwani, Sara. 2020. "Asian American Mobilization: The Effect of Candidates and Districts on Asian American Voting Behavior." *Political Behavior* 44 (1):105–31. doi:10.1007/s11109-020-09612-7.

Sadhwani, Sara. 2021. "The Influence of Candidate Race and Ethnicity: The Case of Asian Americans." *Politics, Groups, and Identities* 1–37. doi:10.1080/21565503.2021.1877749.

Sanchez, Gabriel R., and Edward D. Vargas. 2016. "Taking a Closer Look at Group Identity: The Link between Theory and Measurement of Group Consciousness and Linked Fate." *Political Research Quarterly* 69 (1):160–74. doi:10.1177/1065912915624571.

Sarkar, Preetam, Lohith Kum, Chanda Dhumal, Shubham Subrot Panigrahi, and Ruplal Choudhary. 2015. "Traditional and Ayurvedic Foods of Indian Origin." *Journal of Ethnic Foods* 2 (3):97–109. doi:10.1016/j.jef.2015.08.003.

Schildkraut, Deborah J. 2012. "Which Birds of a Feather Flock Together? Assessing Attitudes about Descriptive Representation among Latinos and Asian Americans." *American Politics Research* 41 (4):699–729. doi:10.1177/1532673X12466582.

Sen, Colleen Taylor. 2004. *Food Culture in India*. Westport, CT: Greenwood Press.

Shah, Sono. 2020. "Essays on co-racial Campaign Contributions." *PhD diss*. University of California, Riverside.

Sims, Jennifer Patrice, and Remi Joseph-Salisbury. 2019. "'We Were All Just the Black Kids': Black mixed-race Men and the Importance of Adolescent Peer Groups for Identity Development." *Social Currents* 6 (1):51–66. doi:10.1177/2329496518797840.

Sims, Jennifer Patrice, Whitney Laster Pirtle, and Iris Johnson-Arnold. 2020. "Doing Hair, Doing Race: The Influence of Hairstyle on Racial Perception across the US." *Ethnic and Racial Studies* 43 (12):2099–119. doi:10.1080/01419870.2019.1700296.

Tate, Katherine. 1994. *From Protest to Politics: The New Black Voters in American Elections*. Cambridge, MA: Harvard University Press.

Waring, Chandra D. L., and Bandana Purkayastha. 2017. "'I'm a Different Kind of Biracial': How Black/white Biracial Americans with Immigrant Parents Negotiate Race." *Social Identiites* 23 (5):614–30. doi:10.1080/13504630.2016.1271739.

Watts Smith, Candis. 2014. *Black Mosaic: The Politics of Black Pan-Ethnic Diversity*. New York: NYU Press.

Wong, Janelle, S., Karthick Ramakrishnan, Taeku Lee, and Jane Junn. 2011. *Asian American Participation: Emerging Constituents and Their Political Identities*. New York: Russell Sage Foundation.

Appendix

Table A1. Differences in Mean Support for the Joe Biden/Kamala Harris Ticket among Three Experimental Groups.

Kamala Harris experiment t-test results				
Scenario	1	2	Difference	p-value
Black & Indian v. Non-Mixed	0.638	0.682	−0.044	0.095
Black & Indian v. Black	0.638	0.685	−0.047	0.150
Black & Indian v. Indian	0.638	0.717	−0.079*	0.015
Black & Indian v. Tamil	0.638	0.643	−0.005	0.868

Note: $*p < 0.05$, $**p < 0.01$, $***p < 0.001$

Table A2. Kamala Harris Experiment t-test Results among Respondents High in Racial Resentment.

T-tests results among respondents high in racial resentment				
Scenario	1	2	Difference	p-value
Black & Indian v. Non-Mixed	0.587	0.599	−0.012	0.838
Black & Indian v. Black	0.587	0.571	0.015	0.850
Black & Indian v. Indian	0.587	0.675	−0.088	0.282
Black & Indian v. Tamil	0.587	0.559	0.027	0.739

Note: $*p < 0.05$, $**p < 0.01$, $***p < 0.001$

The Future of Black Feminism and Black Women Political Elites: A Reflexive Interview with Duchess Harris

India S. Lenear

ABSTRACT
Black feminist politics have traditionally been theorized outside formal political institutions, necessitating a nuanced and capacious account of what Black feminist politics can be in formal political environments. Situating *Black Feminist Politics from Kennedy to Trump* in conversation with recent political changes, I explore the future of Black feminist politics in formal political institutions in an interview with Professor Duchess Harris. Ultimately, Harris recommends leaning into understanding Black women political elites as unique and incomparable to each other while also being attentive to how Black feminist politics may appear in formal political institutions.

Introduction

The increase in political representation of Black women in formal political institutions is higher than it has ever been in US history. Following the nomination of Judge Ketanji Brown Jackson to the US Supreme Court, there have been celebrations because Judge Jackson may be the first Black woman to sit on the Supreme Court. Additionally, if confirmed, Judge Jackson will be the first former federal public defender to serve on the Supreme Court. Similarly, there is a record number of Black women winning their electoral races for the US House. Twenty-twenty set a new record regarding symbolic representation when 117 Black women ran for the US House and 25 won House seats (Dittmar 2021). While there is an increase in Black women's representation, this does not automatically establish the presence of Black feminisms in either theory or praxis within formal political institutions. Whereas Black women have acted as insurgent political elites within these formal institutions, much more work is needed to decouple and to complicate assumptions of Black feminist politics and strategies from Black women. Here, Black feminist politics refers to resisting and working against White hetero-patriarchal and capitalist norms for the benefit of the most marginalized. The idea that Black feminist politics are present in formal political institutions is a central theme in my interview with Professor Duchess Harris because this a central claim in her book *Black Feminist Politics from Kennedy to Trump* (Harris 2019).

What does the increase in Black women in Congress mean for Black feminism in American politics? Representation is important. However, Black faces in high places do not guarantee substantive representation of Black politics. Likewise, just because there is a record high number of Black women in Congress and the current vice president is a Black woman does not indicate that Black feminism is being represented in formal institutions. However, the record number of Black women in Congress and other formal political leadership roles does allow for a nuanced conversation regarding the visibility of Black feminist politics, Black women, and a general need to complicate the narrative of Black women as political actors (Brown 2014). The meta-level questions that undergird this article are as follows: *How will the current political environment influence and be influenced by Black feminist politics? What is next for Black feminist politics?*

Duchess Harris: Black feminist scholar

In trying to explore and answer these questions, I interviewed Dr. Duchess Harris, who is an American Studies and Political Science professor at Macalester College. Harris received her PhD in American studies with a minor in feminist studies from the University of Minnesota in 1997. Harris later earned a Juris Doctor degree in 2011 from the Mitchell Hamline School of Law. Professor Harris has earned countless awards and grants for her work and leadership, including the 2021 Thomas Jefferson Award from the Robert Earll McConnell Foundation, the 2019 Association of Black Women in Higher Education's Presidential Award, and the 2017 Mellon Creating Lifelong Learners Grant. Duchess Harris is a preeminent and interdisciplinary scholar of Black feminism and Black politics and who is well known for her book *Black Feminist Politics from Kennedy to Clinton* and its newer editions. Dr. Harris has also written and edited several books, articles, and essays including *Black Girl Magic Beyond the Hashtag: Twenty-First Century Acts of Self-Definition* (Jordan-Zachery and Harris 2019), *Racially Writing the Republic: Racists, Race Rebels and Transformation of American Identity* (Baum and Harris 2009), *Black Lives Matter and the Price of the Ticket* (Harris 2016), and *Are Michelle Obama or Gabourey Sidibe Our Only Role Models?* (Harris 2010). Additionally, Dr. Harris has penned a collection of books, *The Duchess Harris Collection ABDO*, for children and teenagers that cover a range of topics on US history. Recently, *The Duchess Harris Collection ABDO* has been targeted by conservative lawmakers who do not want topics such as race and sexuality taught in primary schools.

Moreover, Duchess Harris (2009) initially wrote *Black Feminist Politics from Kennedy to Clinton* to create a clear historical and political account of Black feminists' attempts to intervene in American politics after 1961. This book chronicles Black feminists, namely Black women, as political actors and highlights their resistance from "dominant culture and Black men." Harris frames the first edition of this book as a political history of Black feminist organizing. She focuses on Black feminist organizing through the Combahee River Collective and the National Black Feminist Organization and its transition into formal politics via Kennedy's inclusion of Black women on his Commission of the Status of Women. Professor Harris highlights the precarious position of Black feminists who are often demonized, betrayed, and forced to conceal parts of their identity in order to "curry the favor and support of one audience over another" (Harris 2009). While Harris explores the various experiences of Black women in formal political institutions, she also maps on powerful references to socio-cultural text and events such as *The Color Purple* by Alice Walker, *For Colored Girls Who Have Considered Suicide/When the Rainbow Is Enuf* by Ntozake Shange, Anita Hill's Testimony at the Thomas Confirmation Hearings, and the forced relinquishing of Vanessa Williams' crown and title of Miss America into her analysis of political institutions. Professor Harris carefully brings the reader through American history providing vivid political and social context while illuminating Black women's activism and resistance to political institutions. Carefully tracing this history of Black women's political behaviors, Harris situates Representative Barbara Lee's dissenting vote to become involved in the Iraq war as a signifier of the road to come for future "feminist identified" Black women in politics. Lastly, Harris pays significant attention to party politics and its subsequent influence on Black women and concludes with recommendations for cultivating new types of political involvement that fosters political success.

Black women political actors as Black feminists?

With the changing political climate and the emergence of more Black women and Black feminist politics into the American political system, Harris expanded the book into new editions that consider Black feminist politics under the Obama and Trump administrations. In these newer editions of the book, Harris provides more contemporary examples of Black feminist politics in representation and party politics. Each edition of the book aims to see Black women as political actors more clearly and works to further the study of Black women, regardless of their respective political arena. These new iterations of *Black feminist politics since Kennedy* add significant contributions to the study of Black women. First, by continuing to highlight Black feminist politics and resistance, the newer editions also address the changing political environment. In the second edition, *Black Feminist Politics from Kennedy to Obama* (2011) carefully grapples with the complexity of Black feminist politics during the tenure of the first African American President. Specifically, Harris makes note of two Black women, Desiree Rogers and Shirley Sherrod, that had disappointing experiences under the Obama Administration, which ultimately led to their resignations. While the explanations for their departures from the Obama administration differ, Harris critiques President Obama for providing very little protection for these Black women. Professor Harris notes that the unfair treatment and lack of protection for Black were surprising but perhaps expected given "Obama's overall record on African American women within his administration, and race in general, the surprise is diminished. In fact, the reaction just seems standard" (Harris 2019).

Centering *Black Feminist Politics from Kennedy to Trump* (2019), Harris and I discussed several overarching themes that she argues were new contributions to Black feminist politics in the American political system. Namely, Harris emphasized that Black women political elites are not innately Black feminists. This is a theoretical premise that Harris believes scholars should pay more attention to. Professor Harris emphasizes that this theoretical innovation is useful in assessing the presence of current Black feminist politics under the current administration as well as future presidencies.

Black feminist politics

Professor Harris develops a rigorous methodology to identify Black feminist politics. Harris borrows from the Boston chapter of the National Black Feminist Organization (NBFO) and the Combahee River Collective (CRC) to define Black feminist politics during the Kennedy administration and to also set the standard of Black feminist politics. The National Black Feminist Organization was founded in 1973 and disbanded in 1976. The Combahee River Collective began meeting in 1974 and dissolved in 1980. The NBFO was committed to addressing how "Black women have suffered cruelty in this society from living the phenomenon of being Black and female, in a country that is both racist and sexist" (Springer 2005). Likewise, the CRC have articulated their politics as "actively committed to struggling against racial, sexual, heterosexual, and class oppression, and see as our particular task the development of integrated analysis and practice based upon the fact that the major systems of oppression are interlocking" (Springer 2005). While both organizations aid in Harris' operationalization of Black feminist politics, it is vital to recognize that neither organizing body directly addressed or engaged with electoral politics. The CRC were Black lesbian feminists who were invested in theorizing from their lived bodily experiences.

To be sure, these organizations developed a Black feminist political ethos outside of a formal political structure. They did not theorize what a Black feminist position in or to electoral politics would be or what it would look like. There are, however, illustrative aspects of the NBFO and CRC organizing work and statements that lend themselves to imagining or extending their ethos to electoral politics. The essay takes up what an application of Black feminist politics as outlined by the NBFO and CRC would look like within electoral politics and once Black women enter into formal politics.

With this in mind, and as we cast a broader net in understanding the various ways Black feminist politics can be seen in formal politics, it is helpful to describe how Black feminist scholars have defined and characterized Black feminism. Deborah King's (1988) articulation of Black feminist politics and ideology is fundamentally concerned with the visibility and self-determining practices of Black women. King challenges "the interstructure of the oppressions of racism, sexism, and classism" (King 1988, 72). Likewise, she positions Black women as powerful and independent subjects. This articulation of Black feminism considers arguments by other Black feminist scholars that warn against conceptualizing Black feminism as being only defined by the nature of being a Black woman (Collins 1990, 2000). King's understanding of Black feminism pays close attention to the roots of where Black feminism emerges via Black women's experiences while also engaging in broader political and social commitments of resisting and dismantling interlocking systems of oppression. Black feminism and

Black feminist politics are not only concerned with the conditions of Black women but also grappled with the intricacies of political power. The scholarly and practical examples of Black feminism combine to offer a theoretical context to examine Black feminist politics within formal political institutions.

In Conversation with Professor Duchess Harris

I conducted an interview with Processor Duchess Harris via Zoom in January 2022. This was our first professional interaction, and as a PhD student who studies Black feminist politics, I was familiar with her work. During our conversation, I sought to better understand how she understood Black feminist politics to operate and influence formal politics. Namely, I asked Harris how we should see the influence of Black feminism in electoral politics, and if we could expect the emergence of so many Black women in formal politics to increase the power of Black feminist politics in formal politics? Harris replied:

> I think that part of it is that it travels in the different directions. So, I feel like Black feminists engage Black women elites, but I don't know that Black women elites engage Black feminism. What I mean by that is, how we tend to claim Black women elites as our own. A perfect example of this is when Biden and Harris are running on the ticket and a lot of Black women took it upon themselves to compare Kamala Harris to Shirley Chisholm, who was an elite but a very different kind of elite. And to say that they are similar is really a disservice to the Black feminist tradition and to history.

Here, Professor Harris forcefully notes that the power of Black feminist politics emerges from grassroots politics and organizing. Black feminism has historically been situated outside of formal politics because of the rampant marginalization that Black women faced. Black women have endured single-axis identity-based marginalization that failed to fully incorporate them as Black women. For example, their gendered identities were marginalized in Black nationalist organizations as were their racialized identities in feminist organizations. Not only were Black women marginalized in the White male-dominated political arena, they were also discriminated against in the Black male-centered Civil Rights and Black power movements as well as within White women's feminist activism and organizations. Black women have always had to create their own intellectual, political, and physical spaces (Collins 1990; Giddings 1996; Wallace 1982).

This single-axis approach to identity politics was visible as Black women began to be elected in formal politics. Representative Shirley Anita St. Hill Chisholm, the first Black woman elected to Congress, did adopt Black feminist politics into her representation style. Chisholm's extraordinary political work would set the tone for every Black woman that preceded her (Chisholm 2010). Professor Harris belies the assumption that *any* Black woman that enters electoral politics will follow Chisholm's footsteps and engage in a Black feminist politic is inaccurate. To be clear, Harris is not saying that there are no Black women elites who engage in Black feminist politics. Instead, Harris is troubling the practice of generalizing Black women elites and pushing scholars and the broader community to engage current Black women elites on their terms (e.g., Brown 2014). Professor Harris cautions scholars, activists, and political pundits from collapsing analytical categories to compare Black women elites across time and political arenas. This flattens the dynamic experiences of Black women elites, which leads to misrepresenting the individual Black woman elite's personal political practice. Simply put, all Black women political elites are not Shirley Chisholm, nor are they all Black feminist.

To further substantiate this claim, Harris states that "just because her mom was friends with Cedric Robinson doesn't mean that Kamala embraces that. A lot of us have done things differently than our mothers have, but Shirley Chisholm was trying to implement a Cedric Robinson politic." Here, Harris is countering the urge to compare Vice President Kamala Harris and Shirley Chisholm using their immigrant backgrounds as a basis for similarity. Harris is using Dr. Cedric Robinson, an influential political scientist who is renowned for his work on Black Radicalism and Racial Capitalism, as a means for teasing out the ideological differences between Vice President Harris and Shirley Chisholm. To

Harris' point, Shirley Chisholm's political behavior is very different than that of Vice President Harris' behavior and comparing the two elites flattens their experiences and behaviors. Chisholm was the first Black woman to be elected to office to represent a working-class New York neighborhood (Chisholm 2010). Chisholm's political and social commitments as a daughter to immigrants are not transferable or comparable to Vice President Harris' experience as a daughter of immigrants. While being the daughter of immigrants is an important factor that must be considered, Harris is ultimately arguing that scholars engage and study Black women political elites on their own merits.

Next, I asked Harris what brought her to this work. I wanted to understand the conditions she experienced that prompted her to write an extensive account of Black feminist politics from 1961 to now. She described her experience as an undergraduate student at the University of Pennsylvania and how she felt after reading Paula Giddings' (1996) book *When and Where I Enter*. Harris describes her experience of reading the book and wanting to know what happened to Black women's political and social activism after 1961, where Giddings ends the book. In undergrad, Harris was mentored by Dr. Mary Frances Berry, an esteemed American historian, lawyer, and activist who was appointed Assistant Secretary of Education under President Jimmy Carter and later became commissioner and vice chairman of the United States Commission on Civil Rights. During our conversation, Harris recalls asking Dr. Berry what Black women were doing politically after 1961, and what text could she read that addressed this question. Harris states:

> Dr. Berry didn't have an answer for that, which was astounding to me, because I at the time I was 20 and she was Mary Frances Berry. I thought she had an answer for everything. She was the first Black woman I met who had both a PhD and a JD, so, I was blown away by her. So, when I started thinking about this question, a little bit more than 30 years ago, there weren't Black women elites. So that's how I'm getting to answer this here.

This response by Professor Berry helped to place Professor Harris on her current scholarly and professional trajectory. This quote illumines two points: First, the study of Black women's politics was and to an extent remains under explored (Cohen 2003); Second, there are capacious opportunities to study Black women and Black feminism. Studying both Black women and Black feminism is an expansive lifelong project that requires care, attention, and time. As Paula Giddings (1996) made clear in *When and Where I Enter*, the scholarly endeavor of finding the Black women that history has forgotten takes time and is a full commitment. This can also be expanded to include in the study the expansive opportunities that await the exploration of Black feminism. There are so many debates within Black feminism and feminist theory dialogs, namely around intersectionality (Alexander-Floyd 2012; Cooper 2016; Nash 2014, 2019; Puar 2011) that exemplify the overflowing capacity of studying Black feminism. In sum, Harris notes that there is currently "so much work being done, and so much more to do."

Furthermore, in *Black Feminist Politics from Kennedy to Trump*, Professor Harris highlights how Black women continue to navigate liminal spaces. I asked Harris about Black women's experiences under Clinton, Obama, and Trump. More pointedly, I engaged with her analysis regarding the lexicon of "Welfare Queen" and its variations. I asked Harris how she understands the significance of Black women elites being named "queen" and if this trope can be avoided? Harris replied:

> America is committed to seeing Black women in negative ways. So, when you have the lexicon of the welfare queen that Ronald Reagan invents, and then you have the "quota queen," and God rest Lani Guinier like that is how she is referred to, when she's actually talking about gerrymandering. But the people who are reading her work don't even understand that. Then you have the "condom queen," and people talking about Joycelyn Elders, because she's the first Black woman Surgeon General, and actually wants to talk about safe sex practices at a medical meeting. It's not like she's at an elementary school. She's at a medical meeting! And it's also in the height of HIV. The fact that Black women are demonized for being brilliant, really often is the cross that we have to bear.

The controlling image of "welfare queen," coined by Ronald Reagan, has haunted Black women for decades and continues to limit and constrain Black women's experiences and opportunities (Collins 1990, 2000). Harris notes that the conscious action of referring to Black women elites within the same vein of the "welfare queen" is a committal to not only seeing Black women as negative, but it is also an investment into misinterpreting and harming Black women. Reconstituting a lexicon that is informed by misogynoir works to negate the agency and autonomy of Black women. In using Black feminism as an analytic, this concept actively recenters and recovers Black women on their own terms. The mistreatment of Lani Guinier and Dr. Joycelyn Elders by the media and former President Clinton's administration demonstrates the need for a Black feminist analytic. A Black feminist politic considers the institutional actions that have obscured these two Black women, via these racialized and gendered attacks. This is just one example, but Black women political elites continue to be viewed through negative stereotypic lenses that require a Black feminist analytic. Indeed, examples of misogynoir lobbied against Black women are not contained by time and have traveled across decades, which required Harris to write a second and third edition of the book. Black feminist politics is not a linear timeline.

Conclusion

The current political landscape is requiring a deep interrogation of Black feminist politics. There are no easy comparisons to historical, current, or future Black women elites. Professor Harris argues that a comprehensive understanding of Black women elites and Black feminist politics requires nuance. Additionally, scholars must engage in the process through an ethics of care (Nash 2019) that explores the dynamism of individual Black women political elites. Furthermore, Duchess Harris encourages scholars to push the boundaries of Black feminism by exploring other political behaviors that speak to Black feminist principles. To do so, scholars should decouple Black women from Black feminism. This requires an investment in deeply understanding Black women elites as individuals.

To Harris' point, there are simply not enough Black women political elites to generalize them for the sake of an analysis. This aligns with and furthers the claims of many Black women scholars who have continuously invested in understanding and complicating measures of Black women as political actors (Cohen 2003, 2004; Prestage 1991). As Dr. Jewel Limar Prestage, renowned Black woman political scientist, activist, and mother of "Black politics," noted in 1991, "because African American women have only recently been granted access to the political arena as voters and officeholders in significant numbers, there is a paucity of information about them in these roles and even less about their nontraditional actions that predated these roles" (Prestage 1991, 89). Thirty-one years later, there is still much more work to be done to understand Black women as political actors and Black feminist politics in formal and informal environments.

Disclosure statement

No potential conflict of interest was reported by the author.

References

Alexander-Floyd, Nikol G. 2012. "Disappearing Acts: Reclaiming Intersectionality in the Social Sciences in a Post–Black Feminist Era." *Feminist Formations* 24 (1):1–25. doi:10.1353/ff.2012.0003.
Baum, Bruce David, and Duchess Harris, eds. 2009. *Racially Writing the Republic: Racists, Race Rebels, and Transformations of American Identity*. Durham: Duke University Press.
Brown, Nadia E. 2014. *Sisters in the Statehouse: Black Women and Legislative Decision Making*. Oxford ; NY: Oxford University Press.

Chisholm, Shirley Anita St. Hill. 2010. *Unbought and Unbossed*. Washington, DC: Take Root Media.

Cohen, Cathy J. 2003. "A Portrait of Continuing Marginality: The Study of Women of Color in American Politics." In *Women and American Politics: New Questions, New Directions*, ed. Susan J Carroll. Oxford, UK; NY: Oxford University Press, 190–213.

Cohen, Cathy J. 2004. "Deviance as Resistance: A New Research Agenda for the Study of Black Politics." *Du Bois Review: Social Science Research on Race* 1 (1):27–45. doi:10.1017/S1742058X04040044.

Collins, Patricia Hill. 1990. *Black Feminist Thought: Knowledge, Consciousness, and the Politics of Empowerment*. 1st ed. New York: Routledge.

Collins, Patricia Hill. 2000. Black Feminist Thought: Knowledge, Consciousness, and the Politics of Empowerment. Rev. 10thanniversary ed. New York: Routledge.

Cooper, Britteny 2016. "Intersectionality." In *The Oxford Handbook of Feminist Theory*, eds. Lisa Jane Disch and Mary E. Hawkesworth. New York: Oxford University Press, 385–406.

Dittmar, Kelly. 2021. *Reaching Higher: Black Women in American Politics 2021*. Center for American Women and Politics: Rutgers University.

Giddings, Paula. 1996. *When and Where I Enter: The Impact of Black Women on Race and Sex in America*. New York: W. Morrow.

Harris, Duchess. 2009. *Black Feminist Politics from Kennedy to Clinton*. New York: Palgrave Macmillan.

Harris, Duchess 2010. "Are Michelle Obama or Gabourey Sidibe Our Only Role Models?" *HuffPost*, September 15. https://www.huffpost.com/entry/are-michelle-obama-or-gab_b_717607 (May 11, 2022).

Harris, Duchess. 2011. Black Feminist Politics from Kennedy to Obama. New York, NY: Palgrave Macmillan.

Harris, Duchess 2016. "Black Lives Matter and the Price of the Ticket." *AAIHS*, September 16. https://www.aaihs.org/black-lives-matter-and-the-price-of-the-ticket/ (May 11, 2022).

Harris, Duchess. 2019. *Black Feminist Politics from Kennedy to Trump*. Cham, Switzerland: Palgrave Macmillan.

Jordan-Zachery, Julia S., and Duchess Harris, eds. 2019. *Black Girl Magic beyond the Hashtag: Twenty-First Century Acts of Self-Definition*. Tucson: University of Arizona Press.

King, Deborah K. 1988. "Multiple Jeopardy, Multiple Consciousness: The Context of a Black Feminist Ideology." *Signs* 14 (1):42–72. doi:10.1086/494491.

Nash, Jennifer C. 2014. "Institutionalizing the Margins." *Social Text* 32 (1):45–65. doi:10.1215/01642472-2391333.

Nash, Jennifer C. 2019. *Black Feminism Reimagined: After Intersectionality*. Durham, NC: Duke University Press.

Prestage, Jewel L. 1991. "In Quest of African American Political Woman." *The ANNALS of the American Academy of Political and Social Science* 515 (1):88–103. doi:10.1177/0002716291515001008.

Puar, Jasbir. 2011. "'I Would Rather Be a Cyborg than a goddess': Intersectionality, Assemblage, and Affective Politics." In *Inventionen*, eds. Isabell Lorey, Roberto Nigro, and Gerald Raunig. Zürich: Diaphanes, 253–70.

Springer, Kimberly. 2005. *Living for the Revolution Black Feminist Organizations, 1968-1980*. Durham, NC: Duke University Press. Amazon Kindle ebook.

Wallace, Michele. 1982. "A Black Feminist's Search for Sisterhood." In *All the Women Are White, All the Blacks Are Men, but Some of Us Are Brave: Black Women's Studies*, eds. Gloria T. Hull, Patricia Bell-Scott, and Barbara Smith. Old Westbury, NY: Feminist Press, 5–12.

A Conversation with Mary Hawkesworth on Intersectionality, Political Science, and Challenging the Discipline

Catherine N. Wineinger

ABSTRACT

This is an interview with Mary Hawkesworth conducted by Catherine Wineinger. In this interview, Hawkesworth discusses her work on congress-women of color, what inspires her to produce intersectional scholarship, the pushback she has received in the discipline, and the importance of building feminist networks of solidarity.

I had the great pleasure of speaking with Mary Hawkesworth about her pathbreaking research and her experiences in academia. In this interview, we discussed Hawkesworth's work on congresswomen of color, what inspires her to produce intersectional scholarship, the pushback she has received in the discipline, and the importance of building feminist networks of solidarity.

Mary Hawkesworth is a renowned feminist theorist and a Distinguished Professor Emerita of Political Science and Women's and Gender Studies at Rutgers University. She served as the Director of the Center for Women and American Politics (CAWP) from 1998–2001, the Director of the Graduate Program in Women's and Gender Studies from 2001–2004, and the Chair of the Department of Women's and Gender Studies from 2007–2010. She has also served as Editor in Chief of *Signs: Journal of Women in Culture and Society*, the leading journal in feminist scholarship, from 2005–2014.

In addition to these accomplishments, Hawkesworth was the recipient of the 2004 Heinz Eulau Award for best article published in the *American Political Science Review* (APSR). Her article, "Congressional Enactments of Race-Gender: Toward a Theory of Raced-Gendered Institutions," brought to light processes of gendering and racialization in the United States Congress through in-depth analyses of the experiences of congresswomen of color (Hawkesworth 2003). The award committee at the time stated that "a fresh look at race and gender dynamics in Congress promises to encourage creative thinking about how best to address problems of discrimination that are so graphically portrayed [in the article]" ("APSA Awards" 2004, 958).

Indeed, I first read this article as an undergraduate at the University of San Diego in Karen Shelby's feminist theory class, and it transformed my own thinking in critical ways. Not only did it introduce me to new theoretical concepts; it also introduced me to new ways of conducting political science research. I began to see how qualitative and interpretive methods can be used to center the lived experiences of women of color in a way that highlights often-overlooked dynamics within political institutions.

In our conversation, Hawkesworth highlighted the significance of methodological diversity. Intersectional analysis in political science is possible when feminist scholars push back against the disciplinary norms that have long been established by White men. What follows is the transcript of this interview, which has been edited for length.

Catherine Wineinger (CW): As a feminist theorist, what initially drew you to this type of work?

Mary Hawkesworth (MH): That's a great question. It requires time traveling. When I first started taking classes in political science as an undergrad at the University of Massachusetts, there was no such thing as a field of Women and Politics, there was no such thing as feminist theory. And at UMass, they had not yet offered even one women's studies course. So this is antediluvian – this was a whole different world.

It was, however, at the end of the 1960s when the behavioral revolution in political science was riding high. The behavioral revolution was insisting that it was doing neutral, value-free, empirical research at the same time it was denouncing all the things I found most interesting in the discipline. I was a political theory person – that's what drew me to it; I liked the huge questions. So from the get-go, I had this very clear sense that what was masquerading as "objective science" was really pushing a very particular way of thinking about the world that allowed you to see some things but prevented you from seeing other things.

Within the political theory frame, the only things that got taught were written by Euro-American White men: we read the classics. They always started with Plato – maybe one teacher would do something on the pre-Socratics – but Plato through Marx was pretty much the framework. And in all of that work, you'd read these fascinating claims about human nature. And then, snuck 100 pages in, they'd say something derogatory and misogynist about women. In Aristotle, for example, you'd be reading along about the "inherent equality" of rational beings and then all of a sudden, he refers to slaves and insists that "Those who devote their lives to earning a living are incapable of living a human existence."

I was beginning to understand bias in various ways: one, methodological; one, in terms of race and gender. Even the framework that we now call Eurocentrism had not yet been analyzed. We had inklings, but no vocabulary, no conceptual tools. And we were young women who experienced all kinds of sexism in the academy and in life. I started reading feminist works in my free time for sanity's purposes – some of the radical feminist works that were published in the early 1970s, starting out with just mimeographed copies, stuff by *The Furies*, stuff that would just set your brain on fire.

I started being engaged in feminist life in terms of protesting on the streets – anti-Vietnam War mobilizations and early demands for women's rights. This was the period when the whole notion of domestic violence was first being politicized; where rape, as a systemic issue, was first being discussed in feminist street politics; where beauty codes were being problematized. Amidst all that excitement about early feminism, you would go into your classes and it didn't connect – ever. If I asked professors questions like, "How do you make sense of a theorist's statements about women, given his claims about human nature when they are diametrically opposed? If you're supposed to believe that 'universal claims' are universal, how can a theorist cut out half of humanity?" The professor would look at you like you were hopeless – saying, let us talk about "real issues" like war and peace, friend and foe.

My undergraduate studies were shaped by contradictions. I was a good student. I could memorize anything I needed to memorize; I could write essays that answered the questions asked. But I had a real clear sense that much more needed to be said about the human population to even test the validity of these universalizing claims.

When I got my first job at the University of Louisville, there was a very fledgling women's studies community just organizing. There was one woman, Lilialyce Akers, who was teaching "Sex Roles" in those very early days, a precursor to "Sociology of Gender." There was another scholar in the English department, Lucy Freibert, who was introducing women's literature.

I decided to introduce a course on feminist theory, taking this great street literature that had been amassing over the decade of the 1970s and teaching it as a course. My department chair said, well, you can put it out there, and if anybody signs up for it, you can teach it, but if nobody signs up for it, you have to be prepared for that. I said, alright then.

So that's how I started at the very beginning. Just as part of a tiny nucleus of young feminist faculty who were, at the same time, dealing with issues of rape on campus, sexual harassment on campus, trying to politicize issues to make the university a woman-friendly place as opposed to an actively misogynist and scary place. We were doing that kind of work on the side, and pulling together a course that was part feminist critique of "great thinkers" – all men – and part wonderful radical perspectives of young feminist thinkers.

And of course, the minute you started working with these texts, the enormous racial bias within feminist writings instantly came to the fore. And it became clear that there were all these really tough, tough issues of racism that nobody thought it legitimate to talk about. So, one of my colleagues suggested that we start a "difficult dialogues series" where White women and Black women would come together – some were faculty, some were staff, some were students – to talk about all kinds of painful issues that separated White feminism from Black feminism and from "Womanism" and hindered our ability to work together, even when we you had shared goals.

A good decade before [Kimberlé] Crenshaw started publishing her pathbreaking work that gave us the language of intersectionality, I was working hands-on through really painful issues of racism and how it crops up in a million ways – not just in the content of university coursework, but in power hierarchies within universities. And it became clear to me that my training as a political theorist, my training as a political scientist, didn't leave any space to address those issues. I guess I would say that I was of that early generation, struggling to try to come up with a language to make certain kinds of inequalities visible and to figure out how to recognize that the category Woman is marked White and fails to apply to all kinds of racialized and classed people. How do you move from that realization in published texts to being able to show, in some palpable way, that this exclusionary bias exists in the world now?

We were fighting against a completely naturalized discourse in political science – the idea that race and sex are just physical characteristics, totally apolitical, and they have nothing to do with the world of politics that we are supposed to be studying. When we discussed the politics of embodiment, we were constantly being told that we were committing category mistakes: "No, no, no you're talking biology, *we're* talking politics." The challenge was how to show – whether you're doing analysis of public policy proposals or whether you're talking about how institutions operate – that the issue is not exclusively race and sex as biological essentialism, but active processes of racialization and gendering that create hierarchies. That policies, politics, and institutions are actively engaged in making those differences, accrediting those differences, granting differential rights and opportunities on the basis of those differences.

Small communities of feminist scholars would share work with each other, get feedback from each other. Somebody like Crenshaw would come up with one good word, "intersectionality," and we'd go, "Yeah! There's the word!" It's hard to imagine now, how much work went into the struggle for the right vocabulary, for innovative concepts. That's how I came to these questions: partly through teaching new material, partly through dissatisfaction with what my disciplinary training allowed, partly through massive anger at the maltreatment of talented women in the academy.

CW: I always tell my Women and Politics students that feminist theory is rooted in feminist *activism*. It's eye-opening hearing about how activism has influenced you, personally, and about the struggles you've faced in the discipline. And that's what my next question is about.

So much of your work is rooted in understanding how social and political power hierarchies are created and reinforced through the decisions of policymakers as well as everyday institutional practices and interpersonal interactions. So this is more of a two-part question. The first is: why are these power dynamics so important to understand? And second, why do you think they've been traditionally overlooked in political science?

MH: Those are great questions. I'm going to start with why they are overlooked first. And it's because the mainstream methodology does not allow you to see them.

I'll use the Congress study as an example. I was hired as a full professor to be the Director of the Center for American Women and Politics at Rutgers in '98. CAWP was started in '71, and already had an international reputation for pathbreaking research on elected women in politics, mostly state and federal level in the US. They had gotten funding to do elite interviews with congresswomen. These were in-depth interviews – many of them ran for 60 to 90 minutes. As the new Director, I inherited reams and reams of interview data from the 103rd and 104th Congresses that needed to be published as a final report. I started devoting time to reading all of these interviews.

I found it absolutely fascinating that there were differences in the kinds of experiences reported by Black congresswomen; by Patsy Mink, the only Asian American congresswoman; and by Latinas in Congress – reports that differed from what the White congresswomen said. On many points, the congresswomen agreed completely. But then I would hear – because I was listening to as well as reading these transcripts – congresswomen of color articulate dissatisfaction, unique claims about mistreatment, marginalization, racial harassment.

I took careful notes, thinking something has to be written about this. But to publish in this area, I had to learn a lot more about Congress, because I have never been a person who studied Congress. I started reading everything I could get my hands on about Congress and I discovered study after study insisting that race has no effect on legislative behavior. Once nature of constituency and party affiliation were controlled for, Congress scholars insisted that race has no effect; gender has no effect.

This is how methodology can make it impossible to see certain things. If you're doing roll call analysis, you will never see major effects based on race and sex because the numbers of congress-members of color and congresswomen are too small. It's the "small N" problem. When you use a method that literally makes it impossible to ask certain questions, you can never get different answers. The more I read about Congress and its operations, the more I could see that every method being used to study Congress made it impossible to make sense of what congresswomen of color were saying in these interviews.

The methods accredited by the discipline itself made it impossible to understand marginalization of some of the most powerful women in the country. The one thing I found that convinced me that I was on the right track was Wendy Smooth's research, which documented similar reports of margin-alization this at the state level. She too was interviewing incredibly powerful, talented, successful Black women state legislators who were saying the same thing.

These congresswomen were incredibly successful in their jobs – they were producing legislation, serving their constituents, doing great work – and yet they were feeling miserable. And so, I decided I was going to see what I could do to come up with a way of using the interview data to show that if you moved outside of the narrow behavioral range of analysis, you could take questions like this on. I used my training as a political theorist in textual analysis to engage the interview data. Situating their statements in the context of critical race theory and historical analyses of earlier African American men who served in Congress, I conducted a hermeneutic analysis of women of color in Congress. And I have to tell you that lots of my friends said, "You are out of your mind."

By analyzing patterns in the statements of the congresswoman of color, I sought to show that their experience challenged received views about how Congress works. I knew full well that people were going to say that this evidence was anecdotal. So I needed to add supplemental analysis to make a persuasive case. On one hand, interpretive analysis of the words of Congresswomen of color made visible the kinds of experiences that were rendered invisible by behavioral studies. Documenting that methodological bias was important, but I wanted to take up a multi-method approach so critics could not reject this evidence by claiming that everything that I was seeing was just one erratic comment by one Black woman who was probably having a bad day.

I turned to a sustained case study of "welfare reform" legislation, which was taken up in both the 103rd and 104th Congresses. Because the 103rd was Democratic controlled, and the 104th was Republican controlled, I could show that forms of "racing-gendering" reported by the Congresswomen of color could not be attributed to partisan party politics. Congresswomen of color themselves insisted that what they were talking about was not just a matter of partisanship; it was not Republican versus Democrat; it was institutional racism.

That's how the article got crafted. By the time it was drafted, the Perestroika movement for methodological pluralism was raising a ruckus in political science. Absent Perestroika, I would never have sent this article to the *APSR* because it would have gone nowhere. But I thought, if ever there were going to be a chance for a fair review, this would be it.

To cut a long story short, it went through five rounds of review and revisions. Five! It managed to get accepted, and then, much to my total astonishment, it won a prize for the best article in the *APSR* that year, which helped validate it against the claims of so many very well-trained political scientists who still think this is not political science. I also heard from some Asian American scholars that that paper is the first time that any reference to Asian Americans in elective office was ever published in the *APSR*, which I thought was astonishing.

You asked: why can't we see these power relations? The discipline's hegemonic methods don't allow certain questions to be asked or explored. Why should we press these issues? Because so much hangs on it. I don't want to suggest essentialist claims; it's not that all Black women will do X or all Asian American women will do Y, but to the extent that life is made miserable for diverse elected officials, they can be driven out of office while the institution claims to be governed by norms of "equal treatment." If we can make processes of racialization and gendering visible, then they become actionable – then there's hope for social change.

CW: Your work is intersectional in nature. It highlights the experiences of women within multiple interlocking systems of oppression. Intersectionality is a framework that's increasingly being used by scholars in political science. I'm curious what it was like conducting this type of work 20 years ago, and what it's like now. What have been some of your biggest challenges? Was there any backlash to this type of work?

MH: Well, Cathy, you probably noticed that I moved my line from Political Science to Women's and Gender Studies at Rutgers. And almost all of my work has been with feminist scholars. I decided to accept the editorship of the leading feminist journal in the field, not a political science journal. I love reading widely across all those disciplines because I think I've gotten better and better at intellectual innovation in intersectional ways because of the things I was reading across so many disciplines that opened new interpretive possibilities.

I have always belonged to the Foundations of Political Theory subsection, but most of my work has been through Women and Politics Research, feminist theory circles, so it's a kind of specialization which I have not regretted for a minute because I've met such wonderful scholars and I've learned such amazing things – things that still don't touch mainstream political theory.

Postcolonial scholarship, decolonial scholarship, the kinds of things that really take racialization and gendering to heart and see how they play out in the world now, as well as in documents from the past – those things are still not taught in traditional political theory. I'm very fortunate to have had the career I had; I don't regret any of the decisions I've made, but I don't think that the field of political science is remotely open to intersectional analysis or feminist analysis or critical race theory.

I think that the field is still pretty hostile. The Task Force on Political Science in the 21st Century Report showed that, except for Rutgers, there's no other place in the United States where you can get a doctorate in Women and Politics research. Most departments do not offer courses at the undergraduate or the graduate level, so this scholarship, as important and transformative as it is, is not being taught. The field still has, I think, a huge way to go.

CW: I also have a question for you about some of the practical implications of the post-Trump era. We've seen increasing diversity among women in Congress. Since 2018, we've seen an increase in the number of Black women elected to Congress, as well as the election of the first Muslim women, the first Native American women, the youngest woman, etcetera. At the same time, though, we've also seen increasing backlash and violence in response to that diversity.

Given your research on raced-gendered institutions, what do you think these changes mean for women of color in Congress and the environment they have to navigate? Do you think the institution has fundamentally changed, or is changing, in any way?

MH: Again a great question, and a really complicated question. It would be insane to suggest that there has been no change over the past 50 years. Things have changed, and we now have some spectacularly talented younger congresswomen, as well as very astute political strategists who are thinking about how to organize this Progressive Caucus to try to push for the agenda that they share and move away from being quashed by more centrist or conservative Democrats.

There clearly has been some amazing change. On the other hand, in the United States, which portrays itself as the leading democracy in the world, only 27% of US Congressmembers are women. Issues of race, racial equality, and Black Lives Matter are finally on the political agenda, but this has produced a virulent attack on critical race theory. The women who are in Congress are subjected to vicious insults, ranging from racist and misogynist memes to the death threats. Mona Krook's work on violence against women in politics documents this growing phenomenon. Each inch toward equality has been accompanied by incredibly violent backlash. Hate is politically mobilizing in the contemporary US.

We cannot declare victory and say we're just doing swell. We have to admire the courage of people who are willing to go into politics and fight these difficult battles. They are tough. That was exactly the point of the Congress article – that Congresswomen of color are doing the work but not under the same conditions; they're bearing the brunt of racialization, whether it's as vile death threats or whether it's constant microaggressions every single day. And it's not just in the halls of Congress; it's on social media and in everyday life, too. But *that* racing-gendering pervades the halls of Congress is crucial to recognize – there is no bubble of pure equality in the nation's capitol. Congresswomen of color are fighting huge battles on a daily basis.

CW: Absolutely. As an APSA Congressional Fellow, I worked for Congresswoman Rashida Tlaib.

MH: Oh, wow.

CW: Yeah, it was a really amazing experience. And it was also a firsthand experience, not just in terms of learning about the legislative process, but also in terms of seeing what you've long highlighted in your work. I saw up close how Congress is raced-gendered – how Congresswoman Tlaib's experiences differ from her colleagues. I'm also thinking about the death threats we would receive, which wasn't something I was fully prepared for.

Those experiences are shaping my current research agenda, which is actually related to my last couple of questions. A lot of the work that scholars are doing today, including myself, builds on the work that you and other scholars pioneered on the concepts of intersectionality, raced-gendered institutions, and embodied power. What are some trends and scholarship in this area that you're happy to be seeing? Do you think we're at least headed in the right direction?

MH: I love what I've been reading. One of the magnificent things is there is so much great work being produced that you can't keep up with all of it. Just in the past year we have our first feminist editorial team at the *APSR*, and the difference is phenomenal. The *APSR* is now full of articles I want to read – across all the subfields–US politics, comparative politics, international relations. They're asking new questions, they are reframing received views, they're showing how in all kinds of domains – voting behavior, election rules, gerrymandering, what goes on in standard operating procedures within organizations – how the law is being twisted to appear neutral while producing differential effects. Same in the courts – it's in every field.

Recent feminist scholarship has expanded understandings of politics at every level. One of the things that the discipline never wanted to accredit is that all aspects of life are political. And now we have young scholars showing how politics is playing out and how the processes of racialization and gendering that are operating and being documented in all these different terrains really is all about power. And power is supposed to be one of the main concepts our discipline studies.

It does my heart good to see these wonderful articles and books. The *LGBTQ Politics* Reader that came out that is some 2,000 pages. Finally! Creative, innovative, rethinking of all kinds of established theory, consider the globalization studies, the militarization studies – it's just amazing work. And for the first time we're getting little toe holds. In *Perspectives on Politics*, in the *APSR*, in *Political Theory*, we've had two successive feminist editors. It was a huge change in what's being published. So yes, wonderful work.

My big question is whether this scholarship is getting read by anybody but us – the feminists? How do we get over that next hurdle of making it a requirement that all political scientists be familiar with this pathbreaking research? Because new scholarship refutes established views. To refuse to read these refutations is to violate the norms of "science" that's supposed to be open to contestation all the time.

CW: That was going to be the second part of my question, which is, what still needs to be improved? How can we ensure that the discipline is both inclusive and paying proper attention to the racialized and gendered experiences of women of color, in particular? Incorporating this work into syllabi and curricula is definitely one thing. I'm curious if you think there's anything else we can do as political scientists.

MH: Well, one of the hopeful points is to look at the Western Political Science Association. They introduced a norm as early as 1975 that every other year there'd be a rotation of gender in the presidency. And that came out of political activism by the Women's Caucus for Political Science-West.

The Caucus has fought multiple battles to change the institution of political science, but change requiring women to be in power every other year starts to make headway in controlling the program. The year before assuming the Presidency, the President-elect is Program Chair, putting together panels, where scholars have to read each other's work in order to engage. It's going to take a long time to change our field because white men still control the discipline of political science.

But I think you have to use the norms of the discipline to make headway toward institutional change. Political scientists follow Karl Popper in conceiving science as a matter of conjectures and refutations. Well, you can't refute something if you don't read it. And you can't refute it if you don't understand the terms of discourse. So "Scope and Methods" courses should have to include feminist methodology. And feminist methodology is so diverse that it would have to include some readings by feminist scholars in every method included on the syllabus. It is not acceptable to have one week on something *called* feminism. Every series of readings for every single method should include some excellent feminist scholarship. Whether it's feminist ethnography or voting behavior studies or legislative institutional studies, including feminist work would give grad students and undergrads a chance to see that the world isn't just the 16% of the global population that happens to be White, or half of the population that happens to be male, or the tiny percentage who comprise elites. Political science should investigate the whole world out there. The discipline claims to be studying the political world; we've got to hold their toes to the fire to ensure they fulfill that promise.

There are lots of folks working on that agenda in interesting ways. Appointing feminist editors of major journals is huge because when your career publication prospects turn on passing muster with people who are saying, "But look, you're only talking about White men," there's an incentive to change built in there.

CW: Yup. How the tables have turned!

MH: Exactly.

CW: I have one final question. You've had this amazing career – and not just because of the awards and the recognition that you've received. I think a truly great career is measured by the voices you help to uplift and the people you mentor and inspire. One of the reasons your work is so inspiring is that it's grounded in women's lived experiences. And while it uncovers the process of marginalization, it also emphasizes resistance and the power of women within these systems of oppression. This type of work has always taken courage, and it continues to take courage. What advice do you have for younger scholars who are continuing to pursue these avenues of research and are continuing to focus, in particular, on the experiences of women of color?

MH: I think you need networks of solidarity. Whether you forge those networks through a supportive professional space, or whether you do it online through affinity groups, or a network of scholars who read your work and give you positive feedback, you've got to have a cohort of people who affirm your work when you're in a discipline where you're going to face a lot of people saying, "You're not really studying what's important."

The Women's Caucus for Political Science has been hugely important to me in my career. I've met so many great feminist scholars. You've got to have a network of support. There's no way in the world you can sustain your energy and your creativity if you don't have other scholars who are reading your work and reading it openly and fairly – and critically, because you need the critiques to make things better. So, find supportive colleagues and seek solidarity.

Disclosure statement

No potential conflict of interest was reported by the author(s).

References

American, Political Science Association 2004. "APSA Awards Presented at the 2004 Annual Meeting." *PS: Political Science & Politics* 37(4):955–62.

Hawkesworth, Mary. 2003. "Congressional Enactments of Race-Gender: Toward a Theory of Raced-Gendered Institutions." *The American Political Science Review* 97(4):529–50. doi:10.1017/S0003055403000868.

Moving beyond Niceness: Reading bell hooks into the Radical Potential for the Discipline

Alex Moffett-Bateau and Jenn M. Jackson

ABSTRACT
In honor of bell hooks' legacy, we engage with her Black feminist scholarship to parse out what she offers to the study of Black politics. We explore the ways hooks rebuffed compulsory calls for niceness and obligatory congeniality via respectability politics. By interrogating the politics of the Black middle class, we locate hooks' intellectual works as a repudiation of a "politics of niceness" that seeks to maintain the violent status quo of white capitalist heteropatriarchy. We then draw out why the rejection of a politics of niceness matters within broader discussions of race, power, politics, and oppression.

"Black folks who 'love Blackness,' that is, who have decolonized our minds and broken with the kind of white supremacist thinking that suggests we are inferior, inadequate, marked by victimization, and so on, often find that we are punished by society for daring to break with the *status quo*. In our jobs, when we express ourselves from a decolonized standpoint, we risk being seen as unfriendly or dangerous."

bell hooks, *Black Looks* (1992, 17)

There are many lessons we can learn from Black feminist scholarship and movement making. In particular, the work of bell hooks has been critical in shaping a generation of feminists with a critical eye to white heteropatriarchy and the ways capitalism shapes every aspect of our day-to-day lives (hooks 1981). Further, bell hooks provides a Black feminist critical intervention around the performative femininity the Black middle class requires of AFAB (assigned female at birth) Black women. These performative feminine requirements function to remind and enforce the puritanical dogma that proscribes the hierarchy of women and who is of most value in US white supremacist heteropatriarchal capitalist culture.

In this essay, we describe these performative feminine requirements as "the politics of niceness." The politics of niceness requires Black AFAB humans, and all Black women, to perform a personality and politics of "hyper-niceness," in a hopeless attempt at countering stereotypes of the "mean," "aggressive," angry, and "hyper-sexual" Black woman (Smith 2000; Guy-Sheftall 1995). The politics of niceness attempts to contain the intellectual knowledge production of Black women and AFAB humans, to subjects that do not disturb or disrupt Black hetero-patriarchy, Black capitalism, Black wealth hoarding, and anti-Black sentiment toward poor Black people, and AFAB people whose skin complexion is literally darker than a paper bag.

By rejecting respectability politics (Higginbotham 1993) as well as a politics of niceness, within her body of intellectual, creative, and political work, bell hooks held the Black middle-class (among others) accountable via a radical Black feminist politics of community care. bell hooks rejected white mainstream feminism, because its vision of liberation was not interested in a radical effort to deconstruct and destroy all systems of hierarchy, oppression, Black antagonism, and anti-Blackness. Her work understood white mainstream feminism, and Black liberalism, as solely interested in having "equal access" to white supremacist, hetero-patriarchal, and capitalist forms of power (hooks 1994). Further, the fixation on social norms that reproduce gender, racial, ability, and sexual hierarchies has long made mainstream white feminism, and Black liberalism, an untenable model for Black femmes and women. Likewise, bell hooks rejected Black liberalism as simply interested in "diversifying," and being included within, white supremacist, hetero-patriarchal, and capitalist forms of power. hooks was not interested in equity or diversity movements seeking to include Black middle-class actors in existing political, academic, or cultural seats of power. Her rejection of the Black intellectual middle-class and its politics of wealth and social capital accumulation by increasing its proximity to whiteness meant hooks was repeatedly censored and excluded from her peers within the world(s) of Black knowledge and cultural production (hooks 2014). However, as more people in the US are considering non-normative and extra-systemic political engagement, we argue hooks' body of intellectual work instructs on the road ahead.

In the following sections, we first explore hooks' concept of truth-telling as a form of political praxis. Next, we examine hooks' critique of the Black middle class and Black liberalism, which both, too often, leave the Black working class and the Black poor out of its analysis and advocacy (hooks 1994). We close with a brief reflection of the ways that the Academy would do better to engage with hooks' work rather than relegating her to the informal, self-help section of our scholarly imagination.

Rejecting the politics of niceness: truth-telling as political praxis

One of the most critical contributions bell hooks offers us as scholars, activists, and co-strugglers is the importance of truth-telling in our social, political, and emotional lives. In *Sisters of the Yam*, hooks (2005) situates truth-telling as a form of political praxis. This praxis is a crucial component of engaged scholarship and transformative social advocacy. For hooks, the veil of untruth functions to perpetuate problematic ideas and beliefs about Black people and other marginalized populations. As such, it is through truth-telling that Black people work to free themselves of harmful systemic violence and elucidate the true nature of Black life in the United States. She writes, "White supremacy has always relied upon a structure of deceit to perpetuate degrading stereotypes, myths that Black people were inferior, more 'animalistic'" (hooks 2005, 12). The deceit hooks mentioned here is substantively and intentionally different from the types of gossip, riddles, and tricks associated with communities of color who have long used verbal traditions to ensure their survival (Cohen 2004; Hanchard 2010; Kelley 1996). Rather, the deceit of dominators in this context is an active process of public misremembering and historical rewriting meant to mask the true nature of white supremacy and its implications for Black life. Hortense Spillers (1987) refers to this naming and labeling process as "American Grammar," and Black feminists for generations have encouraged us to tell our own truths despite these violent and harmful social conditions. Truth-telling, then, is not simply an act of courage in the face of great challenge, it is an interruption of a set of logics that seek to criminalize, eradicate, and systematically label Blackness as outside of the justifiable confines of citizenship. It follows that truth-telling about the nature of white capitalist heteropatriarchy is an active form of resistance against the existing status quo and a gesture toward a more liberatory future.

For hooks, truth-telling is about struggling against what she calls dissimulation, which leads us to greater opportunities for healing in the community. Dissimulation is the process by which individuals are socialized to conceal their true thoughts and ideas to remain in line with a perceived status quo. Dissimulation is complicated because it has been critical to both Black survival and to creating traumatic relations within Black communities. According to hooks (2005, 15), "dissimulation makes us dysfunctional." By learning to disassociate with the true nature of ourselves and our feelings, we have lost touch with our inner selves and our inner knowing. And, in many ways, this loss of authentic self-identity leaves open space for the integrationist and assimilationist byproducts of white supremacy. Without a firm anchor of the truth of Blackness and its expansiveness, dissimulation provides a veil to cloak the true nature of Black life, while performance takes priority. Under a politics of niceness, this superficial performance is often in alignment with whiteness and middle-class identity. In many ways, the performance of Blackness (or a particular form of it) is precisely what hooks (1994) derides in her analyses of well-to-do Black people. Likewise, in her rejection of the culture of dissimulation, hooks is suggesting that performance is wholly insufficient in addressing the underlying systemic problems Black people face under a white heteropatriarchal capitalistic system of order.

Thoughtfully, hooks theorizes that dominator logics under white supremacy are the impetus for Black performance, our need to survive in the face of unceasing anti-Blackness, and persistent surveillance of Black life, outstrip our capacity for confronting those systems. These conditions are the crucible within which the politics of niceness is formed and reinscribed. Here, hooks builds upon Evelyn Brooks Higginbotham's (1993) canonical theorization of respectability politics. Higginbotham's framing was rooted in the notion that Black American comportment to a set of proper and respectable social mores and behaviors might help to fight against negative stereotypes of Black people. "The politics of respectability emphasized reform of individual behavior and attitudes both as a goal in itself and as a strategy for reform of the entire structural system of American race relations" (Higginbotham 1993, 187). This form of racial coping was an intentional survival tool meant to subvert existing racial hostilities facing Black Americans in the post-Reconstruction Era and throughout the twentieth century. hooks extends Higginbotham's respectability framework as she interrogates the internalization of the racist messaging and systemic discrimination. As such, rather than strategically undermining the status quo, niceness calls Black people to ignore overt racism and discrimination in favor of garnering greater proximity to wealth, whiteness, and perceived power (hooks 1994). Likewise, it encourages Black people to move away from a set of liberatory politics capable of challenging the existing status quo (hooks 1992). While the politics of niceness do not explicitly serve Black people's wholeness, authenticity, and identity formation, it does empower some Black people to assimilate into a performance of Black identity absent the sharper edges. A Black identity performance whose primary function is to protect their access to the very systems seeking to annihilate them (hooks 1994). Instead, hooks' centering of truth telling despite societal pressure to capitulate to dominator logics and frameworks is an overt rejection of these systems. Moreover, her contributions here are a helpful lens through which to examine the ways that the Black middle class often espouse the politics of niceness in order to gain greater proximity to whiteness and further distance itself from poor and working-class Black people.

A critique of anti-Blackness within the Black middle class

Throughout her life, hooks continued to reject the politics of niceness, wherever and whenever its expectations were presented. She argued that the struggle toward liberation required strict account-ability from herself and her peers. In *Black Looks*, hooks writes that members of the Black middle-class (like herself), had a responsibility to maintain radical transparency and accountability, so they did not fall prey to white supremacist, patriarchal, or capitalist logics that would facilitate exploiting more vulnerable Black communities for their own financial gain (hooks 1992). One of the sites of account-ability via cultural criticism hooks became infamous for was her insistence that pop singer Beyoncé was a terrorist (hooks 2014). hooks argued Beyoncé was a "slave" to the white supremacist, patriarchal, and misogynist capitalist logics that organize popular culture in the United States. Other scholars have debated hooks' infamous contention; however, our point here is simply that hooks had no qualms with holding any and everyone accountable when it came to the politics of Black liberation (Weidhase 2015). She was also critical of many Black middle-class men who made films in the 1990's, in particular directors like Spike Lee (hooks 1994). hooks argues that Hollywood maintained an "obsession to have white women film stars be ultra white" in order to maintain a distinct "separation between that image [of white women] and the Black female Other; it was a way to perpetuate white supremacy. Politics of race and gender were inscribed into the mainstream cinematic narrative from *Birth of a Nation* on" (hooks 1992, 119–120). We contend you can extend her argument a step further. Anti-Blackness, white supremacy, patriarchy (misogynoir in particular), transphobia, queer phobia, and global capitalism, are inscribed into, and perpetuated by, Black cultural and academic products, created by the Black middle-class. It is no accident that the Black poor, and the Black working class (particularly secondarily marginalized Black non-men) are largely depicted as inept, incapable, undesirable, and unworthy, within much of mass-produced Black film, literature, and some academic disciplines.

In 2022, we are still dragging the baggage of the "post-racial Obama era," behind us. As hooks (1992, 10) astutely notes, "racial integration in a social context where white supremacist systems are intact undermines marginal spaces of resistance by promoting the assumption that social equality can be attained without changes in the culture's attitudes about Blackness and Black people..." As a result, we have prioritized the presence of Black people ("ideally" in positions of leadership) within as many white elite institutions in the United States as possible, as the *premiere*, foremost, and most critical site of Black struggle in the country. "I conclude that many of us are motivated to move against domination solely when we feel our self-interest directly threatened" (hooks 1994, 290). She explains that many who espouse liberationist politics do not do so for the purposes of collective uplift and freedom but to end what they deem personally harmful (hooks 1994). Here, hooks rejects self-interest as an impetus for a liberatory politic as it does not address the underlying systems and collective nature of white supremacist violence. For hooks, it is critical social change be radical and transformative rather than shallow and performative. Like many other Black feminists, this sentiment is echoed when Audre Lorde reminds us, "the master's tools will never dismantle the master's house" (Lorde 1984). To extend this argument, social movement theorists have shown that the best way to dismantle radical insurrection is via absorbing the leadership of those movements into the existing power structure (McAdams 2010). The United States did not reject white supremacy or embrace a radical ethic of community care when it allowed John Lewis, Barbara Jordan, or Shirley Chisholm into the Legislature. The US federal government simply tied their livelihood, their community standing, their perceived power, and their economic stability, to a false promise they could change the very foundations our government is built on. Instead, the institution of Congress changed their social relationships, their connection to Black people, their values, and their politics. By the end of their political careers (and in some cases their lives), their political commitment was to the health of the institutions of power they served, and they were no longer of explicit service to the Black communities who elected them.

Despite this real political history, the general public seems to accept without debate the idea that transformation has not happened within institutions of power, because the *wrong individuals* are currently occupying the seats in the building. There has yet to be a real reckoning with the meat and potatoes of hooks' intellectual work on Black liberation. For hooks, institutions of power, built on the foundation of white supremacy, cannot be rehabilitated, they cannot be saved. We want to believe marginalized people are somehow morally superior. We hope that by simply being added to the payroll, the *right* Black middle-class individuals will erase the patriarchal, misogynist, homophobic, ableist, transphobic, classist, colorist, and white supremacist founda-tions that institutions of power are built on. But as hooks reminds us, this is simply not true (hooks 2000). Black people, particularly those closest to whiteness, are just as indoctrinated into white supremacy, capitalism, neoliberalism, patriarchy, misogyny, imperialism, transphobia, able-ism, and queer phobia. We can look to recent and current Black mayors like Lori Lightfoot, Keisha Lance Bottoms, or Eric Adams for example. All three have aligned themselves with police departments and the wider carceral state in support of punitive policies that disproportionately punish the Black poor. All three consistently blame the "cultural habits," of the Black working class and the Black poor, for their suffering. We could go on with a multitude of other examples, but the key takeaway here is that hooks was disciplined throughout her life about holding those with power, accountable despite the specter and expectations of the politics of niceness.

We are often seduced, in one way or the other, into continued allegiance to systems of domination—imperialism, sexism, racism, classism. It has always puzzled me that women and men who spend a lifetime working to resist and oppose one form of domination can be systematically supporting another. (hooks 1994, 299)

As hooks argues, it is only through active and intentional work to decolonize our minds, values, intellectual ideas, and political commitments, can members of the Black middle-class eschew the seductive power that systems of domination offer each and every one of us (hooks 1992). It makes complete sense then that throughout the 2020 Summer Uprisings following the police killing of George Floyd, young Black people reported regularly hearing from elders who told them to "stop wasting time in the streets and go run for office." Or "if you don't vote, you don't have a right to complain." But what those elders are actually saying is, "running for office, voting, participating within formal systems of government as defined in the United States, are acceptable, respectable, white-proximate means of engaging in power, which *might* help, when you are inevitably misread as 'unfriendly or dangerous.'" The idea that being Black middle-class status could help lessen the likelihood anti-Blackness results in deadly outcomes (hooks 1994).

Of course, anti-Blackness ensures the Black middle class will never be able to access the forms of protection whiteness provides to its adherents. In *Invisible Visits*, Tina K. Sacks does a brilliant job of showing why Black middle-class women have a disproportionate likelihood of experiencing medical neglect and medical trauma, across race, gender, and class status (Sacks 2019). However, Black elders have always told little Black girls like us how important it is to "dress-up" when we leave the house as a form of protection (Laymon 2018). Because, as hooks points out in *Outlaw Culture*, when you are visibly Black and middle-class it is generally understood, on a day-to-day basis, you will likely deal with less racial violence and harassment if you fall within acceptable gender and race norms (hooks 1994).

> Rather than using coercive tactics of domination to colonize, [white supremacist logic] seduces Black folks with the promise of mainstream success if only we are willing to negate the value of Blackness ... we are collectively asked to show our solidarity with the white supremacist *status quo* by over-valuing whiteness, by seeing Blackness solely as a marker of powerlessness and victimization. (hooks 1992, 17-18)

Further, hooks argues that middle-class Black folks, proximate to whiteness, who can successfully embody the desires and expectations of whiteness, are best placed to take advantage of white supremacist capitalism by commodifying white stereotypes about what Blackness looks like (hooks 1994). Ultimately, you do not have to look much further than "liberal," "social justice," or "democrat" Twitter. Many of the AFAB Black humans who can successfully commodify their social justice activism, disproportionately come from Black middle-class families. They are often biracial, young, and/or have lighter complexions and less kinky hair. People with darker complexions who can break through the colorism barrier also often come from the Black middle class and tend to have a preexisting and meaningful proximity to whiteness. Significantly, this over-valuation of whiteness and negation of Blackness within Black academic, and Black cultural production spheres, is why white people who want to masquerade as Black people are generally the most successful when they work/volunteer for Black legacy civil rights institutions (Rachel Dolezal), academic departments (Jessica Krug and CV Vitolo-Haddad) or within the cultural/activist production spaces (Satchuel Cole).

The over-valuation and prioritization of whiteness, as a qualifying characteristic for being fully admitted into the Black middle class (for reference see the book *Our Kind of People* by Lawrence Otis Graham), in addition to the hyper-valuation of lighter skin and straighter hair, means that the Black middle class is extremely susceptible to white people who want to be reborn as Afro-descendent people from the United States. The critique hooks' makes of the way Black middle-class cultural, financial, and political values have usurped the diverse values of Black folks in the US across all classes, and prepares the way for hooks' broader political critique of the Black middle-class writ large (hooks 1994).

> Decolonized progressive Black individuals are daily amazed by the extent to which masses of Black people (all of whom would identify themselves as anti-racist) hold to white supremacist ways of thinking, allowing this perspective to determine how they see themselves and other Black people. Many Black folks see us as "lacking," as inferior when compared to whites. (hooks 1994, 10-11)

For hooks, anti-Black self-hate is an internal problem with very real political consequences (hooks 2005). No matter who holds these anti-Black views, hooks understands those views to be a result of consistent exposure to white supremacy, absent decolonizing self-work (hooks 2005). The collective hatred toward Black non-men, poor Black people, and Black trans people is a result of accepting white supremacy as a cultural product, global export, and national identity (hooks 1992). The solution is both very simple and yet incredibly complex. As bell hooks (1992, 20) instructs us, "loving Blackness as political resistance transforms our ways of looking and being, and thus creates the conditions necessary for us to move against the forces of domination and death and reclaim Black life." Ultimately, the only path to liberation for *everyone* is through a radical commitment, and full acceptance of the inherently diverse human values of Black people, Black culture, and Black communities. Her rejection of the Black, "anti-racist," middle-class, "obsession with whiteness." Further, hooks' explicit critique of the Black middle-class and its politics of wealth and social capital accumulation via proximity to whiteness meant hooks was repeatedly censored and excluded by her peers within the world(s) of Black knowledge and cultural production (hooks 1994, 173, 2014).

It must also be noted that hooks' rejection of the politics of niceness and her insistence on rigorous, critical, and honest, accountability was a political and intellectual risk she knowingly made. hooks argued throughout her life that her membership in the Black middle class, as well as the Black cultural and Black academic production class, required her to hold herself and her peers to rigorous accounting. Ultimately, hooks paid a significant price for her refusal to give in "to the post-1960's notion that material success is more important than personal integrity" (hooks 1992, 18). As she went on to discuss during one of her most infamous speeches at the New School, her political, and subsequent, intellectual choices meant she would never be rewarded by her peers via a MacArthur Grant or disciplinary awards (hooks 2014).

> Evidently, many Black folks, especially the bourgeoisie, find it difficult to believe that we are not all eagerly embracing an American dream of wealth and power, that some of us might prefer to live simply in safe, comfortable, multi-ethnic neighborhoods rather than in mansions or huge houses, that some of us have no desire to be well-paid tokens at ruling-class white institutions, or that there might even exist for us aspects of Black life and experience that we hold sacred and are not eager to commodify and sell to captive colonized imaginations. (hooks 1994, 174)

But hooks' embrace of radical Black love required grace, as well as honest and transparent accountability. For hooks, radical Black love meant she was harshest in her critique of herself, her peers, and her colleagues. She rejected a politics of niceness and instead embodied an ethic of radical Black love throughout her personal, professional, and political lives. The sacrifice hooks made, while she was with us, should not have been required, but it could help us get to a comprehensive understanding of liberation from white supremacy. In short, to get to a queer Black feminist future, we must love a diverse and fully human Blackness, while destroying whiteness.

Conclusion

Reflecting on the central claims of this essay, we suggest that the politics of niceness is much more than performing agreeableness for the purpose of personal likability, wealth accumulation, or interpersonal credit-taking. And, we argue that it also extends beyond the politics of respectability, which is rooted in both survival and tactical resistance to systemic racism and stereotypes. Instead, the politics of niceness regulates our abilities to navigate the complex social environment around us all, demanding we water ourselves down, avoid "difficult" topics, and otherwise remove any potential political disagreements that may lurk between civil individuals, specifically involving white Americans. Extending this concept to our analysis of the political, academic, and cultural power of the Black middle class offers us a lens through which we may all be held accountable for the systemic inequalities that remain intact in modern society. Moreover, it provides a framework for dismantling the system from every potential angle.

It thus follows that hooks was not concerned with being nice. She was concerned with struggling toward freedom via a Black feminist radical accountability, despite the potential costs. Like many Black feminists before her, she was clear that the stakes for Black scholars, activists, and movement makers were strenuous and demanding of Black women, AFAB people, and femmes (feminine presenting people) in ways that are unique and specific. Audre Lorde echoes this sentiment in her essay "Man Child" when she notes that young Black children who are raised by Black lesbians are exposed to a form of mothering that primes them against stereotypes and misogynistic ideas about Black women (Lorde 1984). She, like many Black feminists, points out that Black women's experiences and orientations to power allow us to see systemic disprivilege and violence more clearly as we are often the victims of those very systems. Here, both hooks and Lorde are underscoring the ways Black women rest at multiple margins of identity simultaneously, and are often the primary individuals concerned with issues of justice and liberation for all people, a sentiment articulated by a number of Black feminist thinkers and scholars (Collins 2002; Combahee River Collective 1977; Guy-Sheftall 1995). Given these conditions, hooks' rejection of the politics of niceness is simultaneously a rejection of assimilation and integration logics that ask nonwhite, non-middle class, non-abled, and non-straight people to lean into mainstream (white heteronormative) ideals.

One of the primary concerns we have in penning this essay is the general lack of engagement with hooks' work not only in the Political Science discipline but across the Academy. hooks' work has spanned decades but has only recently been acknowledged for its canonical contributions to the study of Black femininity, love, and the politics of doing justice to Black people in public. What is more, hooks' scholarship contains a radical potential to interrogate the political work and intentionality of both our scholarship and activism. In this era of "scholar-activists," we challenge researchers across disciplines to more deeply engage with hooks' calls for accountability. In writing this reflection, we hope that it encourages more scholars to interrogate the systems, institutions, and leaders, which actively work to limit access to the critical works of Black Feminists like hooks. Our academic lack of engagement with Black feminist thinkers only further reinscribes the inequalities and hierarchies hooks struggled against for a generation. In so doing, we continue to perpetuate the status quo hooks spent her entire life writing and working against.

Disclosure statement

No potential conflict of interest was reported by the author(s).

Funding

The author(s) reported that there is no funding associated with the work featured in this article.

References

Cohen, Cathy J. 2004. "Deviance as Resistance: A New Research Agenda for the Study of Black Politics." *DuBois Review: Social Science Research on Race* 1 (1): 27–45.

Collins, Patricia Hill. 2002. *Black Feminist Thought: Knowledge, Consciousness, and the Politics of Empowerment.* New York: Routledge.

Combahee River Collective. 1977. *The Combahee River Collective Statement* 1(1983): 264-274.

Guy-Sheftall, Beverly, ed. 1995. *Words of Fire: An Anthology of African-American Feminist Thought.* New York, NY: The New Press.

Hanchard, Michael. 2010. "Contours of Black Political Thought: An Introduction and Perspective." *Political Theory* 38 (4):510–36. doi:10.1177/0090591710366379.

Higginbotham, Evelyn B. 1993. *Righteous Discontent: The Women's Movement in the Black Baptist Church, 1880-1920.* Cambridge, MA: Harvard University Press.

hooks, bell. 1981. *Ain't I a Woman: Black Women and Feminism.* Cambridge, MA: South End Press.

hooks, bell. 1992. *Black Looks: Race and Representation.* Cambridge, MA: South End Press.

hooks, bell. 1994. *Outlaw Culture: Resisting Representations.* New York: Routledge.

hooks, bell. 2000. *Where We Stand: Class Matters.* New York: Routledge.

hooks, bell. 2005. *Sisters of the Yam: Black Women and Self-Recovery.* Cambridge, MA: South End Press.

hooks, bell 2014. *Are You Still a Slave? Liberating the Black Female Body, a Conversation with Bell hooks.* A panel discussion facilitated by bell hooks at Eugene Lang College, The New School for Liberal Arts. New York, NY. May 16, Accessed April 1, 2022. https://youtu.be/rJk0hNROvzs

Kelley, Robin D.G. 1996. *Race Rebels: Culture, Politics, and the Black Working Class.* New York: Free Press.

Laymon, Kiese. 2018. *Heavy: An American Memoir.* New York, NY: Scribner.

Lorde, Audre. 1984. *Sister Outsider: Essays and Speeches.* Trumansburg, NY: Crossing Press.

McAdams, Doug. 2010. *Political Process and the Development of Black Insurgency.* Chicago, IL: University of Chicago Press.

Sacks, Tina K. 2019. *Invisible Visits: Black Middle-Class Women in the American Healthcare System.* New York: Oxford University Press.

Smith, Barbara. 2000. "Establishing Black Feminism." *Souls: Critical Journal of Black Politics & Culture* 2 (4): 50–54.

Spillers, Hortense J. 1987. "Mama's Baby, Papa's Maybe: An American Grammar Book." *Diacritics* 17 (2):65–81. doi:10.2307/464747.

Weidhase, Nathalie. 2015. "Beyoncé Feminism' and the Contestation of the Black Feminist Body." *Celebrity Studies* 6 (1):128–31. doi:10.1080/19392397.2015.1005389.

Index

Note: Page numbers followed by "n" denote endnotes.

Adida, Claire L. 115
American activism 89
American Bar Association (ABA) 49–51, 102, 106
American Political Science Review (APSR) 135, 139–41
American political system 129, 130
anti-Blackness 119, 122, 144, 145, 147
Asian American Political behavior 115–17

Bejarano, Christina 116
bereaved Black mothers 86, 87, 95
Black communities 3, 4, 12, 87, 96, 123, 144, 146, 148
Black Congresswomen 66–68, 75, 138
Black feminism 128–33
Black feminist politics 128–33
Black maternal bereavement 86
Black maternal politics 85–97
Black middle class 143, 145, 147, 148
Black mothers 86, 89, 90
Blackness 26, 117, 144, 145, 147
Black sororities 74
Black women 2–5, 7, 12, 49, 60, 61, 68, 73–76, 80, 129–33; geography 68–73; presence in congress 80–81; *see also individual entries*
Black women judges 48–62; evaluating 50–51; experiences on the bench 51–53; experiences with legitimacy, authority, and competence 56–58; experiences with litigants and attorneys 56; experiences with not being called their appropriate name 58–59; experiences with (dis) respect 54–56; and white men in courtroom 59–60
Bourdieu, Pierre 93
Brown, Michael 86, 92, 94
Butler, Judith 86

California 9, 28, 38, 40, 73, 114, 118, 123
Capuano, Michael 24, 25–29
Carew, Jessica D. Johnson 90
Carroll, Susan J. 2, 5

Carter, J. Scott Jr. 116
Citrin, Jack 124n3
Collins, Patricia Hill 86–88, 94
Colorado 38, 40
colorism 86, 114, 115, 117, 118, 122
communal socialization 3
competence 55–57, 59
congressional midterms 17–31
Crenshaw, Kimberlé 50
Cross, Christopher 52
cultural expectations 2

Dancey, Logan 110n3
Davenport, Lauren D. 115
Davis, Jordan 91–93, 97
decision-making process 5, 10
Deckman, Melissa M. 89
Delta Sigma Theta Sorority 7, 11, 74
Democratic National Convention 91, 114
dissident citizenship 5, 6
Dittmar, Kelly 90
Dolan, Julie 89
Dowe, Pearl K. Ford 74, 94

education 4, 9, 22, 39, 75, 76, 102, 103, 132
election results, breakdown 29
electoral politics 19, 86, 97, 130, 131

federal judgeships 102, 103, 109
Fix, Michael P. 50
formal political institutions 128, 129, 131
formal politics 129–31
Frazier, E. Franklin 87
Fulton, Sybrina 85, 86, 89, 91, 93, 94

Garcia, Jennifer R. 124n3
gender 2, 3, 18–20, 26–28, 30, 31, 49–51, 60, 80, 102, 147
gendered racial socialization 4
gender-race groups 108, 109
Georgia 8, 11, 18, 28, 38, 39, 68, 93, 123

INDEX

Giddings, Paula 132
Greene, Stacey 116
grief 88, 89, 95
group consciousness 3, 116
group identities 29, 118

Hardy-Fanta, Carol 73
Harris, Duchess 50, 128–33
Harris, Kamala 114–24
Harris-Perry, Melissa V. 87
Hawkesworth, Mary 91, 135–42
Haynie, Kerry L 76
Hernández, Katerí Tanya 119
Higginbotham, Evelyn B. 145
home socialization 3
hooks, bell 143–49

Indian American perceptions 114–24
intersectionality 18, 42, 50, 51, 132, 135, 137,
    139, 140

Jacob, Harriet 89
Jayawardene, Sureshi 117, 119
Johnson, Gbemende E. 50
judicial experience 103, 106

Kansas 36, 38, 40
Karnig, Albert K. 73
Kelley, Robin D.G. 1
Killen, Kimberly 91
King, Deborah K. 130

leadership 4, 5, 8, 10, 12, 28, 30, 76, 80, 115, 146
Leape, Lucian L. 62n14
Lemi, Danielle Casarez 115–19
Leslie, Gregory John 115
Levy, Morris 124n3

Martin, Trayvon 86, 92, 93
Martinez, Josiane 29
Masuoka, Natalie 115
maternal politics 85, 90–92, 97
Matos, Yalidy 116
McBath, Lucy 86, 87, 91–93, 96
McClendon, Gwyneth 115
McSpadden, Lezley 86, 91, 94
Means, Taneisha N. 50
Minnesota 26, 38, 40, 41, 129
mixed candidates 115–18, 123
motherhood 4, 88–91
Moyer, Laura 102

Nelson, Kjersten R. 110n3
Nevada 35, 38, 39
Nicholson, Harvey L. 116
non-mixed conditions 117, 120

nonwhite women 102–6, 108–10
Nteta, Tatishe M. 124n3

occupational background 75–76
Ono, Yoshikuni 50

Pinderhughes, Dianne 73
political actors 27, 29, 89, 90, 128, 129, 133
political catalyst 86
political identities 2, 89, 118
political moment 88, 90, 91, 96
political participation 4, 7, 8, 10–12, 74, 96
political praxis 144
political science 18, 129, 135–37, 139, 141, 142
political socialization 3, 4, 74
politics of niceness 143–46, 148, 149
Pressley, Ayanna 17–31; *versus* Capuano
    25–29; case study analysis 20–24; opposition
    24–25

qualifications 102
queer women, US state legislatures 35–44

race-gender groups 102, 105
racial minority judges 50
racial polarization 9
radical imagination 2, 4, 5, 7, 8, 12
recusal requests 48, 52–54, 58, 59
resources dissident citizenship 10–12
respectability politics 86, 88, 92, 95, 145, 148
Restar, Arjee 116
Rice, Samaria 95
Richardson, Allissa V. 88
Richardson, Elaine 4
Ringsmuth, Eve M. 110n3

Sadhwani, Sara 116
Sanbonmatsu, Kira 2, 5, 116
Sierra, Christine Marie 73
Simien, Evelyn M. 19
single states: with fewer minority lawmakers
    42–43; with more minority lawmakers
    41–42
Smooth, Wendy 4, 91
social identities 59
socialization 2, 4, 8, 12; process 3, 4, 10, 12
Speight, Suzette L. 4
Spillers, Hortense J. 144
state legislatures 24, 35, 36, 38, 40, 41, 44, 73, 74
stereotypes 2, 87, 90–92, 96, 114, 123, 148, 149
Stout, Christopher T. 124n3
Swers, Michele L. 89
symbolic empowerment 17, 19, 21

Tarsi, Melinda R. 124n3
Texas 38, 39, 48, 68, 123

INDEX

Thomas, Anita Jones 4
Tyson, Timothy B. 89

Unah, Isaac 50

Washington 4, 5, 22, 23, 27, 38, 40, 41, 49, 50, 73
Welch, Susan 73
white cisgender 38–42
white male norm 101, 102, 104

whiteness 26, 144–48
white supremacy 7, 93, 95, 144–46, 148
white women 3, 4, 6, 50, 51, 86, 87, 89–91, 101, 104, 105, 108
Williams, Linda Faye 3
Williams, Rhaisa Kameela 86, 87, 94
Wong, Cara J. 124n3

Zilis, Michael A. 50